Translation and Nation

TOPICS IN TRANSLATION

Series Editors: Susan Bassnett, *University of Warwick* and Edwin Gentzler, *University of Massachusetts, Amherst*
Editor for Translation in the Commercial Environment:
Geoffrey Samuelsson-Brown, *University of Surrey*

Please contact us for the latest book information:
Multilingual Matters, Frankfurt Lodge, Clevedon Hall,
Victoria Road, Clevedon, BS21 7HH, England
http://www.multilingual-matters.com

TOPICS IN TRANSLATION 18
Series Editors: Susan Bassnett, *University of Warwick* and
Edwin Gentzler, *University of Massachusetts, Amherst*

Translation and Nation

Towards a Cultural Politics of Englishness

Edited by
Roger Ellis and Liz Oakley-Brown

MULTILINGUAL MATTERS LTD
Clevedon • Buffalo • Toronto • Sydney

Library of Congress Cataloging in Publication Data

Translation and Nation: Towards a Cultural Politics of Englishness
Edited by Roger Ellis and Liz Oakley-Brown
Topics in Translation: 18
Includes bibliographical references and index
1. English literature–Foreign influences. 2. Literature–Translations into
English–History and criticism. 3. Translating and interpreting–England–History.
4. National characteristics, English, in literature. 5. Language and culture–England–
History. 6. Nationalism–England–History. 7. Nationalism in literature.
I. Ellis, Roger. II. Oakley-Brown, Liz. III. Series.
PR125.T73 2001
820.9–dc21   00-050113

British Library Cataloguing in Publication Data

A CIP catalogue record for this book is available from the British Library.

ISBN 1-85359-518-7 (hbk)
ISBN 1-85359-517-9 (pbk)

Multilingual Matters Ltd

UK: Frankfurt Lodge, Clevedon Hall, Victoria Road, Clevedon BS21 7HH.
USA: UTP, 2250 Military Road, Tonawanda, NY 14150, USA.
Canada: UTP, 5201 Dufferin Street, North York, Ontario M3H 5T8, Canada.
Australia: P.O. Box 586, Artarmon, NSW, Australia.

Typeset by Florence Production Ltd.
Printed and bound in Great Britain by the Cromwell Press Ltd.

Contents

About the Contributors

Roger Ellis is a Senior Lecturer in English at Cardiff University. He has published on Chaucer, the Middle English mystics and St Bridget of Sweden. Since 1987 he has organised International Conferences on Medieval Translation, and has edited the Proceedings, now part of a Series (published by Brepols) which he also co-edits, *The Medieval Translator*.

Rainer Emig is Professor of English Literature at the University of Regensburg, Germany. His publications include *Modernism in Poetry* (Longman, 1995). His book on W.H. Auden is due to be published by Macmillan in 2000.

Christa Knellwolf is Research Fellow in the Humanities Research Centre at the Australian National University. She is the author of a book on Alexander Pope and gender, *A Contradiction Still*, published by Manchester University Press, and she is co-editor of volume 9 of The Cambridge History of Literary Criticism. Work in progress includes a book on the aesthetics of empiricism.

Liz Oakley-Brown is a former student of Cardiff University and was recently awarded her Ph.D. for her thesis on English translations of Ovid's *Metamorphoses* (1480–1717). As well as continuing her research on translations of the *Metamorphoses* by women in England, she is also editing Caxton's translation of the *Metamorphoses* for publication in *The Medieval Translator*.

Hugh Osborne's doctoral thesis was on Anthony Trollope. He has lectured in Victorian Literature at Cardiff University and, in 1998, was co-organiser of the International Symposium on Lewis Carroll held at the university.

Acknowledgement

The editors are extremely grateful to Professor Susan Bassnett for all the help she gave them at the different stages of the production of this book.

Introduction

> In the limits to which it is possible, or at least appears possible, translation practices [*sic*] the difference between signified and signifier. But if this difference is never pure, no more so is translation, and for the notion of translation we would have to substitute a notion of *transformation*: a regulated transformation of one language by another, of one text by another. We will never have, and in fact have never had, to do with some 'transport' of pure signifieds from one language to another, or within one and the same language, that the signifying instrument would leave virgin and untouched. (Derrida, 1987: 20)

During the last twenty years, with the publication of texts like those by Jacques Derrida and his translators,[1] George Steiner's *After Babel* (1975), Susan Bassnett's *Translation Studies* (1980, revised 1991) and *Constructing Cultures* (1998), Edwin Gentzler's *Contemporary Translation Theories* (1993) and Lawrence Venuti's *The Translator's Invisibility* (1995) and *The Scandals of Translation* (1998) – to name only some of the more important – the marginal position that has defined translators and their texts throughout much of the post-Romantic period in England has come under increasing and sustained challenge. Indeed, the quotation above from Derrida suggests that what is actually meant by 'translation' is now open to debate, making the critical practices employed in the discussion of translated texts as varied as the definition of the term. As José Lambert has explained, 'not only texts but also text fragments and discursive patterns may be imported into the target literature', thus rendering any simple definition impossible (Baker & Malmkjær, 1998: 131). Recently, Susan Bassnett has argued that 'by pretending that we know what translation is, i.e. an operation that involves textual transfer across a binary divide, we tie ourselves up with problems of originality and authenticity, of power and ownership, of dominance and subservience' (1998: 27). Rather than looking at translation as a process of equivalence, a process which moves meaning unproblematically from source to target language, many writers in the area of translation studies are now perceiving translation as a textually dynamic enterprise: a textual mode affected by ideological imperatives as much as any other. However, writers on translated texts

1

still need to free themselves from the dominant critical approach, a web of binarism that enmeshes the object of study and, to change the metaphor, continues to fetishise the original, even when no 'original' can be definitively traced, as often happens with vernacular translations of classical texts. Such an approach needs to give way to a critical practice which encourages an interpretative focus on the translated text's historical and cultural specificity:[2] vernacular texts, as this volume will show, have particular significance in terms of identity, representation and subjectivity.

The foregoing remarks provide a framework for much of the impetus and critical background which informs the five essays of this volume. The idea for this book came about some years ago when its editors were gathering material for their section on the 'British Tradition' for the *Routledge Encyclopedia of Translation Studies* (Baker & Malmkjær, 1998: 333–46). That project brought quickly to the fore an understanding of how issues of English identity, representation and subjectivity were constructed through and in the processes and products of vernacular translations. Yet, although translation and subjectivity had been thoroughly considered in terms of post-colonialism and post-structuralism, for example in Eric Cheyfitz's *The Poetics of Imperialism* (1991), Tejaswini Niranjana's *Re-siting Translation* (1992) and Michael Cronin's *Translating Ireland* (1996), there were few publications which focused specifically on the construction of Englishness through vernacular translation. To make good this omission, the editors invited contributions under the heading which became the title of this book: *Translation and Nation: Towards a Cultural Politics of Englishness*. All the essays in this volume, therefore, are concerned with the cultural and political implications of translation and the construction of English subjectivities at particular historical moments.

The book is not intended to be definitive; rather, it suggests ways of looking at the interpellation of the English subject – a subject formed through a variety of matrices, including those of nation, gender, religion and class – through texts that engage with translation in differing ways.

The opening essay by Roger Ellis, 'Figures of English Translation 1382–1407', focuses on the cultural and political implications of translation in texts produced in the quarter-century preceding Archbishop Thomas Arundel's ban against unlicensed Bible translations in Britain (1409). Moving through a wide range of texts, including works by Geoffrey Chaucer, John Trevisa and the author of the so-called Prologue to the Wycliffite Bible, Ellis shows the growth of a desire to see 'England as a notional geographical and linguistic entity', so that writing in English could offer a challenge to the domination of Latinity and its association with a clerical elite. However, the violent responses of religious and secular authorities prevented the borders of a distinctively English identity from being drawn until the sixteenth century.

Although fissures can be detected in the Middle Ages, the decisive break with Catholicism was not achieved until the Reformation; it is this period which is considered in the second essay by Liz Oakley-Brown, 'Translating the Subject: Ovid's *Metamorphoses* in England 1560–67'. Although translations of the Bible remained as contentious in the sixteenth century as they had been throughout the fifteenth, the argument in this essay considers not Bible translations but the seemingly unrelated English translations of Ovid's *Metamorphoses* in the 1560s. Oakley-Brown argues that these texts are sites where the identity of the emergent Protestant subject can be rehearsed in the seemingly less radical arena of classical translation. By closely reading translations of Ovid's text produced in the opening decade of Elizabethan rule, the essay explores the complex transformation of the English subject as it shifted from Catholicism to Protestantism.

Significantly at the centre of this volume is Christa Knellwolf's essay, 'Women Translators, Gender and the Cultural Context of the Scientific Revolution'. Men have largely shaped the canon of translation in England; women have more often been regarded as readers and patrons than as producers.[3] This can be seen in the fact that four out of the five essays here feature translations, and writing about translations, exclusively by men. But, as Knellwolf shows, there are always other genealogies to be considered, and her chapter looks at the ways in which translations of scientific texts, including Aphra Behn's and Elizabeth Carter's versions of, respectively, Bernard le Bovier de Fontenelle and Francesco Algarotti, affected the subject of science in late seventeenth-century and eighteenth-century England.

The following chapter, Hugh Osborne's 'Hooked on Classics: Discourses of Allusion in the mid-Victorian Novel', centres around a period in which literary translation had really become a 'secondary' mode of literary expression compared to 'original' composition. Nevertheless, through an exploration of writings by Trollope and other contemporaries, Osborne argues that the practice of classical allusion and quotation – translated and untranslated – exposes an 'implied discourse on Englishness', dependent on translative strategies, in which the English middle-class, male, subject in the mid-Victorian period can be constructed.

The first four essays in this book look at the construction of Englishness through translative strategies which operate within the boundaries of the nation state itself. Knellwolf's essay, of course, widens the frame of reference by considering the ease with which texts migrated from England to Italy, thence to France, and back again. Like Knellwolf's paper, the final chapter of this volume, Rainer Emig's essay '"All the Others Translate": W.H. Auden's Poetic Dislocations of the Self, Nation and Culture' moves across conventional geographical divides to consider the effects of translation, cultural and textual, upon an English subject living in Germany in the early 1930s, and further shows how this exile affected the constitution of the English self in later translative projects by Auden. Emig's essay brings the discussion into the twentieth century and, in that sense, fittingly rounds off the volume; but his essay also rounds off the book in a more important way. As his discussion makes clear, the complex treatments of translation and nation in Auden's output really encompass the cultural politics of Englishness that every text discussed in this volume has engaged with on some level.

It should be apparent from the foregoing comments that this volume offers readers examples of the different critical approaches that can be fruitfully followed when studying translation. While it is true that each chapter serves as an important introduction to the particular subject under discussion, the editors are confident that the book as a whole is more than the sum of its parts. Scientific translation, for example, figures in the papers of Ellis and Knellwolf, and women readers and translators of Newton's *Principia* in the papers of Knellwolf and Osborne. Translation from the classics appears in the papers of Oakley-Brown, Osborne and Emig, and Ovid's *Metamorphoses*, the principal subject of Oakley-Brown's paper, enjoys a walk-on part in the papers of Osborne and Emig. Bible translations figure centrally in the paper of Ellis, but subsequent translation projects like those studied by Oakley-Brown and Knellwolf can hardly be understood without reference to them. Translation as playful self-display figures prominently in the papers of Osborne and Emig; Emig's paper widens our use of the term by considering translations of one art form (engraving) into another (opera). Identified with desire and ignorance, women generally get a bad press in this volume as consumers/producers of translations. Translation as a site of debate is perhaps the most obvious common thread: Ellis's paper describes an actual debate, in 1401 at Oxford; Knellwolf's, a rush to print in 1738, by the Frenchman du Perron de Castera, to savage the Italian translation of Newton by Algarotti the previous year; Osborne's refers to the celebrated debate between Matthew Arnold and Francis Newman, in 1861–2, over the best way to translate Homer, at much the same time as a debate was raging over 'the advantages of a "liberal education" . . .

over against a classical education'. Licensing and censoring of translations, an obvious response by authority to material deemed subversive
– so in Ellis's paper, whose end point is the banning of unlicensed Bible
translations in 1409 by Archbishop Arundel – is also apparent in
Knellwolf's study of Behn's translation of Fontenelle and Du Perron
de Castera's of Algarotti, where the former practised 'an almost imperceptible form of censorship' and the latter 'describe[d] his task as the
carrying-out of an enlightened censorship'.

By and large, translation appears in this volume as a reaction to a
perceived intellectual/cultural lack, which the translator hopes the translation will make good: that same lack which, as Copeland (1991) has
shown, fuelled the translation projects of Latin authors like Horace and
Quintilian. In this sense, the English 'nation' of the book's title is always
being constructed out of pre-existing material found in other cultures
and languages: in French (in the Middle Ages and, again, after the
Restoration, throughout the eighteenth century); in German (from
the nineteenth century on); in Italian (from the high Middle Ages to the
end of the sixteenth century); above all, in Latin and Greek, Latin from
the Old English period on, Greek from the sixteenth century. These debts
are well documented in the papers in this volume: to Latin, in the papers
of Ellis, Oakley-Brown and Osborne; to French and Italian, in Knellwolf's
paper; to German, in that of Emig.

But England has shown itself, from earliest times, as vigorous a
coloniser as ever it was colonised: English self-definition, that is, cannot
be understood without reference to the imposition of English culture, first
throughout the British Isles, and later across the globe. Considerations of
this sort give particular point to Knellwolf's study of translations
of Newton into Italian and thence into French, against a backdrop of
ongoing French resistance to English intellectual pretensions. Translations
of Newton in the eighteenth century can then represent those processes
of colonisation which are so important a part of the English story, and
which other studies have so well documented.

All which may confirm, as Emig states, that:

> culture itself is shown to be the results of translations, and these
> translations are depicted not so much as inevitable forces of history,
> but as individual acts that rely on their social and political contexts.
> Inside these contexts they often fail, and the consequences of these
> failures can indeed be fatal. But equally fatal is the attempt to ignore
> translation as a crucial prerequisite of the formation of identity, be
> it personal, national or indeed cultural.

Notes

1. Almost any text by Derrida and his translators could be cited here. Gayatri Chakravorty Spivack's Preface to *Of Grammatology* cites (1979: lxxxvii) the extract from *Positions* used as the epigraph to this introduction. See also Evans, 1994: 32 and Bassnett, 1996: 11.
2. A single example of this desideratum is the study of English versions of Ovid's *Metamorphoses* in the early modern period. See Oakley-Brown, 1999 for a more detailed discussion.
3. See Simon, 1996 for an excellent introduction to the subject.

Chapter 1

Figures of English Translation, 1382–1407

ROGER ELLIS

In 1409 the Archbishop of Canterbury, Thomas Arundel, issued a ban, drafted in 1407, against unlicensed Bible translations in England.[1] His action was the culmination of a process with numerous precedents in the last twenty years of the fourteenth century, most notably the Blackfriars Council of May 1382, at the end of which Arundel's predecessor Archbishop Courtenay issued a promulgation forbidding unauthorised explication of the Scriptures in either Latin or the vernacular.[2] Like Arundel's constitutions, Courtenay's edict had as its target the Oxford academic – by then, the heretic – John Wyclif and his Oxford-trained disciples, who had early appreciated the value of, and need for, vernacular Biblical translations as part of a thorough-going programme of church reform. In the increasingly dangerous times between those two proclamations – times punctuated by the deposition of Richard II and the usurpation of the throne by Henry Bolingbroke (Henry IV) in 1399, as also by the civil statute *De heretico comburendo* [*On the burning of the heretic*] in 1401 – not only was a large number of translated and original works produced, but also an important debate was joined about the possibility and justification of <u>vernacular translation</u>, which we can use as a snapshot of the state of translation up to that time and beyond.

For these debates there was good precedent, as we shall see, in the various prefaces produced by St Jerome to accompany his Bible translations.[3] Jerome does not figure directly in the prefaces produced by Geoffrey Chaucer (*c.* 1343–1400) to accompany his many major translations. But he does figure in other works studied in this chapter: in the preface (1387) by John Trevisa (*c.* 1342–*c.* 1402) to his translation, for his patron the Duke of Berkeley, of the *Polychronicon* of the Chester monk Ranulph Higden (d. 1363–4); in the so-called General Prologue (1395–7) to the second version of the Wycliffite Bible translation; in an anonymous Wycliffite Tract in support of the latter, produced sometime between 1401 and 1407 and deriving from a contribution to the debate in 1401 by the orthodox Oxford academic Richard Ullerston (d. 1423); and in a set of anonymous tracts in defence of Biblical translations in English, preserved in a manuscript dated between 1400 and 1430 (MS Cambridge University Library Ii.vi.26).[4] As striking as the writers' invocation of Hieronymian models, though, was their general recourse to home-grown precedents, many of them derived from the *Polychronicon*: which has the bonus of allowing us a backward glimpse at the situation of translation in England earlier in the Middle Ages.[5]

The figures referred to in the title of this chapter are therefore twofold: first the translators themselves, though this is not an essay, as such, about their translations; secondly, the figures, Biblical and other, home-grown and European, whom they cited in support of their projects.

Chaucer

The debate was not restricted to the academic circles most closely associated with Wyclif. Echoes can be clearly heard in the work of the court poet Geoffrey Chaucer, though Chaucer's theorisings have little feel of an actual debate about them.[6] Like Trevisa, Chaucer had the added benefit, which the Wycliffites soon lost, of friends in high places for whom translation projects could function as a form of self-publicity, and who might therefore be prepared or persuaded to give the exercise their support. This, I take it, is one reason why Chaucer's *Treatise on the Astrolabe* directly names Richard II as 'lord of this langage' (56; cf. Crane, 1999: 55 n. 63).

There is, nevertheless, if submerged, a clear debate going on in the work of Chaucer. This debate is fuelled above all by that fear of error or excess – that transgressing of boundaries – which Horace and Cicero had boldly made matter of virtue in a translation and which St Jerome had turned into a (negative) moral imperative (Copeland, 1991). An authoritative original, it is assumed, needs to be transmitted unchanged to its target readership with no other changes than 'oure tonges difference' requires (*Troilus and Criseyde* I.395). This religious model of translation carries the consequence that expert readers must be invited to oversee the translated work and correct it as necessary (*CT* VIII.84). Such readers may find fault with an original which adds to its original (by way of proverbs, *CT* VII.955–6; in other ways, *Troilus* III.1329), and Chaucer gives them power to 'incresse or maken diminucion' of the text (*Troilus* III.1335).

Clearly implied in all this theorising is a tacit denial of cultural difference. A translator totally identified with his original, and possessed of the linguistic means to carry it over to like-minded readers, will grant readers immediate and unmediated access to its truth. The impossibility of realising such an aim is immediately apparent, though, in the effort needed to bridge the gap between the language of the original and that of its new readers. Chaucer has a number of ways of expressing this understanding. Most radical is his use of the Gospels, in the prologue to the *Melibee*, to provide a precedent for the divergences of a translated text from its original. The evangelists, he tells us, vary in their presentation of the Passion: 'somme of hem seyn moore, and somme seyn lesse'. In their work, truth is therefore operating at the level not of their individual 'tellyng', where there is a clear 'difference' between them, but of the divine 'sentence' [meaning] they were inspired to utter (*CT* VII.943–52). Chaucer uses the trope to guarantee a translation's identity at the level of 'sentence' with its original, even as he allows for differences to operate in its actual expression. But he also allows the inference to be drawn that truth does not have to be monolithic, monological.

The implications of this relativising of the sacred text were evidently not lost on Chaucer. The *Troilus*, for instance, having worked to collapse the gap between present and past, in the already-noted comment to Book I, openly acknowledges it in the prologue to Book II. Here, writing of his Boccaccian original as if it were written not in Italian but in Latin, and, moreover, as if it were contemporary with the events it is describing, Chaucer confronts head-on the unavoidable consequence of any attempt to make the past available to the present. Lovers may have managed their affairs as well in the past as they do now, but their example needs mediation – or, what is now almost a shibboleth of the subject, 'domestication' (Venuti, 1995) – to make it relevant. The translation of a thousand-year-old past in *Troilus* has to reckon with words which now seem 'wonder nyce and strange' (II.24). Consequently, even though Chaucer reiterates his belief in the translation's ability to match the original on the level of its *sentence* – for, as the proverb has it, all roads lead to Rome (II.36–7) – the emphasis falls squarely not on that *sentence* but on its new *tellyng*. Chaucer's alleging of the Latinity of his source then works both to elevate the translation, and to allow the inference to be drawn that Latin enjoys no absolute status: this in spite of the fact that, as the lingua franca of late medieval Western Europe, Latin was hugely valuable as a tool enabling the learned to speak directly to one another across vernacular divides.

These understandings come still more clearly to the fore in the preface to the *Astrolabe*.[7] Once again the need for a translation truthfully to represent its original is focused by the trope that all roads lead to Rome (*Astr.* 39–40). This time, though, Chaucer's claim to have preserved the truth of his original in his new version is not simply ironic, because this translation is a working tool, designed to help the reader calculate the movements of the stars. It will be of use only if tailored precisely to an actual location: 'the latitude of Oxenforde' (10). The original text, that is, exists only as differently realised in different locations and languages. In this schema, Latin, the point of departure for Chaucer's version, is not a universal language, the property of a clerical élite, but rather the language of a 'folk' (33), presumably of Italy. The analogy with versions of the treatise in other languages – Greek, Arab and Hebrew – clinches the point: Arab and Hebrew identify the people whose native tongues they are. Hence, Latin versions are themselves dependent on existing versions in 'othere dyverse langages' (34). This awareness of Latin as the penultimate step in a chain of linguistic transmission has immense importance for the discussion. It has striking precedent – as analogue, not source – in King Alfred's preface to his translation of the *Cura Pastoralis* of St Gregory (Swanton, 1993).

This explicit relativising of Latin accompanies an opposing impulse to elevate the status of English: 'these trewe conclusions [will suffice] in Englissh as wel as sufficith to . . . Latyn folk in Latyn' (28–33). This assertion of the equality of English with other languages for the expression of complex understandings was not a new development in vernacular writing. In the early fourteenth century (so Turville-Petre, 1988, 1996), it was almost part of a writer's self-definition. But the only clear precedent for it in Chaucer's work comes with the awareness, at the end of the *Troilus*, that English as a language is compromised by its 'diversite . . . in writyng' – probably the absence of a standard written English – so that it compares unfavourably, in this respect, with the uniform Latin language of Chaucer's illustrious Latin predecessors (V.1792–4). The *Astrolabe* has another, equally specific, negative to contend with: its first reader is a 10-year old boy, the writer's own son, 'lyte Lowys' (1). Consequently, the text has to undergo a double transformation, first into English and then into the 'light' and 'naked' English which a 10-year-old can understand. Hence the title given the work in several copies, 'brede and milke for children'. To make sure the child can understand what he is reading, Chaucer must not only simplify his language, eschewing 'curious endityng and hard sentence' (45) in favour of 'rude endityng', 'naked wordes' and 'lighte Englissh' (26, 43, 51), but also repeat himself, so that, having read 'a god sentence' twice (49), the child is more likely to remember it: a 'superfluite of wordes' (43) readily paralleled elsewhere in Chaucer, as we have seen.

These comments are more important than they may at first appear, not least because the *Astrolabe* survives in more copies than any of Chaucer's other works except *The Canterbury Tales*. In particular, as we shall see, the terms Chaucer uses to categorise his translation ('light', 'naked', 'rude'), and his own role as translator ('lewd'), are regularly used, earlier in the century (Turville-Petre, 1996: 35–6), as also by Chaucer's contemporaries, to characterise vernacular translation generally. This overlap is possible because a translation undertaken for a child can function as a metaphor for the whole process of translation: able to speak and read only their mother tongue, the *illiterati* are as children compared with their intellectual betters. Consequently, translation aims to help these metaphoric children to grow up, and to develop a competence in areas of thought to which hitherto they have had no direct access.

In this metaphorical schema, the obvious father of the people is the King, who has the power to unite the people around himself – 'alle that him feith berith and obeieth', as the preface says, 'everich in his degre, the more and the lasse' (57–9). Chaucer may well have been looking across the Channel to the courts of Charles V and VI, in hopes that Richard would follow their drive to shift the centre of European literary gravity northwards from Italy to France: what Lusignan (1989) has called *translatio studii*. Get the King on line, and you make it more likely that your support for the vernacular will not fall foul of the growing ecclesiastical reaction against it. Not just a patron, Richard is to authorise a vernacular (English) court culture for which there has been no sustained precedent in England almost since the time of King Alfred. So, at least, I read the earlier-noted address to Richard in the preface as 'lord of this langage' (56).[8]

Unfortunately, Richard was showing himself signally unable to unite his people around himself. Chaucer's only other direct address to the monarch, in the envoy to the *balade* 'Lak of Stedfastnesse', a poem whose difficulty of dating may witness to the difficulties which dogged Richard's reign almost from its outset, reveals a dispirited awareness that the King is unlikely ever to function as an English Augustus. He must be urged to protect his people ('Lak' 23, 28) and permit nothing that may damage his 'estat . . . in [his] regioun' (25). The implied relationship of king, royal estate, people, and country is in danger of breaking apart; the King himself seems no longer to 'dred God, do law, love trouthe and worthinesse' (27).

In such a situation, the vernacular translator-author may find it simpler, and safer, to assume the mantle of the 'lewd compilator' (*Astr.* 61) who defers to the authority of the ancients ('olde astrologiens', 62). A further sign of this caution is the use of the traditional formula (Tupper, 1917) deprecating 'envie': 'and with this swerd shal I sleen envie' (*Astr.* 64).

The courts of the great are hotbeds of envy, as the prologue to Chaucer's *Legend of Good Women* clearly acknowledges (F 352–60): so the envy to be slain by Chaucer's assumption of the role of compiler is possibly that of contemporaries towards *him*.[9] The figure recalls, however briefly, the dangerous situation in which Biblical translators like St Jerome regularly find themselves.

Trevisa

Trevisa was fellow for a time of the Oxford college, Queen's, which also accommodated Wyclif and the most important of Wyclif's early followers, as well as, later, Ullerston. Consequently, Trevisa was closer to the eye of the storm Wyclif was raising than ever Chaucer was. By the time he came to produce his translation of the *Polychronicon* for the Duke of Berkeley, fortunately, he was well away from the literal epicentre of the debate: like Chaucer, therefore, he gives little sense of the dangerous issue translation was becoming. Nevertheless, the fictional debate that Trevisa creates, in his prologue, between a lord and his clerk, surrogates for his patron and himself, has numerous links with the actual debate(s) of which records have survived. In acknowledgement of the power relations that will sustain the translation, and also, perhaps, of the sense that the issue of translation was still an open question, Trevisa's version of the debate is as playful as a similarly fictionalised debate by Chaucer, in the prologue to the *Legend*.[10]

The lord wins the debate hands down, with much better arguments and much surer control of the minutiae of scholarly debate, notably when he distinguishes the different kinds of need which could justify the production of a translation of a volume of chronicles for lay readers (70–81). And the debate casts Berkeley in a still more favourable light: he doesn't need the translation himself, since he can read Latin – of course, he will be glad of help with the harder bits: who wouldn't? – so he is championing the cause of translation for his Latinless under-lings as an instance of disinterested princely generosity.[11]

Trevisa has another way of creating a positive role model for his noble patron. As part of his argument for translation, he includes a number of precedents, both European and home-grown, which feature prominent royal patrons: Charles the Bald, who commissioned John Scotus Erigena to translate pseudo-Dionysius from Greek to Latin; most importantly, King Alfred, who commissioned the Bishop of Worcester to 'translate Seint Gregore hys bokes Dialoges out of Latyn ynto Saxon' (139–40). Berkeley is in the very best company, therefore, in patronising his dim-witted clerk.

At least from the time of the *Life of King Alfred* written by his companion Asser – or, if we accept arguments to the contrary by Smyth (1995), pseudo-Asser – King Alfred enjoyed a status second only to the legendary Arthur as the founding father of Englishness. In the century after the Conquest, conquerors and conquered alike, with very different agendas and to rather different ends, were eager to invoke Alfred as legitimating their own work. Thus William of Malmesbury, drawing on Asser's work, made much in his *Gesta Regum Anglorum* (*c.* 1125) of Alfred's literary and translational achievements. (The *Gesta* itself acquired foundational status in the high Middle Ages, and its pronouncements – on language, for example – were regularly recycled.)[12] Later in the century, the Anglo-Norman writer Marie de France claimed to be translating her *Fables* not directly from a Latin text but from a version produced by King Alfred (Crane, 1999: 46); shortly after, works produced in English in the west of the country, where traditions of Anglo-Saxon scholarship survived longest, cited Alfred as the fount of popular wisdom (Stanley, 1960). Higden in his *Polychronicon* added to the myth-making with a new story readily seized on by Trevisa and by later contributors to the debate: Alfred founded the University of Oxford!

Most of these stories do have a basis in historical fact. Alfred was a bold and imaginative leader, who saw the vital importance of a thriving vernacular culture as a tool of popular self-identification and a focus for resistance to the Danish invaders. He commissioned and produced translations of Latin religious classics which were, in his own words, in the preface to his translation of the *Cura Pastoralis*, most necessary for all people – specifically, the sons of free men – to know. Those who invoked his example were seeking its authority for their own practices, or the practices they were hoping to persuade their princely readers to adopt.

Unfortunately, Alfred's royal example cast fewer shadows than his widely acknowledged authority might have suggested. In the late tenth century, royalty (King Edgar) combined with ecclesiastical authority (Dunstan, Archbishop of Canterbury) to produce a major set of monastic reforms, and to generate a thriving religious vernacular culture (Brooke, 1961); but, with the coming of the Normans, what had by then become a native vernacular culture, and became for later English writers one of their own founding myths, was relegated to the margins both literally and metaphorically, its place taken by the culture of the invading Normans. Not until the fourteenth century, when Anglo-Norman culture had entered on a period of steady and irreversible decline, was vernacular English culture able to begin mapping out a territory nationally for itself again.

But, even at the height of their influence, the Normans had not been able or interested to produce a national literary culture to rival Alfred's achievements.[13] We have to wait until the reign of Henry V for a concerted effort to generate a national literary culture in the vernacular (Fisher, 1992). But Henry's vernacular Renaissance was a very different affair to that of Alfred five hundred years previously. It had a deeply conservative colour, derived in part from the unity forged between the usurping Henry IV and the archbishop who had shared his exile in 1397, and it found readiest expression in action against the heretics.

For Trevisa, then, the figure of Alfred functions as idealised patron and translator. As translator, Alfred takes his place in the prologue alongside other translators, home-grown and European. The latter are represented principally by translators of the Bible: Trevisa notes five translations of the Old Testament into Greek, and one into Latin by St Jerome. He also notes the Bible's long translation history: from Hebrew into Greek, from Greek into Latin, and from Latin into French.

Trevisa also notes translations into Latin of Aristotle's works of 'logyk and of philosofy' (129). The most important such translations in the Middle Ages were undertaken in the early thirteenth century by possibly the greatest medieval English translator, Robert Grosseteste, Bishop of Lincoln, and Trevisa may well have had Grosseteste in mind at this point. Wyclif and his followers, as we shall see, adopted Grosseteste enthusiastically as role model. Like Trevisa, they encountered Grosseteste most immediately in Higden's *Polychronicon* VII.36 (Southern, 1992: 20 n. 27). Granted, they met him there as a commentator rather than as a translator, but, as modern studies regularly note, the line between translation and commentary cannot be easily drawn and was not clearly observed in medieval theory or practice.

Other home-grown translators, whom Trevisa also probably learned about from Higden (*Polychronicon* V.19), include Bede, who translated the Gospel of St John into English (142–4), and the herdsman 'Cedmon of Whitby' – another founding father of Englishness for nineteenth-century scholarship – who 'made wonder poesyes an Englysch nyȝ out of al þe storyes of holy wryt' (140–2). Trevisa knows even about an anonymous Apocalypse in French and Latin painted on the walls and ceiling of the chapel of Berkeley castle (144–6: French was still clearly a part of aristocratic identity, which may help to contextualise comments about the demise of French as a learned language by Trevisa and other contributors to the debate.)

Another figure proves equally important for Trevisa's argument, as for those who follow him in the debate: preaching in the vernacular.[14] The

Fourth Lateran Council in 1215 had demanded a minimum level of religious knowledge on the part of the laity. Throughout the thirteenth and fourteenth centuries bishops and archbishops, Grosseteste included, had legislated accordingly. Preaching in the vernacular played a vitally important part in the realisation of this aim. But if 'such Englysch prechyng is verrey Englysch translacion, and such Englysch prechyng ys good and neodful', then surely, *ipso facto*, 'Englysch translacion ys good and neodful' (151–3).

This generous understanding of the subject has a number of important ramifications. First, it presents translation not simply in terms of literary culture, like Chaucer, but rather as part of everyday communication. Hence the prologue's opening remarks emphasise not written but spoken languages, and identify the translator with the ancestor of the modern interpreter: 'bytwene strange men of þe whoche noþer vnderstondeþ oþeres speche, such a man may be þe mene and telle eyþer what þoþer wol mene' (18–20). In so emphasising speech and dialogue as the condition of translation, Trevisa is also emphasising the provisionality of translation. Consequently, unlike Chaucer, he is relaxed about the possibility of error in a translation and the existence of multiple versions of a text: 'no synfol man ... makeþ so good a translacyon þat he ne myȝte make a betre' (158–60). Any fault lies not in the inevitable provisionality of any attempts translators make – the *trespas* against which St Jerome had warned – but in a failure to make the attempt: 'what haþ Englysch trespassed, þat hyt myȝt noȝt be translated into Englysch?' (134–5).

This emphasis on speech as both instance and metaphor of translation yields a further striking metaphor, of the deaf mute who, because he has been unable to hear others speaking, cannot learn to speak himself: 'alway deef ys alwey dombe' (6). Translation, that is, aims to give speech to the dumb man. Like Chaucer's implied metaphor of the child who will remain ignorant without instruction, this metaphor addresses the need of readers for direct access to the information they must have if they are to become fully participating members of literate society.

A final point. Trevisa is very positive about the role of Latin as the lingua franca of medieval Europe. In the aftermath of Babel, that cardinal trope of translation theory (cf. Steiner, 1975; Derrida, 1980), which Trevisa himself invokes at the outset, Latin serves artificially to unite Europe linguistically. Hence Trevisa does not see a need to make Latin's cultural superiority the matter for ironic asides, like Chaucer; nor does he tackle head-on the claims of its defenders to its absolute and unmediated status, as the Wycliffites will do.

Trevisa's achievements are hugely impressive. At the same time, they are limited. His project to translate a popular world history was never likely to prove as contentious as the drive to translate the Bible. The contrast – to jump back several centuries – with King Alfred's own translated work for the sons of the freeborn, which included not only the *Consolatio Philosophiae* of Boethius but also, as Trevisa noted, the translation of a large portion of the Psalter, is instructive. If Alfred shares with both Chaucer and Trevisa his radical understanding that, in a translation, 'ælc mon sceal be his andgites mæðe . . . sprecan þæt he sprecð' [each man must speak what he speaks according to the measure of his understanding] (Stanley, 1988: 362), he enjoyed an advantage as monarch denied to them, of being able to set the clerical agenda. And the very real threat to the kingdom from without, in his time, a very different affair from the perceived threat from within, at the end of the fourteenth century, may go some way to explaining the greater freedoms Alfred enjoyed.

The Prologue to the Wycliffite Bible, Chapter 15

With the so-called General Prologue to the Wycliffite Bible, particularly the frequently anthologised Chapter 15 of that Prologue, we come much closer to the eye of the storm.[15] The Prologue has very close links with the arguments of Chaucer and Trevisa. For example, it echoes Chaucer's distinction between the single truth of a translated 'sentence' and the variations in its 'tellyng', with the added important point that if a text is 'englissh[ed] aftir þe word' its 'tellyng' may be so 'derk' as to obscure its truth (55–6): hence the need for a translation which will be as 'trewe and opin' (68) as its original on the level of 'sentence', and remain close to the original on the level of its 'lettre'. And the Prologue shares Trevisa's acceptance of multiple translations of the same text, since, in the words of Grosseteste, 'where oon seide derkli, oon eiþer [*tr.* or] mo seiden openli' (156–7): by implication, a reader should be able to compare versions so as to get closer to the truth of the original. Yet here, too, there is a subtle shift in emphasis, which we might see as taking the battle more directly to the enemy. Where Trevisa saw multiple versions as a way of counteracting error in an individual text, the Wycliffite Prologue sees them collectively as a way of guaranteeing truth.

Along with Grosseteste, the Prologue shares several other role models with Trevisa: notably, Sts Jerome and Augustine, and Bede and King Alfred, the latter this time only as the translator of the Psalter. The Prologue goes further than Trevisa in acknowledging the existence of versions of the Bible in contemporary European vernaculars, Bohemian, French and Breton (165–6). Clearly, the specific project of a Bible translation required the gathering of as much Biblical precedent as possible.

Only one non-Biblical precedent is offered: the translation of 'bokis of deuocioun and of exposicioun' (166–7). Given the importance this phrase will acquire in later contributions to the debate as a possible marker of heresy, this widening of the terms of the debate may show how opposition was increasing to the project. Inevitably, both parties found themselves fighting each other's fires on an ever-widening front.

The one modern authority cited is the earlier-noted Grosseteste. There is no doubting Grosseteste's importance as a role model for the Wycliffites (Southern, 1992: 308). Grosseteste produced translations which his contemporary, the Franciscan Roger Bacon, himself no mean student of Greek and Hebrew, commended as roundly as he criticised existing Latin translations of Greek texts (Deanesly, 1920), and Grosseteste insisted on 'taking the Gospel to ordinary people' (Southern, 1992: 309). Wycliffites could also readily identify with him as an uncanonised saint who fell foul of the highest ecclesiastical authority. Lastly, though he does not name him as an authority, the author of the Wycliffite Prologue may also have had Bacon in his sights, when he insists, twice, on the need for a translator to be well versed in source and target languages, as well as in 'þe sentence of holi scripture' (86–7, 88). Bacon had criticised existing translations of Greek scientific texts on very similar grounds.[16]

The Prologue courts comparison with Grosseteste in part because, like much of Grosseteste's own work, the Bible translation was a collaborative venture. 'Diuerse felawis and helperis' (27) worked as textual critics of the Latin original to produce, as the base for their translation, a text 'sumdel trewe' (29); then studied the corrected Bible with its glosses to determine how best to translate its details; then 'counseile[d] wiþ elde gramariens and elde dyuynis of harde wordis and harde sentencis, hou þo miȝten best be ... translatid' (32–3); lastly, assisted with overseeing the completed translation and correcting it as necessary. This very considerable achievement allows the author of the Prologue to take the argument for translation a major step further than either Chaucer or Trevisa had done. Far from conceding error in the translation as a disqualification, the writer asserts, like Wyclif before him, that most copies of the Latin Bible 'han more nede to be corrected ... þan haþ þe English bible late translatid' (74–5).[17] His intention has been to produce a version whose 'sentence' is 'as trewe and opin in English as it is in Latyn, eiþer more trewe and more open' (68–9). Those versed in both English and Latin, and in the 'sentence of holi writ and English togidere' (68), will be able to confirm his success, or, if he has failed, to produce a version 'as trewe and as opin, ʒea and opinliere' (88–9) than the Latin, which is often 'derk' to literal and other senses. Such a version is, in principle, much 'sharplier and groundlier' than any of the productions of 'manie late [*tr.* recent] postillatouris eiþir expositouris' (93–4); it will even be 'openliere and shortliere' than the 'þe elde greete doctouris' (92–3), like Augustine and Jerome, for whom the Wycliffites had a great regard. The terms in which these criticisms are made are consistent with others in the Prologue, and almost without parallel in Chaucer or Trevisa.

The voices raised in opposition to the project are scarcely better informed than was the clerk in Trevisa's preface: some of the sillier arguments given them match those Trevisa gave his clerk. There is an interesting difference in tone, though, between the two. As we saw, both Chaucer and Trevisa played games with the opposition; the author of the Wycliffite Prologue eventually loses patience with them, labels them 'worldli clerkis' (131), and finds their 'lewid' objections worthy only of 'stilnesse eiþir curteys scorn' (134). This difference in tone may have more than one cause, but pretty certainly it points to the increasing dangers of arguing for translation in the mid-1390s. Those who seek to have a copy of the Bible may have to pay for it with their lives (23).

In such a context, not even the 'falsnesse and necligence of clerkis' (169) can explain sufficiently the absence hitherto of a Bible translation. Deeper causes are to be sought, in a penalty God may have imposed on the entire people for their 'olde synnes' (170). Here we may have another version of Trevisa's playful view of the 'trespas' of the English language or people, which previously prevented the undertaking of translation. If so, the colouring is much darker. The passage carries something of the doom-laden tone of the twelfth-century historian Henry of Huntingdon (Patterson, 1991: 87–8), who popularised the idea of English history as a series of plagues – invasions by Romans, Picts and Scots, Angles, Danes and Normans – which God allowed because of the sins of the people. Higden, followed in this respect by his translators Trevisa and Bokenham, saw the corruption of a previously pure language which resulted from these invasions as matter for regret (Taylor, 1966: 61–2; Sisam, 1921; Burnley, 1992). By contrast, Trevisa, in his Prologue, and the author of the Wycliffite prologue, both seem to have seen the invasions as, if dangerous, an opportunity to be welcomed. At all events, if they are echoing Henry of Huntingdon's narrowly religious view of history, they also seem to see translation as in some ways undoing the effects of a previous curse: not a curse, as opponents would try to paint it, but a blessing.

In one important respect, the author of the Prologue makes common cause with Chaucer and, so far as anything can be argued from his silence on the point, against Trevisa: that is, in his awareness of England as a notional geographical and linguistic entity with its own distinctive religious traditions in which all have a stake. Hence the insistence in the Prologue both on 'English' as verb and adjective, and on the first person plural pronoun. With one exception ('oure lewid men', 18), the writer uses the latter regularly as a mark of shared identity ('we English men', 15, 'oure peple', 143; 'oure rewme', 25). Turville-Petre (1996) has shown how, earlier in the century, the first person plural possessive pronoun, when applied to the nation, marked out for writer and readers a linguistic identity which was emphatically not French. Here I think something very similar is happening: only, this time, the 'symple creature' who has translated the Bible for his 'lewid' and 'symple' compatriots identifies himself with them, rather like Chaucer with his infant reader in the *Astrolabe*, to assert an identity against that which 'worldli clerkis', the 'late post-illatouris eiþir expositours' of Holy Writ, have claimed for themselves on the basis of their needlessly sophisticated Latin learning.

As with all arguments, of course, the writer sometimes paints himself into a rhetorical corner. To invoke the authority of the Fathers, for example, even as he declares his own version superior to theirs, is to leave a question mark, however delicate, over his self-presentation as a 'symple creature' and an idiot (131). Again, the writer properly challenges the opposition's claim that the worth of a translation depends on the moral state of a translator, since, as Jerome witnesses, even the translations of 'open eretikis' (112) have been approved by the Church. Since holiness, like authority in translation, depends on a person's proximity to and distance from the source of holiness, the translators of the Septuagint, miraculous though their translation was, are not as holy as the Old Testament figures whose words they translated.[18] Followed to its logical conclusion, as it is by the opponents of Bible translation, this wonderfully preposterous argument would result in the silencing of modern translators altogether, and the writer is forced to argue for a greater than usual holiness on the part of the present translators of the Bible as a guarantee of their project: they need 'to lyue a clene lif and be ful deuout in preiers and haue not [their] wit occupied aboute worldly þingis' (184–5) so that the Holy Spirit will preserve them from error. Such argumentation leaves unchallenged the whole premise of the argument. If the writer's understanding of the temporal dimension of translation is more nuanced than that of his opponents, then, it is still (if differently) compromised.

Or again: the writer shows himself well aware of the translated status of the Vulgate Bible, and shares with Trevisa the sense that Latin is merely one link in a linguistic chain reaching back to the Hebrew. Indeed, at the time when St Jerome was producing his translations, Latin was merely a language like English, 'comoun' to those who lived in the country around Rome, and the ancestor of the 'Latyn corript' which the commoners speak at present in Italy; just so, 'Saxon' was the 'comoun langage' of England in the time of Bede (138–45). Yet, while providing marginal glosses where the Hebrew originals differ from the readings of the Latin (75–8), the writer accords authority *de facto* to Latin as the language of the version from which he is translating, so that his practice inevitably undercuts his theorising. We can see readily enough why he did so: the ubiquity of the Vulgate in the liturgy, and more particularly the Church's use of a translation of the Psalter 'of oþere men þat hadden myche lasse kunnyng and holynesse þan Ierom' (81–2), mean that, even were it feasible, it would not be realistic to imagine starting afresh with an entirely new version.

The Oxford Debate: The Opposition

Thus far we have using the term 'debate' broadly. Much of the material that remains to be considered originated in the context of an actual debate in Oxford, in that same dangerous year, 1401, that saw the passing of the statute *De heretico comburendo* and the burning of the Lollard priest Sawtre. There is therefore nothing narrowly academic about the debate. At least two voices were raised in opposition, the Franciscan William Butler and the Dominican Thomas Palmer; the major speaker on the other side was Ullerston.[19]

Butler argues on two main fronts, linguistic and social. The latter arguments are more fully developed. For the laity, the best way to know God is through meditation and prayer (406), through the church's administration of the sacraments (407), through a pure heart (409) and through faith (411): above all, through knowing only those things necessary for salvation (412). It is for the *perfecti* to scrutinise the divine mysteries (411) and to know what their subordinates need (410). Using very familiar bodily metaphors, depending ultimately on 1 Cor. 12, Butler finds it absurd for other parts to presume to do the seeing which is the job of the eye; just so, it is for the belly to provide the other parts of the body with what nourishment they need once it has digested the food (416).

This understanding of a rigidly hierarchical view of social relations yields a very different image of the monarchy to the one Chaucer was advancing. Characterised as 'christianissimus' [most Christian], the monarch's function, for Butler, is twofold: to support religious authority

and prohibit public debate about the Christian faith (414); and to drama-
tise in his own person the ideal response of reverence to the preachers
of the Church.

Biblical metaphors favoured by Butler reinforce this general understanding, and focus especially (417) on the familiar idea of the laity as
ignorant children who cannot digest solid food (1 Cor. 3.2). Other figures
include the Ethiopian eunuch converted by Phillip's preaching in Acts 8
(417), whose bodily lack functions as spiritual metaphor and parallels
that, earlier noted, of deafness; and the Jews, newly returned from exile,
and read to out of the Law by the priests (413): the laity need to hear
the Bible rather than to read it for themselves.

Palmer contributes a scholastic *quaestio* on the subject, with 18 arguments in favour of translation followed by an equal number against, the
former then answered, point by point, at the very end. Sandwiched
between these arguments come the main arguments against the proposition, followed by a set of 11 in favour of it, and a further set of 4
arguments against translation.

The opening arguments in favour of translation include many that we
have seen, or will see, elsewhere. Vernacular translation is authorised by
the parallel case of preaching (arts. 1, 8: 418–9) and by the precedent of
Biblical translations in other languages (arts. 5, 11, 14, 16: 419–20), including Anglo-Saxon (Bede, arts. 6: 419). It is a necessity if the age-old equation
of English and barbarian, noted, for example, by Bede, is not to be perpetu-
ated (arts. 1, 5, 11, 16, 17: 418–20). A deaf mute cannot hear the preached
word of God, and therefore needs access to the written word so as to know
how to live properly (arts. 8: 419; cf. Trevisa's use of the same trope).

The closing arguments in favour of translation are less well-organised,
but they depend, in the main, on the fact that Christ himself taught most
secret and difficult truths to his followers. If these utterances were public
property, leading the Jews to seek to kill him, it would seem that holy
things were indeed given to the dogs and pearls cast before swine, and
so, by extension, and following the curious logic that informs other
contributions to the debate, it is in order to produce a translation of the
Bible for the laity. In the same way, and yet more strikingly, when he
instituted the Eucharist Christ allowed himself to be eaten even by Judas,
who was shortly to betray him. 'Qui potest, capiat' (432: Matt. 19.12) [let
him take it who can], indeed! One needs to read well against the grain
to find positive role models in these Biblical figures, though other writers
use the same Bible text in support of their arguments, and its general
idea of making what sense you can of a difficult text has a ready parallel,
as earlier noted, in Alfred.

   Palmer's opposing arguments are based mainly on literary and linguistic grounds. As with Butler's comments, they operate a covert hierarchy in favour of spiritual interpretation at the expense of the literal interpretation preferred by the Lollards. Even if trained in grammar and able to read Latin, the laity will not be able to reach the higher levels of spiritual understanding unassisted. How, if they barely understand Latin grammar, should the 'simplices' – a term which possibly alludes to the already-noted Wycliffite self-definition – avoid error in translating from Latin? Palmer can accept the need for a deaf mute to have in writing those things he needs to secure his salvation (436): more than that he will not allow.

   A similar hierarchy operates in favour of Latin and against languages like English which do not have a grammar. Since English does not have what Palmer recognises as inflections, and does have a large number of monosyllabic words like 'ston, bon . . .', a translator would need to use circumlocutions to express some of the complex meanings found in Latin (in its grammatical inflections, presumably: 427).[20] Translations from Latin can be allowed only when the target language can replicate Latin in respect of its grammatical relations: translation into a 'linguam . . . barbaricam' [barbaric tongue] like English is therefore ruled out.[21] Or, rather, such translation is to be undertaken by the clergy only orally, and only of that material absolutely necessary for the salvation of the laity.

   There are, it is true, differences between Palmer and Butler. Palmer reacts differently to the unstable 'now' in which translation operates. Butler allows for translation only in a past when the paucity of believers seemed to justify the production of written texts in the vernacular. Palmer can see an unspecified time when things until now hidden will be revealed: the ban operates merely 'quoad tempus' [for the time]. On the other hand, this 'tempus' may last until the Second Coming and the Last Days, which will do away with the need for all translation. So the difference is really only one of emphasis.

   Ullerston's contribution to the debate reports fully a set of arguments against translation before providing its own arguments in favour. As he reports it, this opposition has opened fire on the same two fronts, linguistic and socio-political, as Butler and Palmer. The linguistic arguments depend upon a distinction between the principal languages, Latin, Greek and Hebrew, and the lesser languages ('minus principales et famosas', fos. 195r[a], 198r[b]), including English. Latin functions as a sort of linguistic gold standard. Like Greek and Hebrew, it is grammatical; that is, it has a grammar which is formally taught. The lesser languages do not have such a grammar, and their thinness ('peniuriam', fo. 196r[a]), exposed by comparison with the richness of the superior language, makes translation all but impossible. Similarly – the speaker is quoting Roger Bacon – an English translator would be forced to make up new things in his translation ('noua fingere', fo. 195r[b], cf. fo. 196r[b]), as a logician would have to do in the absence of equivalent terms for his science in the target language. Modern students of translation (Bassnett, 1991; Lefevere, 1992a/b) have no difficulty accommodating this idea, but conservatives have never seen it as matter of virtue.

And Latin could be used on other grounds, too, as a stick to beat this heretical dog with. Didn't Roger Bacon savage translators whose Latin translations of Greek texts revealed an insufficient knowledge of source and target languages, as well as of the subject matter of those texts (fo. 195r[b])? If translation even into Latin could be criticised, criticism of translation into the lesser languages from Latin must apply with yet greater force. Moreover, translations into Latin from Greek resulted in a general neglect of Greek among Latin readers; wouldn't it follow that translation from Latin into the vernacular would be accompanied by the demise of Latin as the language of European scholarship (fo. 196r[b])?

Further proof is to hand in the decline of French as the medium for teaching Latin grammar to schoolboys, now that English is being used for the purpose (fo. 196r[b].). This observation is traditional, though the speaker's use of it is not. The use of French among *gentil* folk, and its decline as a learned language in England, had been receiving comment since at least the turn of the fourteenth century. Higden had noted the impairment to the English language that resulted in part from the greater social prestige attaching to French, with children of the *gentils* taught to speak French from their cradles, and country bumpkins taking pains to speak French to be better thought of;[22] and with schoolchildren, against the custom of all other nations, forced to abandon their own language and study their Latin grammar in French, a practice first introduced by the Normans after the Conquest. Higden's nationalistic fervour contrasts strikingly with the present speaker's regret at the decline of the learned vernacular. This change, according to Trevisa, started after the Black Death, and was associated with the grammar teaching, first, of John Cornwall, and then a widening circle of teachers (Bland, 1992), so that at the time of Trevisa's writing (1385) 'in al þe gramerscoles of Engelond childern leueþ Frensch and construeþ and lurneþ an Englysch' (Sisam, 1921: 149); similarly, *gentil* folk were no longer teaching their children French. But Trevisa offered a more measured view of the change than Ullerston's opponent. He found both gain and loss in the change. Positively, children learned their grammar much more quickly; negatively, they knew no more French than 'here lift heele' [their left heel].

Apparently, French, even the provincial French spoken in England, could function as a sort of lingua franca: consequently, its demise is, according to Ullerston's opponent, on a par with the anticipated demise of Latin, if ever writing in the vernacular takes hold.

The second ground of objection is the familiar one of hierarchy. Translators of the Bible ought in principle to have a specific mandate to instruct the laity by preaching to them. It would dangerously disturb established order should the simple faithful ('laici ... et simplices') – worse still, the peasantry ('rusticus'); worst of all, women (fo. 195v^b) – perform the task in their stead. It would derogate honour from priests and disadvantage the Mendicants, and would result in disrespect for scholars and teachers (fo.196r$^{a–b}$). Moreover, the vernacular is critically implicated with the growth of heresy: witness the publication of (unspecified) heretical vernacular texts.

The Oxford Debate: Ullerston

Ullerston's contribution, the longest of the set, is also the most important. He begins, appropriately, with definitions of the key terms in the debate.

'Translation', the main such term, can be understood in several ways, all relevant to the discussion. Literally, 'translation' refers to the physical displacement of an object or person, like the children of Israel, exiled to Babylon because of their sins (2 Kgs. 17.6, 23: such translation provides a fascinating reverse image of the conservatives' view of translation as cause of error). Metaphorically, translation includes the adaptation of one language to another, and even the processes of intralingual communication ('per exponere, reuelare, explanare, seu reserare sensum in verbis latentem', fo. 196v^a [expounding, revealing, making plain or unlocking the sense concealed in words]).

Translation thus includes the interpretation for bystanders of the inspired gift of speaking in tongues (1 Cor. 14), and Joseph's power to interpret dreams (Gen. 40–41). These gifts are no part of Ullerston's present brief: rather, he will consider that knowledge ('noticiam') of tongues which a person can gain by his own efforts (fo. 196v^a). In so arguing, Ullerston may be opposing the view that translation can be justified only if divinely inspired; he will adopt the same position, later, to support his case, much as the author of the Wycliffite Prologue did, and, for that matter, much like St Jerome himself (*Pent.* 29–30). A word thus translated into another language may need to be preserved in writing, as others had argued, 'propter lapsum memorie' (fo. 197v^a) [because of a failing of memory]. Another understanding of the term concerns the copying in one language of a text written in another, where the necessary changes do not affect the *sentencia* of the original. Consequently, a text may be read aloud, or preached on, expounded, or written 'in uulgari' (fo. 207r[b]) [in the vernacular]: effectively, it's all one.

Hence, like Trevisa and Palmer's opponent, Ullerston finds in preaching a ready figure for the act of translation. Didn't Grosseteste say that a priest who could not preach could memorise the bare text ('nudum textum') of the Gospel story for the Sunday and preach that to his people (fos. 198v[a], 207r[b])?[23] If it is lawful to preach the bare text to the people, it is also lawful to write it for them. Ullerston has seen written copies of such sermons, and heard that their auditors expressed clear preference for sermons read from a prepared script. It must also be lawful, therefore, to translate the whole Gospel and other parts of Scripture. One of the highest religious authorities in the land did something similar: William Thoresby, Archbishop of York, had his chaplain John Gaytryge in 1357 produce a tract written in the vernacular containing the articles of the faith and other matters 'necessaria ad salutem' (fo. 198v[b]) [necessary for salvation].[24] Admittedly, as we have seen, this limited recourse to the vernacular, itself the product of the Church's drive for a religiously-educated laity, was conceded even by opponents of translation. But they were willing to allow the vernacular only a very limited scope, and then only viva voce. For Ullerston, instruction in the basic elements of the faith was part of a total package of religious instruction which logically required the translation of the whole of Scripture.

Prophecy, as used by St Paul in 1 Cor. 14, further serves to define Ullerston's defence of Bible translation. St Paul is attempting to distinguish the gift of prophecy from that of speaking in tongues. He does so in terms of the superior power of language used to communicate. Those who speak in tongues edify others only insofar as the sounds they make reveal the power of God at work, unmediated, in them: only God knows the meaning of the words they utter. Prophecy, an action undertaken on behalf of the community, mediates the word of God to the community in language it can understand, and is to be preferred.

The Bible provides numerous other precedents. Take, for instance, St John. In the opening words of his gospel, as St Augustine says, St John writes of God not as He is but as best he, John, could: inspired though he was, he could not say all. The impossibility of translation, of which opponents have made so much, did not prevent the evangelist from attempting to 'translate' God into human speech. In so psychologising the human agent of divine revelation, Ullerston makes common cause with Chaucer and, as we shall see, with another of his authorities, Archbishop Fitzralph.

Ullerston also shows first-hand knowledge of other vernacular versions of the Bible. He has learned of a Bible in the Vandal or Slavic tongue used by the Russians; he has seen a copy of the Psalter used by the Armenians. Both churches are in communion with Rome. Neither language is 'grammatical'; Armenian uses a very different script and pronunciation to Greek. Then there was a Fleming called James Merland (cf. Deanesly, 1920: 71–5), who translated the Bible into Flemish. Summoned before the Pope, his translation was examined and approved, and his enemies were confounded: shades of St Jerome, and, as we shall see, of Fitzralph.

Equally important are the home-grown authors of the Anglo-Saxon and later periods. One is Bede. One of two books 'vetustissimo anglico' [in very ancient English] (fo. 198v^b) owned by Ullerston, about meteors and celestial bodies, was produced by Bede or another churchman of the time ('antiquorum patrum') and is well known now to noble readers in a French version (fo. 201v^b). Bede was as venerable as he was saintly (fos. 201v^b, 204r^a, 206v^b), and undertook his translation of the Bible – or just the Gospel of John, according to Higden, whom Ullerston is following at this point – under divine inspiration into the English of his time. Several copies ('nonnulla originalia', fo. 198v^a) survive in monasteries. Bede would not have undertaken his translation had it not been both lawful and expedient. Then there is King Alfred, cited, again from Higden, as author of several translations and commissioning editor of one. Yet another Anglo-Saxon King combines the roles of saint and translator. From Bede's *Historia Ecclesiastica* (III.3), probably by way of the version in the *Polychronicon* (V.xii), Ullerston tells the story of how the saintly King Oswald translated Bishop Aidan's Irish into his own Northumbrian dialect for the sake of the people on whose behalf he had invited the Bishop to his kingdom to preach.[25]

Nearer his own time, Ullerston also cites the Psalter of the fourteenth-century Yorkshire mystic Richard Rolle. Rolle's is the only name to appear in the conclusion, in a context that speaks of linguistic skills ('periciam') and divine inspiration ('spiritus dei duct[u]s') as joint guarantors of the lawfulness of the activity of translation (fo. 207v^b). Ullerston shares Rolle's view that a Bible translation can serve as a crib, even an aid to learning Latin.[26] French translations of the Bible have been so used (fo. 204r^b), so it doesn't follow that recourse to the vernacular will inevitably mean the death of the Latin language.

And then there is, from slightly later in the century, Archbishop Fitzralph ('Ardmachanus'). Ullerston cites him extensively, though never going as far as the Wycliffites, who regarded him as a Saint because of his hostility to the Mendicants.[27] From one of Fitzralph's works, the *De Quaestionibus Armenorum*, Ullerston derives the point that the evangelists and apostles, uneducated men and therefore unable to write *grammatice*, wrote in their own vernaculars: Matthew in Hebrew; John and Paul in Greek; Mark in Italian (fo. 203v[b]). This is to take much further Chaucer's earlier-noted distinction between the 'tellyng' and the 'sentence' of the evangelists: not only their content but their very languages were different. The orthodoxy of the *De Quaestionibus* was vindicated when it was brought before the Roman curia for examination and passed the test with flying colours.

We have already noticed Ullerston's use of another Wycliffite 'saint', Grosseteste. Grosseteste's follower Roger Bacon also appears prominently in Ullerston's reply. Bacon had been earlier cited by Ullerston's opponent, but was too important a witness simply to be left to the prosecution. So, where he can, Ullerston invokes his authority, and, where he must, he challenges it. Bacon's claim, for example, that Latin is the same from Apulia and Calabria to the ends of Spain and even to the Channel ('mare Britannicum'), differing only in its local idiom, allows Ullerston to conclude that these local idioms are in fact different languages.

Previous remarks suggest that Ullerston's awareness of the historical and linguistic contexts of translation was significantly greater than that of his opponents. Ullerston also provides more information about historical and linguistic questions than we find in the prefaces of Trevisa and the author of the Wycliffite Prologue, and almost as much literary awareness as we find in the prefaces of Chaucer: he is readier to acknowledge the existence of secular literature than his opponents. That said, he shares with the Wycliffites an awareness of the dangers of bringing children up on a diet of classical literature, which, according to Bacon, will leave their souls darkened and blinded in adult life. It is a much better pastime to read in the Bible than in 'romanciis vanis et frequenter falsis' (fo. 204r[b]) [romances which are vain and frequently false], or in the 'insaniis et fabulis Ouidianis' [in the madnesses of Ovidian stories] in which they will find a multitude of false gods (fo. 205r[b]). Ready as they are to use such material in their sermons, too few modern preachers warn their congregations of its dangers, though they would do better to do so than to argue against Bible translations.[28]

Ullerston similarly reveals a more nuanced view than his opponents of the relation of the past to the present. If, in the past the lawfulness of Bible translations was never in question, anyone wishing in the present to translate the words and the 'locutiones' of his originals cannot simply follow the ways in which his forefathers wrote ('consuetudinem veterum', fo. 197r[b], quoting St Augustine's *De Doctrina Christiana* (II.12)). All languages change over the course of time: witness the difference between the English of our own time and that of the time of Bede (fo. 204r[b]). Latin has changed similarly throughout its history, and suffers from the same penury relative to Greek and Hebrew (fo. 197r[a]) as opponents claim English suffers relative to it. Against Augustine's criticism of pre-Hieronymian translators of the Septuagint for incompetence, Ullerston produces the weightier argument of St Jerome that they should have translated from the Hebrew.

Not only that. The Vulgate is inconsistent in its translational practices: for example, the two versions of the gospel narrative of the widow's mite differ, one (Mark 12.43) leaving the Hebrew word 'Amen' untranslated, the other (Luke 21.3) offering the translation 'vere dico' [I tell you in truth]. Jerome himself, while asserting that his translation has been faithful to the Hebrew ('hebraica veritate', fo. 202r[a]), accepts that one writer might translate a word which another has left untranslated. Bible translations require 'magnam latitudinem' [great latitude] (fo. 197r[a]), and we have to allow for imperfections in 'our translation'.[29] And if there is nothing unchangeable about either the language or the translational choices of the Vulgate, neither can offer a standard against which other translations, other vernaculars, can be measured and found wanting. Latin has generated a crop of heresies to match any currently encountered in England: if the mere presence of heresy justifies banning writing in the vernacular, shouldn't one also ban Latin writings throughout Europe?

Ullerston's view of the social context of translation is also much more positive and flexible than that of his rivals. He sees the relation of clerics and laity as, in principle, collaborative, not confrontational or hierarchical. Use of the vernacular is more productive of mutual understanding. Moreover, a religiously-educated laity would free the Mendicants from their present work to exercise their apostolic function where it would do most good, against the infidel (fo. 205r[b]). A homily of St Gregory tells of a devout layman, unable to read the Scriptures, who bought copies of the sacred text and persuaded the religious to accept his hospitality on the condition that they read to him out of those copies: in due course he learned the Scriptures properly (fo. 207v[a]: this figure was realised in the fifteenth century, in ways that Ullerston might not have welcomed, in the illicit schools and assemblies of the Lollards (Hudson, 1988)).

Unsurprisingly, therefore, Ullerston makes much of the Chaucerian figure of translation as a tool to make intellectual children into adults. An adult's moral status depends critically on his or her education as a child: in a wonderful chain of linked quotations, Ullerston quotes

Boethius, as glossed by Bede, and recycled in this later form by Bacon, to support the teaching of Seneca's work to children because 'libri Senece sunt morales' [the books of Seneca are moral] (fo. 205r^b). If, moreover, as his opponent claims, children are now learning Latin grammar through the medium of their mother tongue, English, rather than through a tongue they have had to learn, French, translation into the vernacular is clearly alive and flourishing in the grammar school. Well aware how his opponents have used the metaphor negatively, to represent the laity as permanently infantile and semi-bestial, Ullerston deftly turns the image on its head, likening his opponents to children playing a game of follow-my-leader, and opposing translation because someone else in their Order or their College, someone of greater authority, has done so. Like children, they speak 'ex ignorancia' whatever they have heard their elders say; like animals, when one grunts, or barks, they all do.[30]

Ullerston's thinking, then, has much in common with the Wycliffites', and he shares many of their criticisms of the established order. For example, country priests understand Latin hardly better than their parishioners (cf. Deanesly, 1920: 161, 172), and would themselves benefit from a vernacular translation of the Bible. Today's clergy are, in fact, as bad relative to those they lead as the scribes and Pharisees of Christ's own time. Admittedly, this particular comparison, which may have come to Ullerston through criticisms of the Mendicants like those made by Fitzralph (Szittya, 1986), is sufficiently fluid to allow Ullerston to use it against the heretics as well, in a passage lifted from Chrysostom (fo. 207r^b); but it has numerous parallels, and the same wide reference, in Wycliffite writing.

That said, Ullerston is unwilling to follow the Wycliffites all the way into heresy. In particular, he accepts his opponent's association of heresy with the production of vernacular texts ('dispersi sunt periculosissimi tractatus per regnum uulgari continentes errores et hereses', fo. 198v^b) [most dangerous vernacular texts have spread through the kingdom containing errors and heresies]. He also sees the proposed ban on Bible translations as a pious, though misguided, attempt to contain a dangerous situation. And he has no intention of allowing translation to disturb, much less dismantle, the existing hierarchical relations of the Church, the 'terminos antiquos quos posuerunt patres nostri' (fo. 202v^b) [the ancient limits set by our fathers]. The administration of the sacraments will remain the sole responsibility of priests and bishops – as will the actual practice of translation and the elucidation of religious complexities ('sensus scripture subtilissimi', fo. 206v^a). Vernacular Bible translations will provide the uneducated with the bare minimum of religious knowledge, 'grosso modo' (fo. 206v^a), which they need for salvation. In effect, therefore, Ullerston hasn't changed the rules of the ecclesiastical game but, by redefining 'necessity' so as to include the whole text of the Bible, has merely widened the goal-mouth.

This point becomes yet clearer if we consider the role envisaged for women in the translation process. Ullerston's opponent had argued that translation would allow every country bumpkin who wished to, and every old woman, to usurp the preacher's office. In opposing to this crude misogyny a more nuanced view of the relation of the sexes, Ullerston finds himself implicated in an unavoidable double-bind. Jerome, he reports, wrote 28 epistles to holy women addressing very difficult questions, which certainly argues for women's intellectual capacities; similarly, his foundationally anti-feminist *Adversus Jovinianum*, from which Ullerston also quotes (fo. 203r[a]), includes a number of positive role models for women. Yet, in a letter to one of these holy women about the right way for her to read the Scriptures, Jerome urged her to approach the Canticles last, when thoroughly familiar with the rest of the Bible: should she begin her studies with the Canticles, she would risk misreading its erotic metaphors literally. Moreover, any preaching to be undertaken by the laity is to be informal and private, when the wife and her children and servants receive instruction from her husband. Wife is to husband as woman to man, as servant to master, as country yokel to gentlefolk, as laity to clergy.

On the other hand, Ullerston is willing, within these strict limits, to read the evidence generously. It might be beneficial to the whole Church, if not its English branch, that the heretics are writing in English: there is less chance that their errors will spread across the Channel to infect the rest of Europe (fo. 204r[a]). In this comment, as in the earlier-noted reference to the 'mare Britannicum', we can see the negative of Ullerston's appeal to national pride as a motive for and defence of translation. This appeal, which Chaucer and the author of the Wycliffite Prologue were also making, is clearly implicit in Ullerston's choice of English role models and theorists. Hence, Ullerston finds it as lawful for the English to have the Scripture in their own tongue as for the French, Germans, Vandals and Armenians, because of the 'paritate libertatis gentis Anglicane cum ceteris nationibus' (fo. 207v[b]) [equality of freedom of the English people with other nations]. Freedom – from alien rule, presumably – is the defining characteristic of a people: a hundred years previously, in 1295, Edward I had accused the French of trying to do away with the English language (Turville-Petre, 1996); Edward III had argued that the French were seeking to do away 'with the English language and occupy England' (Coleman, 1981: 52). That very freedom is both instanced and defended by the production of an up-to-date English translation of the Bible.

The Wycliffite Tract

With this anonymous work, it's difficult not to smell the smoke of the fires that would in 1410–11 burn the first Lollard layman and copies of Wyclif's books.[31] At the same time, the Lollardy is more a matter of inference than of colours nailed to a mast. The Tract lifts sizeable chunks of Ullerston's material and allows them to be read through Lollard lenses, but it does not seriously distort his evidence.

From Ullerston the Tract takes a number of figures in defence of the new translation. English writers so treated include Alfred and Bede: the latter for his defence of translation so that the English should not be regarded as barbarous, for his advocacy of Seneca's works as an element in the instruction of the young, for his account of King Oswald's activities as translator, and for his own translations, surviving copies of which are written in 'so oolde Englische' that hardly anyone can read them.[32] Authors nearer the writer's own time are treated similarly: Grosseteste for his support of the 'nudum textum'; Rolle for his translation of the Psalter and Gaytryge for his of Thoresby's catechism; Fitzralph for his claim that the Gospels were written in the native tongues of the apostles. Merland's Flemish Bible is also lifted from Ullerston, and the Tract owes to Ullerston its generous understanding of the word 'grammatical': 'gramaticaliche is not ellis but þe abite of riȝt spekyng and riȝt pronounsyng and riȝt writynge' (239–41), in any and every language. Lastly, Ullerston provides several of the Tract's Biblical figures: Paul on speaking in tongues in 1 Cor. 14; Moses and Ezra preaching the Law to the people in their own language, in Deut. 31 and Neh. 8 (the 'ffirst [*read* second] boke, 8° cᵒ' of Esdras); Eldad and Medad preaching outside of the Tent of Testimony.[33] These figures, though not distorted by their move to their new home, harmonise very well with other expressions of Lollard interest.

In the case of Moses and Ezra preaching to the people, for instance, the writer declares the message as plain to its first hearers ('apertily', 30) as it is now to those who can read the Bible's account of it (30, cf. 71). Ezra not only preaches to the people so powerfully that all the hearers are moved to tears (34–5, cf. Neh. 8.9); he preaches to them 'in þe stret'. So too with the figure of Eldad and Medad preaching. At an early stage in the journey of the Israelites through the desert to the Promised Land, the Spirit comes upon the seventy whom Moses has brought with him to the Tent of the Testimony, and they are inspired to prophesy. Two elders, Eldad and Medad, not present with the rest, are similarly inspired. A scandalised observer asks Moses to forbid them to prophesy. Moses retorts that he does not have the power to forbid God to inspire whom (and, by implication, where) he will (79–86, cf. Num. 11.25–6).

The Tract also introduces us to a latter-day *illiteratus* who owned a vernacular Bible: a Londoner called Wyring (or Wearing) owned a Bible in 'norþen speche', seemingly 'too houndred ʒeer olde'. This text may have importance for the writer not just because of its age, but also because of its northern origins. Throughout the Middle English period, the speech of northerners received critical comment from southern writers. William of Malmesbury was the first with such criticisms, in 1125, and his views, repeated and developed by Ranulph Higden in the 1340s (Taylor, 1966: 61–2, 137), were translated by Trevisa in the 1380s and Bokenham in the 1440s (Sisam, 1921; Burnley, 1992). Consequently, it is just possible that the writer of the Tract is appealing – if so, sub-liminally – to regional pride as a motive for producing a vernacular translation of the Bible. If the northerners can do it, why can't we?

Contemporary Jewish attitudes to their own Scriptures provide another striking precedent for the project of vernacular Bible translation (221–8) – though, given ambivalent Christian attitudes to Judaism, the strategy may not have been entirely risk-free. The writer tells how he has much 'comyned with þe Jewis' and knows that the text of their Bible, in their own tongue, is available to 'al [the] myʒty men of hem in wat londe þei ben born', both priests and 'lewde men'. Granted, the priests still have the duty of reading it in 'comyne' so as to fulfil their priestly duties and edify the 'poraille' who are too lazy to study it. Granted, too, that reference to 'myʒty men' might suggest a restriction of vernacular Bibles to those on the upper rungs of the social ladder; Arundel's subse-quent ban on unlicensed Bible translations generally operated with greatest force against the 'poraille'. Nevertheless, there is no gainsaying the radical nature of the writer's proposal. It amounts to a re-imagining of the relations between priests and laity. One could almost conceive of a situation in which a religiously-educated laity rendered the clergy obsolete.

This recourse to the example of the Jews is ultimately inspired by St Jerome, who defended his use of Hebrew versions of the Scriptures by urging critics of his translations to consult with Hebrew authorities (267).[34] We have seen Jerome regularly cited as an authority by earlier contributors to the debate. The Tract puts him to new and telling uses, as an embattled translator under attack from the ignorant: further evidence, if any were needed, of the polarisation of opinion that was taking place. Jerome appears in the Tract not just as translator but also as the author of prologues to his translations of the various books of the Vulgate, quotations from which show him attacked by friend and foe alike. This figure, it is true, also informs Jerome's self-presentation in the *De optimo genere interpretandi*, a text which Ullerston had also used. However, if we except a possible parallel at the end of Chaucer's prologue to the *Astrolabe*, the figure is strikingly absent from the other contributions to the debate, though, of course, it appears in the translated Hieronymian prefaces in the Wycliffite Bible. Hence 'many enemyes' (262–3) attack the Saint for translating the Bible at all, and for introducing errors into the sacred text in his translation: they stir up ill-will to him among 'vnkunnynge men' (264). 'Enueye' (264) fuels their opposition, that same envy which Chaucer's assumption of the role of the 'compilator' in the *Astrolabe* was designed to lay to rest.[35] But Jerome proposes, like the companions of Ulysses, to 'passe [by] wiþ a deffe eere ... þe dedely songes of þe mermaidens', and he 'scorneþ his enemyes' (270–3). This latter phrase may recall the 'curteys scorn' advocated by the author of the Wycliffite Prologue as a reply to the criticisms of the ignorant, but, if so, it shows yet again how far we have come, and in how short a time, from the 1390s and the urbane ironies of Chaucer and Trevisa.

But it's the last section of all which indicates most clearly the thoroughly radical, and politically innocent/impotent, position adopted by the writer. In addition to the Anglo-Saxon Kings Oswald and Alfred, the author also cites King Richard II and his wife Queen Anne. Both were dead at the time of writing. The reference to Richard functions first as a temporal marker, in pointed contrast to Chaucer's reference to Richard in the preface to the *Astrolabe*. More importantly, and given the widespread early resistance to the reign of the usurping Henry IV, it may witness to a feeling that nothing is to be expected of the current secular authorities. It may therefore represent an attempt to energise opponents of the new reign in support of a translation which has been misrepresented as heretical.

The more important figure, both in her own right and for the context created for her, is that of Richard's first wife Anne. Wyclif had himself drawn attention (Deanesly, 1920: 248) to her possession of the Gospels in Czech and German; so too, according to the author of the Tract, Archbishop Arundel himself. As Richard's Chancellor and Archbishop of York, Arundel had delivered the funeral oration on the Queen, and had remarked that

not-wiþstanding þat sche was an alien borne, sche hadde on Engliche
al þe foure Gospeleris wiþ þe doctoris vpon hem . . . [He] comended
hir in þat sche was so grete a lady, and also an alien, and wolde so
lowliche studiee in so vertuous bokis. (296–301)

The writer cannot have been so naive as to suppose that this reminder
of the Archbishop's words would lead Arundel to rethink his hostility
to the Wycliffites.[36] Rather, the author is wanting to add Queen Anne
as a foreigner (he names her so, twice), and possibly also a woman, to
the list of other marginalised and foreign figures who owned or produced
Bible translations: Flemings and Jews.

But, then, by contrast with the other named figures, Queen Anne was
'so grete a lady' that her possession of vernacular scriptures was without
practical consequence, whatever the writer of the Tract might have hoped
for from it. His citation of her merely serves to confirm the gap between
him and the greats whose favour he needs if the vernacular Bible is to
have any hope of succeeding. To put this another way: in his very determination to invoke figures from the margins who might offer a precedent
for the translation, the writer is tacitly admitting that the battle is lost.
We have come a long way from the humour of Chaucer and Trevisa,
and from the ironies of the Wycliffite Prologue.

If there had been a time when victory was still possible, it might just
have been, according to the author, when a bill was presented to
Parliament, with the backing of the Archbishops of Canterbury and York,
to 'annulle þe Bibel þat tyme translatid into Engliche, and also oþer bokis
of þe Gospel translatid into Engliche' (281–3). When the Lords and
Commons understood the drift of the bill, the chief layman after the
King, the Duke of Gaunt, roundly rejected it, affirming with an oath
that, in his own words,

we wel not be þe refuse of alle men, for siþen oþer naciouns han
Goddis lawe . . . in þer owne modir langage, we wolone [*tr.* will]
haue oure in Engliche wo þat euere it bigrucche [*tr.* whoever
begrudges it]. (285–90)

It is well known that Gaunt, for a time, did lend Wyclif and his followers
his very considerable support, in pursuit of political and personal aims of
his own (McKisack, 1959; McNiven, 1987; Hudson, 1988: 111). Whether
or not this account is historically accurate, it generates a striking figure of
royal support of vernacularity. Trying to pit Church against State in this
way might (just) have made sense in the later years of the reign of Richard
II. It could hardly make sense in the reign of Henry IV – even though, as

late as 1410, the so-called Lollard disendowment bill (cf. Hudson, 1988: 114) shows that Wycliffites still had hopes of getting 'the Kyng and . . . the noble lordes' to side with them, by inviting them to asset-strip the monasteries and divide up the spoils.

The Cambridge Tracts

That is not, of course, the end of the story, but what follows, at least throughout the fifteenth century, functions as a sort of prolonged and sad coda to it. On the *pro* side of the debate, an anonymous Wycliffite produced a series of vernacular tracts in defence of translation, in the already-noted CUL Ii.vi.26.[37] Other copies exist of several items in the set.[38] Comparing these copies with those in Ii.vi.26, Deanesly argued for John Purvey, a major first-generation Wycliffite, as author of the whole set, and for a date between 1382 and 1390 for its composition: which would mean that, far from functioning as a coda to this chapter, the tracts should have appeared as a kind of overture to it. But Hudson has offered a later date, in the 1390s, for the creation of one of the texts used to give this early date, and a still later date, after 1407, for the composition of another.[39] For that matter, there is no compelling reason to suppose that all the items in the manuscript were originally composed in sequence by a single writer.[40] Consequently, it seems safer, and simpler, to refer most of the items in the collection, whatever the origins of the individual items, to the interests of the anonymous compiler, so far as the texts themselves suggest them.

The most striking instance of the reworking of an earlier text, though it yields little information about the date either of its composition or of its copying into the manuscript, is item 11, which uses material from the late fourteenth-century translation of the preface to the thirteenth-century Anglo-Norman *Miroir* of Robert de Gretham. Neither translation nor original has yet been completely edited.[41] Gretham produced his work, principally a translation of the Sunday gospels (71–8), at her request, for a noble lady, Aline (99–100), and presumably as a consequence of the directives of the already-noted Fourth Lateran Council.

Gretham's view of social relations is extremely traditional. He describes the three estates of society, 'guaignurs . . . defendurs,/ . . . lettrez, co sune conseillurs' (257–8; cf. ME 'winners . . . defendours, and asailours' [*var.* conseillours], fo. 2ʳ), and their functions, 'pur pestre tuz de sun labur/ . . . pur tuz defendre/ E . . . pur tuz aprendre' (260–2). Or, in the Middle English version,

God haþ sette þe winners for to fede alle wiþ her trauaile, and
þat ben þe commen puple. þe defendours, þat ben þe kniʒtes þat
schul defenden hem and al þe lond fram iuel. And þe asailours
þat ben men of holi chirche þat schuld techen boþe þat on and þat
oþer . . . (fo. 2ʳ)

It is the knightly caste, the *defendours* of this quotation, for whom Gretham
is undertaking his translation, because their women need to be weaned
from their attachment to the lies and vanities of romance literature
(4–44).[42] Generally, though, the preface operates a simpler distinction,
between clergy and laity, the latter represented by labourers. Here
Gretham is at his most traditional. He shares with Butler, and, closer to
his own time, the *Northern Homilies*, the view that the clergy express
their religious function most directly by learning and teaching others
about God, and the laity theirs by dutiful and moral behaviour.[43] Priests,
like rain-clouds, have the duty of cultivating the laity, the earth, by
watering them with 'bons sermuns'; the latter, as God's vine, will then
bring forth a fruit of 'bones oures' (385–8; ME 'wiþ gode prechinges . . .
frute of gode werkes', fo. 3ʳ). Both estates must obey God's command-
ments. The cleric does this by preaching, the laity by listening to his
preaching and cherishing him in God (415–18).

In this extremely rigid and hierarchical view of social relations, it is
for the preacher, regardless of his moral state, to expound texts to his
hearers which would otherwise be dark to them. Gretham's use of
the cloud figure earlier in the preface reinforces this point. This time
it is not the priest who is the cloud, but the two Laws, of Moses and
the Gospel. These require a partnering exposition: Mosaic law through
Old Testament prophets, the gospels through 'le escrit de cristiens' (244),
a phrase which seems to claim for the latter an authority analogous to
that of divinely-inspired Old Testament prophecies. Gretham's self-
presentation is more modest than this phrase might suggest. Returning
to an image with which he started, he declares that he can barely pare
the fruit of Scripture to expose the sweet flesh. Nevertheless, he does
better to share the little talent God has given him and not to conceal it:
to speak truth 'par rustie' than to mislead 'par curteisie' (111–2; cf. ME
'better is for to sei þe soþe boustouslich [*tr.* roughly] þan for to say fals
þurtʒh queyntise', fo. 1ᵛ).

But these idealised relations of clerical writer/speaker and lay
reader/listener are breaking down in the face of widespread ignorance
and ill-will. Clergy are often poorly equipped to teach ('de diuine pagine
est lai', 326 [illiterate with respect to the divine page]); those who can

read Latin may use it as a mark of pride (80–6) and find fault with his work (137–50). Hence, the Biblical images used to present the relationship of priests and laity have a much more critical feel to them than those used, say, by Butler and Palmer. Take, for instance, the familiar Pauline image of the estates as members of a single body. Gretham certainly uses this metaphor. As with Butler, he makes the priests the eyes of the body. He cannot, it seems, conceive of a third estate which might wish to use its own eyes to see with:

> Li oil sunt li ordene
> Ki el frunt de honour sunt pose
> Pur guier tute saint iglise
> En amur, bien fait, en iustise,
> E pur sa uie pur guarder
> E bone essample a tuz duner. (345–50)

> Be þe eiȝen is vnderstonden men of ordre þat ben sette in
> Goddes forheued for to gyen and wissen [*tr.* guide and direct]
> al holi cherche þat ben cristen men. He schuld leden hem in
> loue and gode werkes and in riȝtfulnesse and liue hemseluen
> in clennesse, þat oþer mai take ensaumple at hem to do wele.
> (fo. 2ᵛ)

The Biblical figure underlying this image is not, however, that of St Paul, but the much darker figure of Ps. 69.24, in which the Psalmist calls down a curse on his enemies:

> Lur oilz, fet il, seient obscur
> Qu'il ne ueient point de luur,
> E lur dos seient tut dis curuez. (341–3)

> Obscurentur oculi eorum et dorsum eorum semper incurua:
> her eiȝen schul ben blinde þat hij ne schul se nouȝt, and her
> rigge [*tr.* back] be euermore croked. (fo. 2ᵛ)

If the priests are the blind eyes of the body, blinded by 'pudre de mundein deliz' ['pouder of worldlich delices'], the laity, like a bent back, cannot help but follow them, and both must inevitably fall into the ditch of which Christ spoke (338; Matt. 15.14).

Another Bible text cited by Gretham reinforces this general point: Lam. 4.4 uses the, by now, familiar image of the small child asking for bread – that is, says Gretham, the preaching of God's word – and finding no one to break it for him, since nowadays priests are generally more devoted to the privileges than to the duties of their calling.[44] The priest's failure to teach them, then, produces an ignorant and wicked laity (303–4), all refusing to know their proper place (389). The earlier metaphor of the dark cloud is here ironically realised in a laity so deeply in cloud that they know neither from books nor from their own innate moral sense how to distinguish good from bad, in desperate need of someone to call down a rain of grace upon them. The whole process comes full circle when God punishes his people for their wickedness by preventing those who would speak the truth in his name from doing so; here too we have striking Biblical precedent, in Ezek. 3.26 and Isa. 5.6 (368ff., fo. 3ʳ). Gretham's recourse to the example of the prophets Ezekiel and Isaiah, and to the darker sayings of Jesus and the Psalmist, may give point to his earlier understanding that the work of expounding the Gospel by preaching is akin to that of Old Testament prophecy.

The laity, then, cannot know how to live right lives if the Scripture is not presented to them, as Gretham is now proposing to do, in a language they can understand (French). The limits of that exercise, though, need stressing. For Gretham the priest remains an active mediating presence: readers are not to have the text without its partnering expositions, and these, according to Gretham, are to be 'sentences de maneres' (212, a phrase which I take to refer to the relatively shallow intellectual waters of moral conduct). Yet, limited though the exercise is, and dangerous though the times are in which it is to be undertaken, the possible rewards more than justify the risks. They are, quite simply, the appropriation for the laity of what had previously been restricted to the cloister. Hence the image of shaking the tree of Scripture by expounding its letter so that it will drop its rich crop of fruit and give the hearer something sweet to taste.

I have lingered over Gretham's preface in part because his work helps to contextualise earlier generalisations about the situation of translation, and particularly translation into Anglo-Norman, during the earlier Middle Ages;[45] but also because it enables us to see more clearly the changed cultural context of translation two centuries later. Notwithstanding his complete orthodoxy, Gretham's criticisms of ecclesiastical abuse, and support for vernacular versions of the Scriptures, seem to have secured a ready readership for his work among the Wycliffites. Duncan is unsure whether, or how far, we should think of the Middle English translator as a Wycliffite (cf. Hudson, 1988: 414–15); he is in no doubt that the translation, written in the 1380s or even later, provides clear evidence of the growing dangers facing the producers of vernacular religious translations. His views apply with equal force to the version of the text in CUL Ii.vi.26 (opening words, 'holy writ haþ þe lyknesse').

I say 'version of the text', but it is truer to see 'Holy writ' as a new text that has lifted material from the Middle English translation and created a new context for it.[46] From Gretham by way of the Middle English translation come the images of the fruit tree and the dark cloud, the account of the three estates with the priests as eyes, and the Bible quotation from Lamentations.[47] This is, clearly, a very selective use of Gretham's material, and it has been subjected to radical expansion, alteration and dislocation in the move to its new home. The images of the fruit tree and the dark cloud, for instance, have been altered so that the processes of exposition which Gretham used them to symbolise are now explicitly processes of interlingual translation: the promised sweetness of the fruit cannot profit a person until 'it be drawn and schaken into his owne langage' (fo. 52^r); the rain that enters a person's soul and makes it bear fruit is expressly identified with 'þe voys of his owne langage'; the dark cloud is now the ignorance that results from having the Scriptures only in 'Latyn in Grew or Frensche to an Englische man' (fo. 52^r).

The writer's acceptance of French as a foreign language, on a par with Latin and Greek, has parallels in item 1 of the manuscript, 'Alle cristine peple'. This identifies French as the language of Frenchmen, on a par with 'Latyn corrupte'; this phrase, previously noted in the Wycliffite Prologue, and here identified with the Italian language (fo. 1^v), links Latin and French as useless for the purposes of communicating with his subjects by the King of England (fo. 5^v). This same understanding surfaces still more plainly in item 7, 'þis trettys': Christ's command to his disciples to preach the gospel to all people cannot be met by preaching 'only in Frensch ne in Latyn but in þat langage þat þe pepel vsed to speke' (fo. 43^r). These different comments echo those of Ullerston's opponent about the demise of French, but from the opposite side of the theoretical divide. They witness to a drive to extend the franchise well beyond what writers like Gretham were prepared to allow, or able to imagine.

'Holy writ' develops Gretham's understandings in other striking ways, too: notably, his account of the three estates. It retains the image of the body to describe the interrelations of the estates, but it replaces Gretham's blind eyes and bent back with a more idealised picture: the priests are still the eyes of the community, but knights, absent from Gretham's picture, are the arms, protecting its other members, and the commons are the feet, supporting the rest of the body. In fact, 'Holy writ' envisages a much greater role for the knight in the process of evangelisation than did Gretham; it owes to the Middle English translation its view that knights should defend the commons 'and al þe lond fram iuel' (fo. 2^r). It goes further still. Knights are to 'defende þe louers of it [God's

law] bi her pouer from alle þe enemyes of trouþe' (fo. 52ʳ.), and to preach
to those who 'contrarie to [*tr.* oppose] cristis lawe boþe worde and werke'.
If no repentance follows, knights, 'bi þe charge þat þei han of God [must]
compelle [MS *reads* compelele] hem wiþ charitabl punyschynge to leue
her wicked lyuynge . . . be þei seculeres or prestis' (fo. 53ʳ). Not without
cause, writes St Paul (Rom. 13.4), they bear a sword (fo. 52ʳ). In so giving
the knight power over the other social orders, 'Holy writ' appears to be
arguing for the creation of a religiously-educated gentry to support the
reformers against the clergy, a project shared with other Wycliffite texts.

The account of the priesthood offered by 'Holy writ' is differently
surprising. It takes over directly almost none of Gretham's criticisms of
them; the already-noted text from Lamentations, in fact, provides the
only clear evidence of such borrowing: the text expresses its criticisms
more temperately, for the most part, than the Middle English translator,
and maybe even than Gretham himself. All which may remind us once
more how difficult it can prove to tell orthodox and heretic apart.

Elsewhere in the Cambridge anthology, the criticisms are more strident:
most notably in the reworking of 'A, dere God', a text which may well
have been produced in the aftermath of Arundel's constitutions. Both versions of this text, in CUL Ii.vi.26 and the Epilogue to the Glossed Gospels,
share a strident and doom-laden tone almost without parallel in the other
contributions to the debate studied here. Both copies present the
Wycliffites as Christ's 'trewe prestis', who have embraced 'wilful pouerte
and greet mekenesse' in order to devote themselves continually to
'studiynge and techyng holy writ' (Deanesly, 1920: 460). Ranged against
them in an unholy coalition, and blind to the truth, are 'sum prestis' and
'cristen kyngis and lordis'. The priests 'constreynen cristen men for to
byleue to her lawis, statutis and customes by peynes of dampnacioun,
as they feynen'; they join with secular authority to impose 'bodily peynes'
of cursing and imprisonment. Motivated by 'pride and couetise', priests
'charge more the puple in cost than Crist and his apostlis ordeynden', and
buy and sell ecclesiastical office at the expense of the simple faithful. Their
'newe statutis', sealed with 'deed leed [*tr.* lead] or rotun wex' (461), are
the antithesis of God's word (461).

Clearly, 'A, dere God' is addressing an actual situation, one in which
the monarch and his nobles can no longer be looked to as possible
sources of patronage and protection, and where 'newe statutis' go hand
in hand with the excommunication and imprisoning of the Wycliffites.
It is strictly possible that this coalition of Church and State refers, as
Deanesly thought, to a time in the reign of Richard II;[48] it seems likely,
though, that the version of this text in CUL Ii.vi.26 was produced *after*

the reign of Richard II. The version in CUL turns the priests, three out of the four times when they appear in this short text, into 'prelates [*sc.* bishops] and priests'. It makes the threatened penalties significantly fiercer: not simply excommunication and prison, but slander, pursuit, torture and death (fo. 50ʳ). And, to the 'lawes, statutis and customes' – not only sealed with 'deed leed or rotun wex', but also 'coloured with fals ypocrice' (fo. 50ʳ) – by which 'sum prestis' have bound the faithful under pain of damnation, it adds 'custitucions'. This material, especially the reference to the constitutions, makes easiest sense if we suppose it refers to the time after the publication of Arundel's constitutions.⁴⁹

Occasionally other texts in the Cambridge collection address the actual political context of the debate with similar directness. Item 2 (opening words, 'þus preueþ'), for example, addresses the fears of worldly clerics that an English version of the Scriptures would make 'men at debate and sougitis to be rebel aȝens her soueryns' (fo. 24ʳ): the very condition which Gretham (389–90) and his Middle English translator (fo. 3ʳ) had argued would result from *failure* to make the Scriptures available in the vernacular. Arguing similarly, 'Alle cristine peple' writes how, for ignorance of God's law, 'þe lond is in poynt to be vndon', at risk of being 'chaunged from one nacion to anoþir nacion' (fo. 20ʳ).

For the most part, royalty and the nobility receive very favourable comment in the items of the collection: which might suggest that the texts where they are so treated were written while there was still some hope of enlisting royal support for the project, and even before the deposition of Richard II. Item 5 (opening words, 'Anoþer sentence') offers as royal role models King Josiah, who read to the whole people from the book of God's Law (fo. 37ʳ, cf. 2 Kgs. 23), and Nebuchadnezzar and Darius, who, though pagans, wrote to all peoples 'and langagis in alle erþe' witnessing to the 'signis and miraclis' God had done (fo. 37ᵛ, cf. Dan. 3.98–9, 6.25–7 [Vulgate]). 'Alle cristine peple' provides similarly positive models for the monarch as consumer and producer of vernacular texts:

> ȝif þe kynge of Englond sente to cuntrees [*tr.* regions] and cites his patente on Latyn or Frensche, and not to do crie his lawis . . . to þe peple, and it were cried oonly in Latyn or Frensche, and not Englisch, it were no worschip to þe kynge ne warnynge to þe peple. (fos. 5ᵛ–6ʳ)

Just so, as Gretham had noted, a preacher who addressed his congregation in Hebrew, Greek or Latin would be wasting his time (fo. 6ᵛ).

As in the Tract and the earlier-noted disendowment bill, such writing sometimes follows the common Lollard ploy of enlisting the support of secular authority for the writer's cause so as to drive a wedge between Church and State: the author of 'Alle cristine peple', for example, tells how kings, princes, dukes, earls, barons, knights, squires, 'men of lawe and oþer men of value', are usually better 'letterid' than 'þe moost part of men of holy chirche' (fos. 7ᵛ, 8ᵛ), and argues that 'lewed curatis' would benefit as well as the 'lewed peple' by 'bookis in englisch of needful lore' (fo. 3ʳ). As with Ullerston's contribution to the debate, though, this emphasis on the upper classes as potential readers of translations does not imply a more general readership for vernacular writing. The writer of 'Alle cristine peple' offers a modified version of the three estates: those who can read and understand books of Hebrew, Greek and Latin ('good clerkis and wel letterd men'); those who can read 'but litil or noȝt vnderstonde' (i.e. Latin, fo. 8ᵛ) and who need books in their own language, among their number lords and ladies and 'wymen of religion' (fos. 7ᵛ–8ʳ); those who can neither read nor understand. These last, true illiterates, need not expect to receive the benefits of the translator's work at first hand. For them, the book of Creation must suffice (fo. 1ʳ); from them 'hiȝe materis and priuy materis of þe gospel schulden be hid' (fo. 9ᵛ). Hence, when the writer complains that clerical prohibition of Bible translation will, if successful, make the people as ignorant as the clerics themselves are (fo. 13ʳ), it's clear that he is thinking of the 'gentillis': people for whom it is especially appropriate to have God's law written in books (fo. 21ʳ). Like Ullerston, he has moved the goalposts rather than challenged the rules of the clerical game: he is a long way away from accepting any ideas of universal franchise and unmediated access to Scriptures. Other items in the set show a similar reluctance to make a clean break with the religious *status quo*.

Education is clearly the way forward. For the author of 'Alle cristine peple', as for Ullerston, the grammar school provides both precedent, since it has been set up 'be statute of holy chirche', and role model, since children disposed to follow a career in the Church must learn 'what Englische answeriþ to what Latyn' so that they can translate fluently in later life: in the schools students construe Psalter, Gospel and Epistle in English (fo. 6ᵛ). Current practice is not, of course, an unmixed blessing: we should translate from Latin into English and not from 'Englysche into Latyn corrup as men doin þeise dayis', and as they do in Rome, Italy, France, Germany and elsewhere (fo. 13ᵛ). Otherwise we leave the 'lewd', condemned to say their Pater Noster in Latin, more ignorant than a child saying 'bed' and 'hele', since even a starling can be trained to say the Pater Noster and Creed in Latin (fos. 15ᵛ–16ʳ).[50] Or, as the author of 'þis trettys' says,

if a master of skole knoweþ a sotilte to make his children clerkis
and to spede hem in her lernynge, he hidynge his lore from hem
þat ben able þerto is cause of her vnkunnynge. (fo. 42ᵛ)

Conclusion

Against such argumentation, however, the forces of reaction were much
more strongly ranged. In 1410 the Carthusian Nicholas Love produced
a vernacular Gospel harmony, based on the pseudo-Bonaventuran
Meditationes Vitae Christi, which, with Arundel's enthusiastic endorsement, enjoyed a wide circulation. This text reiterated the hierarchical
relations of clergy and laity, for which Butler and Palmer had argued,
by applying to the laity, once again, the metaphor of babies who could
not take solid nourishment but needed to be fed on milk (Hudson, 1988;
Sargent, 1992). Another text, from later in the century, witnesses no less
clearly to the changed religious climate that Arundel's constitutions had
brought about. *The Myroure of Oure Ladye* is a translation made between
1435 and 1457, for the Brigittine nuns of Syon, of their Office. The translator tells how he has had to secure episcopal permission to translate the
Bible verses in the Office, except for verses from the Psalter, which the
sisters can consult, if they wish, in their copies of the Rolle translation.
Like the author of the Wycliffite Tract, he writes in the anxious expec-
tation of provoking adverse criticism: hence, he uses the figure of the
embattled St Jerome as a key role model (Blunt, 1873: 8). That his expressed
anxiety was not a mere rhetorical flourish we can see still more clearly,
at much the same time, in the person of Bishop Reginald Pecock. Since
Arundel's draconian measures had not reduced the Wycliffites to silence
and had proved only partly successful in returning them to the fold,
Pecock supported the use of the vernacular to argue the toss with the
Wycliffites, rather as Ullerston had recommended. But Pecock's support
of the vernacular led only to a charge of heresy against him. He escaped
the flames only by recanting; his books were burned.[51]

Acknowledgements

I am most grateful to Professor Anne Hudson, Mr Tom Duncan and
Dr Nicholas Watson for overseeing a draft of this chapter.

Notes

1. For an edition of the relevant constitutions, see Wilkins, 1737: iii.314–9; for a summary, Hudson, 1988: 82; for modern translations of the principal Constitutions, Deanesly, 1920: 296, Somerset, 1999: 189–90; for recent comment, Watson, 1995 and relevant articles in Scanlon, 1999.
2. For comment on the Blackfriars Council, see Deanesly, 1920, Staley, 1994, Watson, 1995, Wallace, 1999 Index s.v.
3. These will be cited in the body of the text by line number from the edition of the Vulgate by Weber, 1985, using the following abbreviations: _Pent._ (prologue to Genesis), _Jos._ (Joshuah), _Reg._ (Kings), _Ezra_ (Ezra), _Iob_ (Job), _Psalm._, _Psalm. 2_ (prologues to Psalms), _Isai._ (Isaiah). For comment on the use by medieval translators of St Jerome as role model and authority, see Tupper, 1917.
4. For other comment on figures and texts studied in this chapter, and of the general political context, see Deanesly, 1920, Shepherd, 1969, Hargreaves, 1969, Coleman, 1981, Machan, 1984, 1989, Hudson, 1988, Spencer, 1993, Hanna, 1990, 1996, 1999: 499–500, Strohm, 1998, Wogan-Browne _et al._, 1999; for dating of CUL Ii.vi.26, Deanesly, 1920: 271. Other secondary literature is itemised as appropriate in the following notes.
5. For other material not discussed here, see esp. Wogan-Browne _et al._, 1999, in particular the Prologue to _The Testament of Love_ by Thomas Usk (d. 1388), a work whose importance is barely suggested by its survival in a poor sixteenth-century printing (Shoaf, 1998). For a major work not studied by Wogan-Browne _et al._, the huge Wycliffite sermon cycle, see Gradon and Hudson, 1983–96: 4.71–84; for another, an anonymous translation of Suso's _Horologium Sapientiae_, the _Seven Poyntes of Trewe Wisdom_, see Horstmann, 1888.
6. All citation from Chaucer's works is from Benson _et al._, 1988, and reference is given in the body of the text by book or fragment and/or line number, as appropriate (_Canterbury Tales_ are cited as _CT_; the Prologue to the _Legend of Good Women_ is cited in the earlier (F) version.). Olson, 1999 and Brown, 2000 appeared after the present study was written. 'Lak of stedfastnesse' is discussed by Strohm, 1998: 174–5. Chaucer's comments on translation occur throughout his writings, and are consistent enough with each other to be treated, as here, as a single entity. For a more historicised account of Chaucer's work, see, for example, Patterson, 1991.
7. For comment on this text, see Lipson, 1983; for fuller comment on scientific translation in England 1375–1475, see Voigts, 1996.
8. For earlier instances of identification of the King with the English language, see Coleman, 1981: 52.
9. For detailed comment on the dangers of Chaucer's position as a court poet in the 1380s and 1390s, see Patterson, 1991.
10. On Berkeley, see in particular Hanna, 1989, Green, 1980 Index s.v., Nissé, 1999: 285; on Trevisa, Fowler, 1960, Edwards, 1984; on the debate form, esp. between clerical and lay voices, Somerset, 1999. Quotation from Trevisa's prologue, and line numbers in the body of the text, are taken from the edition of Waldron, 1988. For an annotated edition, see Wogan-Browne _et al._, 1999, and comment _id._ 117–8; for editions in modernised spelling, Pollard, 1903,

Robinson, 1997. For Trevisa's translation of the *Polychronicon*, and Higden's 'original', see Babington and Lumby, 1865–86.

11. For comparable defences of translations from French into English for the Earl of Hereford, from Latin into English for the future Henry V, and from Latin into French for Charles V of France, see (respectively) Coleman, 1981, Strohm, 1998: 187, and Green, 1980.

12. For general comment on William of Malmesbury, see Gransden, 1974, Galloway, 1999; for an edition, Stubbs, 1887–9.

13. For fuller comment see Legge, 1963, Gillingham, 1995, Turville-Petre, 1996, and the relevant chapters in Wallace, 1999, esp. Crane.

14. For further comment on the links between preaching and translation, see Johnson, 1989.

15. Quotation from this work, and citation by line number in the body of the text, are from Hudson, 1978. A recent edition, with modernised spelling, is in Robinson, 1997; an edition of material from Chapter 12 of the Prologue is item 1.15 in Wogan-Browne *et al.*, 1999. For recent comment on this and other Bible translations, see Hanna, 1990, Lawton, 1999.

16. For a modern translation of relevant material, see Robinson, 1997. Professor Hudson doubts that Wyclif or his followers knew Bacon's writings (private correspondence); Bacon was, however, cited in Ullerston's contribution to the Oxford debate.

17. For the Wyclif material, see Gradon and Hudson, 1983–96: 4.72 n. 8.

18. St Jerome similarly found the apostles holier than the translators of the Septuagint (*Pent.* 39–40).

19. For the contributions of Butler and Palmer, see Deanesly, 1920, cited by page number alone in the body of the text; that of Ullerston is preserved in Vienna Hofbibliothek MS 4133, fos. 195–207, as yet unedited and cited by folio number in the body of the text (Professor Hudson has kindly supplied me with both a xerox, and an annotated copy of her transcript, of this work, for which I am most grateful). For detailed comment on these works, and on the Wycliffite Tract to be discussed below, see Deanesly, 1920, Hudson, 1975, Hanna, 1990, Watson, 1995; for general comment, Hargreaves, 1969: 391–2.

20. On the need for circumlocution as a compelling argument against translation, see also Deanesly, 1920: 338 and Hudson, 1988: 445, both quoting *The Chastising of God's Children* (dated by Watson, 1995: 862 in the 1390s). For a striking awareness of the value of native monosyllabic utterance (the uninflected English genitive 'Christ', against the inflected Latin 'Christi') as spoken more easily and more sweet in the hearing, see the late twelfth-century *Life* of Ailred of Rievaulx by Walter Daniel (quoted Baswell, 1999: 131). Opposition to circumlocution in the translation of sacred texts may relate to the needs of liturgical performance: on this point see Lawton, 1999: 472.

21. A similar view was expressed by the Carmelite Thomas Netter (Gradon and Hudson, 1983–96: 4.23).

22. 'Bumpkin' is also used interchangeably with 'English' shortly after the post-Conquest period (Gillingham, 1995: 82). On negative associations of English with lower class and/or rural speech, see also Turville-Petre, 1996: 21, 95, 134.

23. On 'nudum textum' as a phrase beloved of the Wycliffites, see Hudson, 1988; for a single example, Deanesly, 1920: 288.
24. On Thoresby's importance as possible instigator of 'one of the first examples of a major vernacular publication project' (Taylor, in Wogan-Browne *et al.*, 1999: 360), see Hughes, 1988, Wogan-Browne *et al.*, 1999.
25. Ullerston gives the source as Book I Chapter 2 of the *Historia*.
26. For Rolle's view, see the Prologue to the Psalter, item 3.8 in Wogan-Browne *et al.*, 1999; for a modern translation, Allen, 1988.
27. For comment on Fitzralph, see Deanesly, 1920 Index s.v., Szittya, 1986; for Wycliffite 'canonisation' of him, Hudson, 1988 Index s.v.; for a single example, in the Wycliffite *Of Clerks Possessioners*, Matthew, 1880: 128.
28. On preachers' fondness for classical stories in their sermons, a point not directly made by Ullerston, see Owst, 1933; on Wycliffite insistence that sermons ought to include material from 'philosofres bookis' only if their content squares with that of the Gospel, CUL Ii.vi.26 (fo. 26^v).
29. I take this phrase ('translacione nostra') to refer to the Vulgate, but it could equally well apply to the Wycliffite Bible versions. For a possible echo of St Jerome, see Robinson, 1997: 27, 29.
30. Envy under the image of a barking dog is Hieronymian: see *Pent.* 4, *Reg.* 76, *Iob* 37, *Psalm.* 2. 25.
31. Quotation from this text, and citation in the body of the text by line number alone, is from Bühler, 1938. For an earlier edition, see Deanesly, 1920; an extract is edited, as item 2.4, in Wogan-Browne *et al.*, 1999 (and see comment id. 119).
32. On the changing uses of this phrase in the Middle English period, see Ellis, *et al.*, 1998: 9.
33. These figures also occur in CUL Ii.vi.26 (fo. 39^v) and in the Wycliffite *Lanterne of Li3t* (Swinburn, 1917: 11).
34. This observation, from *Pent.*, has parallels in *Reg.* 71, *Ezra* 31, *Psalm.* 2. 28.
35. On envy as the mark of Jerome's opponents, see *Pent.* 4, 39, 46, *Jos.* 28, *Ezra* 4, *Psalm.* 15, *Isai.* 17.
36. On the historicity or otherwise of Arundel's sermon as reported, see Hudson 1988: 248, 417.
37. A fuller and more authoritative account of this material will be available when Dr Hunt's edition of the tracts appears in EETS. For modern editions of some of this material see following note.
38. For an edition of item 7 (opening words 'þis tretty[s]'), and for comment on *Pater Noster II*, with which it shares material, see Hudson, 1978; for the offered date, after 1407, Hudson, 1978: 190 (n. to ll. 94–5). Item 10 (opening words, 'A, dere God') is printed from the epilogue to Matthew in the Wycliffite Glossed Gospels (Deanesly, 1920: 456–61; 'A, dere God' is on pp. 460–61), dated by Hudson to the 1390s (1988: 259). Item 1 (opening words, 'All[e] cristine peple') is partially edited as item 2.5 in Wogan-Browne *et al.*, 1999.
39. For these dates, see previous n.
40. Hanna, 1990: 388 so supposes; Professor Hudson finds compelling reasons to suppose they were not so composed (private communication).
41. For recent comment on the preface, to which several of the following remarks are indebted, and for information about editions of parts of the Old French, see Duncan, 1998. Duncan is preparing with Margaret Connolly an edition

of the Middle English translation, which survives in two main versions, and has kindly supplied me with typescripts of the relevant material from MSS Nottingham University Library Mi LM 4 (W2) and Glasgow University Library Hunterian MS 250 (Anglo-Norman original and ME translation respectively): I quote from the first by line number, from the second by folio number.

42. With this critical commonplace, cf. Chaucer's *Nun's Priest's Tale* (*CT* VII.3211–2).

43. According to the *Northern Homilies*, the priest has responsibility for 'rightwis lare', the people for 'rihtwis fare' (Wogan-Browne *et al.*, 1999: 127, also cited by Turville-Petre, 1996).

44. The author of item 1 in CUL Ii.vi.26 (opening words, 'All[e] cristine peple') cites the same Bible verse, and the same interpretation, in a very similar context (fo. 3ᵛ).

45. For fuller comment about the complexities of a trilingual literary culture in England in the later Middle Ages, see Watson's essay (item 4.2) in Wogan-Browne *et al.*, 1999.

46. *Pace* Hudson, 1988: 424 who describes it as the prologue to the Middle English translation, and Spencer, 1993: 276, who appears to take the same view.

47. Also from Gretham are a comparison of Scripture to a flowery meadow, and another Bible verse, 'Date et dabitur vobis' (Luke 6.38).

48. For evidence in support of this view, see Hudson, 1988: 103 n. 265, Gradon and Hudson, 1983–96: 4.176 n. 17 (letter of Richard II to the University of Oxford; criticisms by Wyclif of the King for authorising episcopal activity against Wycliffites); for evidence against it (the sermon of Nicholas Hereford), Hudson, 1988: 70.

49. For similar material in the Wycliffite *The Lanterne of Liʒt* and *Of Prelates*, the former dated 1409–15, see Swinburn, 1917: 17–19, 100, and Matthew, 1880: 89.

50. For a Chaucerian expression of this idea, see *CT* I.642–3 and relevant n. in Benson, 1988; for a Wycliffite expression, *The Lanterne of Liʒt* (Swinburn, 1917: 56). Ullerston applied the parallel figure, of a chattering magpie, to a priest who reads without understanding what he reads (fo. 204rᵃ).

51. On Pecock, see Watson, 1995, Hudson, 1988, Scase, 1994, Wogan-Browne *et al.*, 1999 Index s.v.

Chapter 2
Translating the Subject: Ovid's Metamorphoses in England, 1560-7

LIZ OAKLEY-BROWN

> In its rejection of external aids to devotion, Protestantism alters
> man's relation to the objective visible world ... [and] to an
> authority outside the self ... In its mistrust of the senses it forced
> man to confront ... the subjectivity of all human knowledge ...
> It privileged an inner state of mind – faith – over wilful action.
> (Lewalski, 1986: 297–8)

Subjects of Ovid

In much post-structuralist thinking, the construction of the subject is perceived as being 'produced from within language' and as depending 'upon
both difference (between the self and the other) and accession to the position of a [provisional] "I" within discourse' (Easthope & McGowan,
1992: 68). In this theoretical context, the translator and the translated text,
thoroughly absorbed in issues of signifying systems and difference, are
pivotal in constructing, and deconstructing, the subject.[1] There have been
many discussions about identity, representation, subjectivity and the self in
early modern England, and yet most fail to bring the subject of translation
explicitly into the debate. Even Stephen Greenblatt's *Renaissance Self-
Fashioning*, one of the most widely cited books in this field, fails to pay close
attention to translation and the interpellation of the subject. Greenblatt has
famously stated that 'self-fashioning is always, but not exclusively, in language' (1980: 9); crucially, at the centre of his book, the reader finds that

> [t]here is no translation that is not the same time an interpretation
> ... [M]en went to the stake in the early sixteenth century over the
> rendering of certain Greek and Latin words. (1980: 115)

In this allusion to the executions of men such as William Tyndale and
Etienne Dolet, Greenblatt describes the political impact of translation,

made visible here through his examples of extreme violence perpetrated against translators.[2] Further on, where Greenblatt notes that by analysing Thomas Wyatt's texts 'we glimpse ... the central place of translation' (1980: 145), he allows for the political significance of translation to be realised in less terrifying ways. And yet, the notion that translated texts are culturally and historically significant for the construction of the subject, in Greenblatt and elsewhere, has remained critically neglected.

It follows, then, that any translated text could be explored for its interpellation of the subject. In this essay, I want to argue that English versions of Ovid's *Metamorphoses*, in particular the anonymous *Fable of Ovid Treting of Narcissus* (1560), Thomas Peend's *Pleasant Fable of Hermaphroditus and Salmacis* (1565), and Arthur Golding's *Metamorphosis* [*sic*] (1567), are arenas for complex shifts in the construction of the English subject at this time.[3] From a critical perspective informed by post-structuralist critical practices, English versions of Ovid's myth are as much about issues of language and translation as they are translations. Ovid's *Metamorphoses* and the English translations of the text are emblematic representations of the desire for presence in language, and are thus sites in which the problematic transformation of the subject, through and in history, can be rehearsed. For the *Metamorphoses* contributes to an ongoing debate about the processes of naming and giving meaning to subjects and objects.

Much of Ovid's text points to the arbitrariness of language and the gap between the sign and the signified:

> Without our cultural and personal derivation, our etiology, the sound of the word has no meaning. Given the etiology, the word acquires a kind of ballast and tendency in its drift. (Greene, 1982: 16)

Although words are given stability through the construction of these histories, the very emphasis of that history serves to undermine meaning. Of course, from the title of the *Metamorphoses* it is obvious that the subject of the work is to be transformation, although the precise nature of the transformation is less apparent. Entries under the term 'translation' in the *OED* provide definitions from as early as the fourteenth century; they describe processes applicable to both bodies and language, aspects which are brought to mind at the very outset of Ovid's text. The opening line of the poem in English, 'My mind is bent to tell of bodies changed into new forms' (I,1), alerts the reader to the many myths in the narrative which prominently feature physical changes of one kind or another to the protagonists, such as the stories of Echo and Narcissus, and Salmacis and Hermaphroditus (III,399–510, IV,274–388, X,503–739).[4]

But Ovid does not merely construct a narrative which will catalogue a variety of corporeal transformations. His is also a text thoroughly concerned with the processes, products and politics of signification, and with the ways in which humankind is made a subject through and in language.

Part of the political project of the *Metamorphoses* is to recount the construction of Rome. Ovid's version of Roman history contrasts strikingly with the epic structure of Virgil's *Aeneid*.[5] As Ovid tells the history of the nation state, from its beginnings in the primeval chaos to its apotheosis in the reign of Augustus Caesar, the reader is presented with a narrative which undermines the teleological structure of the earlier epic.[6] Moreover, this is a text which draws attention to the intertextuality of its own construction. Amongst the two hundred and fifty or so myths enclosed within its narrative frame, Ovid's *Metamorphoses* figures translation in its rewriting of other narratives (Galinsky, 1975: 4).

Not surprisingly, the main precedents for Ovid's text are Greek. As Karl Galinsky has noted, Ovid's poem can be likened in form to the collective poems of Hesiod and Homeric epic (1975: 4). In terms of content, the *Metamorphoses* has some similarities with the *Ornithogonia* of the Greek poetess Boio (or the poet Boios), which deals with the transformations of men into birds, and which was translated into Latin by a contemporary of Ovid, Aemilius Macer. Apart from the three attested *Metamorphoses* by later Greek poets, including Parthenius (*c.* 63 BC), the most well-known Greek precedent for Ovid's narrative is the *Heteroiumena* of Nikander of Colophon (*c.* 2 BC). Particularly from the first century BC through to the beginning of the second century AD, the Romans, as Rita Copeland has shown, acknowledged Greek as 'the more illustrious language [such that] translation from Greek into Latin can be described as a vertical movement from greater to lesser prestige' (1991: 11). However, this hierarchical model had been reversed by the time that Ovid's *Metamorphoses* was produced, and the subsequent cultural and textual supremacy of Rome is affirmed by Horace in the *Ars poetica* (*c.* AD 20):

> Our own poets have left no style untried, nor has least honour been earned when they have dared to leave the footsteps of the Greeks and sing of deeds at home, whether they have put native tragedies or native comedies upon the stage. (cited in Copeland, 1991: 29)

This appropriation of Greek texts by the *Metamorphoses*, not surprisingly, is not acknowledged by Ovid. Moreover, if citations of these interlingual translations are absent, so too are those of Ovid's intralingual reworkings of Virgil's *Aeneid* and of Ovid's own *Amores* and *Heroides*.

Quintilian's *Institutio oratoria* noted the *Metamorphoses* as a text that welded together 'subjects of the most diverse nature so as to form a continuous whole'.[7] The comment is apt. Ovid's *Metamorphoses*, as noted earlier, is framed by a linear, translative impetus that will take the reader from the creation of the world out of chaos to the apotheosis of Augustus Caesar. At the outset, in the first Golden Age (I,89ff.), too well known to need quoting here, linguistic difference is not explicitly invoked, but, from the moment in Book I when Lycaon's contempt for the gods is shown, myths appear which are concerned with issues of signification and translation. Mercury and Iris, the messengers of Jupiter and Juno respectively, mediate between the gods and mortals.[8] Seers and augurs show the necessity for the interpretation of signs as either good or bad omens.[9] And, as Leonard Barkan has noted:

> Many of the great figures of Ovid's poem define themselves by their struggle to invent new languages. That is clearest in the case of meta-morphic victims like Acteon or Io, who must labour to use human language fitting their consciousness once their shape has turned beastly (1986: 247)[10]

Whilst Barkan is astute in his initial observation, these two examples are not completely parallel. For Acteon, transformed into a deer by Diana for spying on her as she bathed, 'words fail his desire' and he is torn to pieces by his own hounds (III,230ff.). Io is in a different plight. First ravished by Jupiter, then changed by the god into a white heifer and, eventually, given as a gift to the jealous Juno, who, in turn, gives her to Argus to guard, Io's initial attempts to communicate are thwarted:

> When she strove to stretch out suppliant arms to Argus she had no arms to stretch; and when she attempted to voice her complaints, she only mooed . . . But instead of words, she did tell the sad story of her changed form with letters which she traced in the dust with her hoof. (I, 647–50)

Eventually, as the above quotation shows, Io is more successful in her efforts to communicate her plight to her father, Inachus. Through speech, symbolic gesture, or written text, the transformed figures like Acteon and Io, and others such as Callisto and Ocyrhoë, all illustrate the desire to translate.[11]

In this context of rewriting and translation, one of the most interesting moments of the *Metamorphoses* occurs when the text configures itself in the tale of Minerva and Arachne, which opens Book VI. In her contest with Minerva, Arachne, the low-born Maeonian weaver who has denied the goddess as her teacher, produces a text full of the 'heavenly crimes' (VI,131) of the gods. Several of these incidents – Jove's abduction of Europa and his violations of Danaë, Aegina and Proserpine (II,858, IV,611, VII,474 and V,391 respectively); Neptune's ravishment of Medusa (IV,798) – appear as part of the main narrative frame of the *Metamorphoses* itself. This narrative *mise-en-abîme* is an effective means for exploring the endless play of signification inscribing and circumscribing Ovid's text. The contest between Minerva and Arachne, however, also emphasises the way in which meaning is held in place by ideological forces. Minerva destroys Arachne's text depicting the nefarious aspects of the gods, and transforms the girl into a spider.

The Latin word *lingua* can be translated as both 'tongue' and 'language'.[12] Significantly, the violent cultural and political implications of translation are taken further in the myths which deal with images of the tongue, the border between the body and language, in the central books of the *Metamorphoses*.[13] After slighting the goddess's beauty, Chione is killed by Diana by an arrow which pierces her tongue and causes her to bleed to death (XI,1). Yet more strikingly, in Book V, Emathion, an old man 'who loved justice and revered gods', and who, 'since his years forbade warfare, fought with the tongue' (V,101), is decapitated by Chromis. The final moment of Emathion's life is thrown into relief as the narrative focuses on the head, which 'fell straight on the altar, and there the still half-conscious tongue kept up its execrations' (V,105). There is a similar image of a semi-independent tongue in the episode of the death of Orpheus, dismembered by the scorned Ciconian women. Orpheus' head and lyre, we learn, floated in the stream while 'mournfully the lifeless tongue murmured' (XI,53).

In this connection, one of the most grotesque and violent images of the *Metamorphoses* occurs in Book VI, when Tereus attempts to conceal his rape of Philomela by further mutilation. He cuts out her tongue. Lingering over the physical torture of the woman, the narrative offers the following description:

> he seized her tongue with pincers, as it protested against the outrage, ... struggling to speak, and cut it off with his merciless blade. The mangled root quivers, while the severed tongue lies palpitating on the dark earth, faintly murmuring and, as the severed tail of a mangled snake is wont to writhe, it twitches convulsively, and with its last dying moments it seeks its mistress's feet. (VI,554–60)

Comparison with the deaths of Emathion and Orpheus shows clearly the explicit nature of the violent act perpetrated against Philomela. The severity of Tereus' violation is conveyed through the personification of her tongue which, metonymically, displaces her body. Denied the capacity of speech, Philomela has to translate her mutilation and rape through the woven image delivered to her sister.

Richard Lanham has observed that the *Metamorphoses* is a terrifying world with anger and violence everywhere (1976: 59). As Ovid illustrates the formation of the nation state of Rome, the narrative is punctuated with violent episodes which focus on the individual, identity and language. However, the narrative voice of the *Metamorphoses*, a 'diffuse authorial self' (36), does not offer these episodes as didactic political propaganda; 'the point is not to hierarchise – there are no hierarchies here, and no perspectives either' (59). Rather, the reader is confronted with a series of situations which encourage interpretations regarding the construction of subjects in terms of nation and gender. Importantly, the type of hermeneutic that Ovid's narrative invites is placed within the context of translation and transformation: a context taken up and greatly developed by translators in the early modern period.

In the religious context of Elizabethan England, translation operates in a radical, not to say iconoclastic, environment, and the textual strategies employed by translators perform a major role in the reformation of Christian frames of signification.[14] In June 1559, eight months after her accession, Elizabeth I issued a set of Injunctions to the 'loving subjects' of England for the 'suppression of superstition' and the planting of 'a true religion':

> to the intent that all superstition and hypocrisy crept into men's heart may vanish away, they shall not set faith or extol any images, relics or miracles ... nor allure the people by any enticements, to the pilgrimage of any saint or image, but reproving the same, they shall teach that all goodness, health and grace ought to be asked and looked for only [of] God ... (Bray, 1994: 335, cf. Duffy, 1992: 565)

According to William MacIntyre, the first fourteen years of Elizabethan rule were the most active in terms of the production of translated texts (1965: 88), and many of the translations produced in the early years of the reign witness readily to the religious imperative revealed by the Injunctions. Translators rewrite source texts according to the ideological perspectives of the target audience (Lefevere, 1992b: 12–13), and the overwhelming project of translation, as it is revealed in the printed texts of this time, is to confront particular systems of signification so as to take newly Protestant England out of alignment with Catholic Rome. These versions of Ovid, published, if not in early response to, certainly in tandem with, the Elizabethan aspiration for a 'true religion' (Duffy, 1992: 568), are framed by a Christian ideology attempting to shift the religious perspectives of its subjects.

As the above extract from the Injunctions suggests, in the break with the past, expressed literally in the destruction of Catholic images, the written text takes on a new significance for the Protestant subject. The pre-Reformation subject of papal Rome had been encouraged to know God through a system of ritual observance and symbolic gesture[15]; the aim of the Protestant subject was to know God through reading Scripture. Thus, the Word of God is also subject to the effects of dissolution and reconstruction which characterise the English Reformation.[16] To enforce this point, the Injunctions dictated a particular translative strategy for religious texts, stating that the clergy should 'diligently study' the New Testament both in Latin and English, alongside Erasmus' 'paraphrasis upon the same, conferring one with the other' (Bray, 1994: 337). Importantly, the textual relationship between the Protestant subject and God was assisted by the production of the Bible in the vernacular. Of the several Bible versions produced at about this time, the most popular was the Geneva Bible (1560), with its frame of Calvinist commentary.[17]

In terms of establishing Protestant ideology in Elizabethan England in the 1560s, arguably the most significant writings were those of John Calvin. Their influence was both attested and assisted in 1561 by the publication of Thomas Norton's translation of the *Institutes*, the 'classical statement of Protestant theology' (Fox, 1997: 60).[18] One of the significant transformations for the Protestant subject derives from the Calvinist belief that humankind is naturally and inherently sinful. This sinfulness means that 'a perpetual disorder and excess is apparent in all our actions' (Fox, 1997: 60). Hence Calvin insists that Christians should do 'away . . . with uncontrolled desire' (*Institutes*, III.xix.ix).[19] In this ideological system, humankind is constantly in conflict with evil desires which threaten to take the human subject out of God's control. Calvinist doctrines propose, therefore, that those desires which come from self-love, such as ambition, personal glory and lasciviousness, should be denied by a devotion to God that prizes spiritual interiority above corporeality (Fox, 1997: 62). Given this Calvinist emphasis on scripture rather than external aids to devotion, desire becomes an important textual dynamic between the Protestant subject and God. Significantly, the affects and effects of desire are displaced onto secular texts, for example, English versions of Ovid's *Metamorphoses*, which had been described in terms of *lascivia* at least from the time of Quintilian.[20]

Narcissus

Recalling the enigma of Ovid's exile, Fausto Ghisalberti observes that Ovid's *Metamorphoses* belongs to the period both of the author's greatest fame and of his greatest disgrace – in AD 8 Ovid was banished from Rome by Augustus for an unknown offence, and spent the final years of his life in exile on Tomis – which makes it a text eminently suitable for adaptation to Christian purposes (1946: 16).[21] Although *The Fable of Ovid Treting of Narcissus* was printed in the same year as the Geneva Bible, at first glance this version of Ovid's myth seems to have more in common with England's pre-Reformation past in its accommodation of the pagan author to a Christian context. In the Middle Ages the numerous moralised Ovids, most notably versions of the *Ovide moralisé* (Boer, 1920, 1954), sought to employ Narcissus as an allegory for the sin of pride; a vernacular example of this treatment of the Narcissus figure can be found in John Gower's *Confessio Amantis* (Harbert, 1988: 86). The use of the word 'fable' in the title of the 1560 text similarly suggests the prescriptive purpose behind the text, one fully realised in the extensive 'moral' following the tale. Nevertheless, the prose 'Argument' that introduces the 192 lines of verse is not overtly didactic in its reading of Narcissus:

> The greate dysdayne of Narcyssus, herein Ramusia Straungely venged, for he heated through huntinge by the drynkynge of a well, supposynge to quence hys thurtse espyed therin the shadowe, of hys face, wherewyth he was so ravyshed that havynge no power to leve hys blynde desyre for the attaynyng of an imposebelytye, ther he starved. (sig. A.ii[r])[22]

Indeed, whilst Narcissus' 'greate dysdayne' is acknowledged, the hermeneutic impetus of the text invites the reader to consider more keenly the youth's 'blynde desyre for the attaynyng of an imposebelytye' which led to his demise. It is thus Narcissus' desire to become one with himself, to become a unified subject, which is thrown into relief in the 1560 translation of the text.

From the perspective of a twentieth-century, post-Lacanian, reader, the publication of Ovid's *Metamorphoses* in English is already associated with the construction of subjectivity and the cathexes of desire.[23] The first vernacular narrative from Ovid's text to be published in Elizabethan England was this 1560 myth of Narcissus.[24] Significantly, then, the initial translation and publication of the *Metamorphoses* in English following the accession of Elizabeth I negotiates the construction of the subject in a way that anticipates certain theoretical positions of modern psychoanalysis – think of Freud's 'On Narcissism'; think of Lacan's construction of the subject by way of the famous episode of the 'mirror stage', where the subject enters the realm of language, the symbolic – and that also signals a clear break with the past.[25] Ovid's myth of Narcissus, taken from Book III of the *Metamorphoses*, delineates the transformation of the youth into the flower which bears his name. As the 1560 version says,

> Liriope had a Sonne by Cephicius named Narcissius, whose contynu-
> ance of lyfe Tyricias a prophete, affyrmed to be longe, yf the knowledge
> of hymselfe, procuryd not the contrary. (sig. A.ii[r])

At the outset, the myth of Narcissus, as it is presented in both Ovid and its sixteenth-century English form, is primarily concerned with issues of the self. The translation of the text into English takes up this interrogation of the subject in a period which is attempting to reform the English subject, and the publication of this myth in English, therefore, is cultur-ally and historically significant in the specific way that it provides an arena for the articulation of this change.

That Narcissus represents a subject in the process of transition is witnessed in his delineation as neither boy or man: 'no chylde was seene so fayre, nor young man better shapyd' (12).[26] The opening part of the narrative develops Narcissus' ambivalent position further by stressing his attraction to both genders:

> A nomber bothe of men and maydes, did hym desyre,
> But bewtye bente wyth proude dysdayne, had set hym so on fyre
> That nether those whome youthe in yeares, had made his make
> Nor pleasaunte damsels freshe of heue [*tr.* hue] coulde wyth him
> pleasure take. (13–16)

This is the only time that the verse explicitly moralises on the figure of Narcissus, attributing to him the common sin of pride. As with the 'Argument', the myth draws attention to the unceasing labyrinth of desire: men and women desire Narcissus and Narcissus desires himself. It is, how-ever, his continued denial of his admirers and of the nymph Echo, taking up the first part of the myth, which leads to the strange revenge of Ramusia:

> Thus here they other nymphes, of woodes and waters borne
> Had he dysceaved, and youngmen yeke, a nomber had in skorne,
> At last wyth handes lyfte up, some to the goddes dyd playne
> That so hys hap myght be, to love and not be loved agayne. (70–3)

Ramusia 'sought to graunte this juste request' (75), and the rest of the narrative is taken up with the demise of Narcissus. A type of mirror appears, in the form of a spring 'that stremes like sylver had' (76), which serves to confound the youth as he stoops to take a drink:

Therewyth he rapt, fell streyght in love, wyth shadowe of his
    face . . .
As image made of marble whyte, his countenance dyd apeare . . .
A face wyth skynne as whyte as snowe, well coleryd wyth bloud
All whych he wonders at, and that he lyketh well
Is even him selfe that wonder makes, with small advice to dwell.
    (89, 91, 95–7)

Although the image offered to the reader is realised in a fragmented blazon, to Narcissus this 'other' figure is perceived as a static whole: a statue 'made of marble whyte'. In Lacanian terms, this is the archetypal depiction of the 'mirror stage': the split between the 'I' that looks and the 'I' that is seen. For Narcissus, his reflected image *'appears* to have the unity and control of itself which the perceiving "I" lacks' (Easthope & McGowan, 1992: 68). Unlike Lacan's infant, however, Narcissus is unable to reconcile the split, and his awareness of his own divided subject confuses the 'I' of the text:

When I doe weep I ofte espy, with sines [*tr.* signs] thy
    countenance steares [*tr.* stirs]
By meuing of thy lyppes, and as I ges I lerne
Thou speakest words, the sence wherof, myne eares can not
    deserne. (138–40)

At this stage, Narcissus believes the image to be another whose words he can translate. 'After many frustrations', Julia Kristeva writes, 'Narcissus gathers that he is actually in a world of "signs" . . . The exertion of deciphering leads him to knowledge, to self-knowledge . . .' (1987: 104). That self, however, is trapped in a semiotic daze. As soon as the question of signs is introduced, the youth utters a phrase in which the construction of the subject, an effect of language, is confused: 'Even this I am I see, my proper shape I knowe' (141). Ovid's version of the line 'I am I see' is 'iste ego sum', a phrase which is 'almost untranslatable' (Nuttall, 1988: 143). Nuttall argues that in the Latin

> Ovid brilliantly exploits the character of *iste,* a pronoun with no exact English equivalent. It is 'a demonstrative of the second person' . . ., a mixture of 'that' and 'your'. Here it expresses very directly the frustration of the whole endeavour: it is as if Ovid can no longer say *tu,* 'you', because there is no clear Other to address; at the same time, however, there is certainly an object, of a kind, associated with the apparent Other Person: the image, after all, is manifestly *iste.* But – finally – even that is identical with the observer: *iste ego sum,* 'I am that you'. (1988: 145)

Nuttall uses Miller's translation of 'iste ego sum', 'I am that you', in order to make his argument clear. In the myth this is the point at which the subject position of Narcissus, always unstable, explicitly becomes unfixed before disappearing. The knowledge which Narcissus obtains, the knowledge which ultimately destroys him, is that the self can never be unified. After his disturbing revelation he declares 'Nowe two to one' (151), and, in the following lines, the verse moves from a consideration of the divided self to the unified subject:

> Hys shape that . . . darkened was . . . when he sawe departe
> Nowe whether doste thou go, abyde he cryed faste
> Forsake not hym so cruelly, hys love that on the cast . . .
> And whylest he thus tormentes, he barred [*tr*. bared] all his
>   cheste
> Before the well with stonye fystes, and beate his naked breste
> Wyth a carnacion hue, by strockes thereon dyd leave
> None other wyse then apples whyte, wyth ruddy sydes
>   receave . . . (153–5, 159–62)

At the outset Narcissus perceives his reflection to be Other. Eventually, however, he acknowledges that the image in the pool is of himself and the observation that it is himself which he 'sawe suffred there' comes at the point of his annihilation. Lacan explains that 'this moment in which the mirror-stage comes to an end inaugurates . . . the dialectic that will henceforth link the I to socially elaborated situations' (1977: 5). In some ways, this depiction of the tormented Narcissus aligns Ovid's youth with Lacan's infant, the child without language, who is a mass of uncoordinated limbs. In Lacan, however, as soon as the infant comes to 'recognise' the figure as another self, the entry into language takes place. In contrast, as soon as the sixteenth-century Narcissus declares 'I am that you', as soon as subject and object become entwined in his speech, the 'I' of the text fades to nothing and Narcissus is denied entry into the realm of the symbolic.

When considered in the religious context of sixteenth-century England, moreover, the phrase 'I am that you' in the vernacular translation seems almost an echo of God's Biblical name in Exodus 3.14, 'I am (who I am).' Hence, it would appear that Narcissus is participating in a kind of bold play with religious commonplace. In attempting to appropriate God's name, however, as Adam and Eve attempted to gain equality with God by eating the apple, Narcissus cannot help, any more than they could, but be punished, and so Ovid's youth fades into oblivion. Nevertheless, Narcissus serves to articulate a break with the past. In *Tales of Love*, Julia Kristeva has written that 'the mythical Narcissus' is a modern character much closer to us. He ... turns sight into origin and seeks the other opposite himself, as product of his own sight. He then discovers that the reflection is no other but represents himself ... Deprived of the One, he has no salvation; otherness has opened up within himself ... Is it then by chance that the images of psychological or aesthetic Narcissi accompany the crises of salvation religions ...? (1987: 121)

At the time that the anonymous *Fable of Narcissus* was published, a crisis was indeed occurring in England regarding the nature of the human subject's relation to God, exemplified in the move from the worship of images to the transcendental signified of the text. Calvin had declared in the opening Book of the *Institutes* that knowing God depends on knowing oneself – indeed, the opening words of the *Institutes* state that 'without knowledge of self there is no knowledge of God' – and yet, as Narcissus shows, the attainment of this knowledge is problematic. The mid-sixteenth century witnessed not 'the death of the One God' but the fragmentation of the subject's relation to the One God of medieval Christendom.

The epigraph to this chapter is particularly relevant here: it notes the transformation of the subject that resulted from Protestantism's attempt to shift perceptions of the self from what John King has called an 'externalisation of religious feelings' to a subjectivity which 'demands inner faith predicated upon spiritual understanding' (1982: 16–17). The Christian subject's move from a perception of the self dependent on its relationship to outward religiosity to one reliant on an inward belief, however, is political:

> early modern Englishmen took for granted ... that the subject is a constructed thing, a 'creature'. One was a creature of God; one might be the creature of a prince ... The sixteenth-century subject was not conceived as the locus of interiority but as a thing of radical and functional contingency. The word *subject* (from the Latin *sub*, or 'under,' and *jacere*, 'to throw') was indissolubly predicated in this period upon subjection. (Gregerson, 1993: 1)

Situated in the context of the Protestant Reformation, the myth of Narcissus serves, in part, as a warning against denying one's subjection to God. It is a myth, moreover, in which the complex shift of self-perception for the Christian subject is constructed. The way to God for the Protestant subject is no longer constructed in the ritualised systems of belief which had characterised Catholicism. God, however, is strikingly absent here and the subject of the anonymous translation of Narcissus is trapped in a seemingly irreconcilable conflict between the visible and the invisible, the self and the other. The depiction offered is that of the archetypal subject of desire.

The world of signs that Narcissus is caught in also articulates a translative dilemma. Caught in the disassembling effects and affects of desire, Narcissus precisely matches the anonymous translator of the sixteenth-century text. *The Fable of Narcissus*, rendered into the vernacular in a period of English history which sought to turn the Christian subject away from the outer to the inner, from the visual to the spiritual, well dramatises the confusion of the Protestant subject. Gordon Braden has observed that the text is 'almost literally unreadable' (1978: 49), and it is apparent from the complex syntactical organisation of the English text that the translator's desire to render the myth into the vernacular is fraught with difficulties. Most noticeably, the translator cannot articulate the divided subject in English. Instead of being given the sense of 'iste ego sum' ('I am that you'), the reader is given 'I am I see'. Rather than realising, as Ovid's Latin does, a divided self, the English text attempts to confirm a unified subject position, and stabilise the divided subject of Narcissus. Throughout the narrative, the reader has been informed that Narcissus desires himself: the explicit 'imposebelytye'. At the precise moment of the revelation of Narcissus' fate, however, the impossibility for the translator lies in his inability to express the confusion of the divided self:

> Corrupt by nature, lost in a maze of sin and pleasure, man cannot escape of his own volition but must have faith in a God he cannot see . . . The narcissistic self traps man in a sinful world. (Lewalski, 1986: 293)

The manner of the Protestant hermeneutic, the promise of reaching God, the transcendental signified, through the understanding of the word, means that, inevitably, humankind is trapped in a 'web of error';[27] a cathexis of desire from which there can be no escape.

Hermaphroditus

It is significant that the Narcissus myth was the first episode from the *Metamorphoses* translated in the reign of Elizabeth I. The Ovidian episode articulates the frustration of the subject caught in a translative dilemma, confounded by desire. It is not surprising that the next metamorphic myth to be translated, and to gain an autonomous English 'voice', was that of the hermaphrodite. The collapse of 'I' and 'other' represented by Narcissus has specifically gendered parallels in the figure of the hermaphrodite.[28] If, as Linda Gregerson has suggested, the 'evolution of desire' begins with the 'mirror stage' (1993: 13), it is only to be expected that the myth of the hermaphrodite, a collocation of the Greek deities who represent the concepts of language and desire, Hermes and Aphrodite, should be chosen after that of Narcissus for translation.

This coupling of Narcissus and Hermaphrodite is well attested elsewhere. Pontus de Tyard's *Douze Fables des Fleuves et des Fontaines* (1586), a set of prose descriptions and verse epigrams originally intended as directions for a group of allegorical paintings in the Château d'Anet, positions the 'Huitiesme Fable de la Fontaine Narcisse' next to the 'Neufiesme Fable de Fleuve Salmace', indicating that the two subjects are to be conceived as pictorial pendants (Wind, 1958: 75; Keach, 1977: 266). Emblems incorporating figures both of Narcissus and of Salmacis and Hermaphroditus are juxtaposed in Nicholas Reusner's *Emblemata* (1581) (Keach, 1977: 266). The similarities between these Ovidian narratives can easily be recognised: each has a male pursued by an ardent nymph. As texts produced in a historical moment in which the identity of the English Christian subject is in question, the myths of Narcissus and Hermaphroditus are seemingly bound together by issues of language and desire, identity and negotiations of subject position.

By contrast with the previously-noted translation of the myth of Narcissus, Peend's *The Pleasant Fable of Hermaphroditus and Salmacis . . . With a Morall in English Verse* offers a far more ordered and considered treatment of its subject matter. Peend's text is divided into distinct sections: 74 lines of prefatory verse, 264 lines of fable, 111 lines of moral, 222 lines entitled *A Pleasant Question*, and finally a section which gives an account of the classical figures employed by Peend so that 'the unlearned myght the better understande' (sig. B.viii).[29] Unlike *The Fable of Narcissus*, with its convoluted syntax, Peend's text is rendered into the vernacular far more coherently. One reason for this, as Peend himself explains in his brief dedication to M. Nycholas Sentleger, is that this translation is 'not altogether under the note and figure according to the text' (sig. A.iii). Through linguistic control, by 'verse' and 'pen', the translator intends to control Ovid's narrative:

> Among a thousand storyes whych
> Are worthy to be scande
> In golden verse by skylful pen,
> I take thys same in hande. (62–5)

This text underscores its didactic purpose through its own translation process. In *The Fable of Narcissus*, desire rendered the subject speechless. Here, the need to master desire is shown in the first hundred lines of the text, in the translator's depiction of Hermaphroditus as a body presented as in a blazon and emphasising its own excess:

> For beauty farre excelling all ...
> Hys shape, it dyd so farre exceed ...
> His noble lyms so fayre to syght ...
> That he might seme *Dame Natures* worke
> As far for to excel: ...
> As to hys fayce it was so fayre,
> And bryght wyth bewtyes shyne:
> That it exceld the glysteryng beames
> In Phoebus face devyne. (3, 9, 15, 17–18, 21–4)

This delineation of Hermaphroditus, long before his meeting with Salmacis, indicates the certainty of his demise. The youth's beauty surpasses even that of Narcissus and Adonis (31–5). And the exorbitant image of Hermaphroditus here offered, thoroughly inscribed through and by images of desire, defines him as a subject under threat of dissolution from the very start. In terms of the fear of desire, however, it is the invocation of Acteon, a figure from Book II of the *Metamorphoses*, which proves most interesting.

Rather unusually, Peend emphasises the similarities between the narratives of Acteon and Hermaphroditus. The *locus amoenus* for both metamorphoses is situated by a pool of water, a connection that Peend makes explicit:

> Much lyke unto a well it was,
> Wherto Acteon drew,
> When Diana, and her Nymphes
> Al naked in the same
> He saw, by chaunce as he dyd seke
> Hys lately coursed game. (93–8)

In Ovid, the unfortunate Acteon is transformed into a stag and torn apart by his own hounds for gazing on the naked body of the goddess Diana. As with Narcissus, the effects of desire here have a violent effect upon the male form. Moreover, the speaking subject, as noted earlier, is shown to be in a state of crisis. Acteon's last words are those he *would have uttered* had he been able to, and they express his desire for a voice: 'He longed to shout I am Acteon, look I am your master' (III,230). Loss of mastery is thus displayed as a loss of language.

Significantly, a trace of Acteon's frustrated cries resonates throughout Peend's translation, picking up the issue of translative mastery apparent in the prefatory letter. And the narrative continues with its theme of violence, most obviously in the description of Hermaphroditus blushing as 'red as blood' (140). This description is derived from Ovid's text, but the Latin source favours metaphors of bodily surfaces: 'the boy blushed rosy red . . . Such colour have apples . . . or painted ivory . . .' (IV,331–2). The effects of desire upon the male body are thus defined in terms of a body bloodied as by some violent act. But the embodiment of desire is explicitly placed elsewhere.

According to Patricia Crawford,

> the sixteenth-century Reformation and Counter-Reformation empha-
> sised hierarchy and authority in churches. Christ in might and
> majesty was worshipped rather than the suffering sorrowing Christ.
> This emphasis upon qualities associated with masculinity rather than
> weakness and femininity had implications for gender relations in
> society . . . [W]omen represented a continuing danger after the Fall.
> (1996: 11, 25)

Crawford's words point to an anxiety about woman in sixteenth-century thought which is inscribed throughout Peend's text. This fear of woman has considerable significance for the translation. God's punishment for building the tower of Babel is the biblical event most usually cited – by modern no less than medieval and Renaissance writers – to explain the diversities of human language. As Alexander Leupin has pointed out, however,

> the history of language's impropriety is sketched out in different
> biblical episodes. When first placed in the Garden of Eden, Adam
> spoke properly and so was able to give all the animals their proper
> names (Gen. 2.19). The original sin and the fall from grace are
> the first biblical events to affect the propriety of Adamic language.
> (1989: 9)

Women are a constant reminder of original sin and fall from grace. But women are also a reminder of man's original linguistic mastery and subse-quent fall from linguistic control: a mastery that men are constantly attempting to regain. It is not surprising, then, that in Peend's translation, a text which confidently displays linguistic control at the outset, the bodies of the male figures are shown to be threatened by the effects of desire embodied in the form of woman: a form which threatens the masculine speaking subject.

Peend has already introduced the image of the goddess Diana, a symbol of chastity, in terms which emphasise the lure of the naked body for Acteon. Diana and her nymphs bathe 'al naked' in the pool which Acteon passes 'by chaunce' (96–7). Like Diana, Salmacis is presented as the dangerous enticement of corporeal desire. No simple figure of passive allurement, however, Salmacis is presented in more aggressive terms:

> Whych even as soone as wyth her eies,
> The yonge man fayre she vewes,
> Strayght set on fyre: The smoldrynge heate
> Doth strike unto her harte,
> And thorow persed by the dynte,
> Of cruell Cupydes darte,
> She strayght desyres with him to join,
> Her lust for to fulfyll. (101–8)

Invested with the forces of desire, Salmacis proceeds to tempt Hermaphroditus. James Runsdorf has argued that Peend extensively uses animal imagery to illustrate the predatory nature of Salmacis' sexuality:

> Peend omits Ovid's likening her to a serpent enwrapping an eagle that has carried it aloft (ll. 361–364) . . .; however, to Ovid's crab embracing its victim (ll. 366–367), he adds a mastiff baiting a bear [199], a hawk pursuing a partridge [203], a pike hunting a roach [230]. (1992: 125)

The overwhelming nature of Salmacis' desires is thus conveyed in these images of hunting: on land, in the sea, through the air. Her passions gradually gain momentum with the unfolding of the narrative, moving from a 'smoldrynge heate' (105) to a condition where

> Her heat affection and desyre
> Not able to susteyne,
> The force of this so fervent flames,
> She doth attempt agayne. (149–52)

For the narrative voice of this translation, the power of desire transforms a 'wekyng Nymph' (261) to one who could 'by force . . . kepe . . . that yonge man at baye' (265). And this negative valuation generally informs the term 'woman' despite women's protestations:

> And yet some women saye, that they
> Be innocentes, got wot.
> This nycy Nymphe doth now display
> Whether it be true or not. (254–7)

The existence of purgatory might have been denied by some Reformation writers but, as Peend's translation makes clear, woman is the hell into which man will fall if he succumbs to her enticements:

> We chaunge our nature clean,
> Being made effemynat.
> When we do yeeld to serve our lust,
> We lose our former state. (83–6)

For Peend, Salmacis and her pool signify a voracious *vagina dentata*. As Stephen Orgel has noted:

> the fear of effeminization is a central element in all discussions of what constitutes a 'real man' in the period . . . In the medical literature it was shown that we all start as women, and the culture confirmed this by dressing up all children in skirts until the age of seven. (1989: 11)

Hermaphroditus is a youth, 15 years old: a liminal figure, like Narcissus, he is neither child or man. In the preceding quotation from Peend's translation, it can be clearly observed that Salmacis represents the threat of effeminisation noted by Orgel. Moreover, Salmacis is another reminder of Eve's actions which resulted in the Fall and the loss of man's mastery over language. So commonplace are such misogynist images that it might seem unnecessary for Peend to provide any more textual evidence of the corporeal desires of woman. In the *Morall* which follows the text, however, he continues the diatribe for a hundred lines. And at the end of his translation, his text falls prey to the very excesses it had criticised, with an extensive coda, entitled *A Pleasant Question*, on the 'mad desyres of women' (sig. B.iii). *A Pleasant Question* narrates 22 ill-fated heterosexual love affairs found in the *Metamorphoses*, the *Heroides* and other romance texts in circulation during the early part of the sixteenth century. These tales, prominent among them those of Thisbe and Pyramus, Dido and Aeneas, and Gysmond and Guistardes, are employed in order to illustrate the dangers of sexual desire.[30]

However, the place and nature of desire is more complex than Peend's translation first suggests. At the beginning of his text, Peend suggests that an enigma surrounds the demise of Hermaphroditus:

> Yet seemes it straunge
> One from hym selfe so flyed.
> Some wolde not thynke that any man,
> Myght chaunge hys nature so,
> That from hymselfe by desteny,
> He myght departe or go. (51–6)

The prefatory lines to Peend's version of the Ovidian myth draw attention to the way in which Hermaphroditus' transformation takes place. Although Ovid clearly points to the agency of others, the gods, in the transformation of Hermaphroditus, Peend seeks to place the blame squarely upon the figure of woman. And yet, the introduction of the figure of Cupid near the beginning of the narrative removes agency from the female form. In the very attempt, then, to identify desire with the figure of woman, the text cannot but undermine its own project.

Tensions about the position of desire are thus inscribed in Peend's translation. At the opening of the text, just like Salmacis herself, the translated narrative 'I' gazes lingeringly upon the body of Hermaphroditus. Peend has tried to separate desire from the masculine domain, and yet it is the translator's (very masculine) desire that has provided the impetus for the translation:

> Wherefore the whylst I shall desyre
> Your Maystershyp to take
> This same, in worthe of worthy warke,
> And full accompte to make,
> That want of wyl is not in mee,
> Though power therto do not agree. (sig. A.iiii)

Laurie Silberman comments,

> his [Ovid's] myth suppresses Hermaphroditus' own desire by assigning it arbitrarily to the female. Hermaphroditus' sexual performance is presented as the object of Salmacis' desire rather than as an attribute of his own. (1995: 93)

In the same way, the translator attempts to suppress his own desire by displacing it on to the body of woman. The controlled syntax of the quoted passage suggests that the translator is clearly not in the same divided state as was the translator of the Narcissus myth. At this point, however, it is useful to recall Peend's inclusion of Acteon in his verse. Instead of making a judgement about the desires of woman, Peend's translation seems to implicate himself, a divided masculine subject, torn, like Acteon and Narcissus, by the forces of desire.

Subjects in Translation

Seven years after the publication of *The Fable of Narcissus* and two years after *The Pleasant Fable of Hermaphroditus and Salmacis*, Arthur Golding's complete translation of the *Metamorphoses* was published.[31] The earlier myths are overtly didactic in their moral discourses of self-love and corporeal desire; in the translators' choices of subject matter, their own anxieties about the disintegrating effects of desire can be readily discerned. Golding's translation of the *Metamorphoses* offers, by contrast, a far more subtle text, exploring and employing the agency of desire in an attempt to bear witness to, and to assist in the securing of, a distinctively English Protestant identity.

Even before his translations from the *Metamorphoses* were published, Golding was strongly associated with contemporary Continental reformers. His first publication in 1562 was a translation from the Latin of an anonymous pamphlet *A brief treatise concerning the burnynge of Bucer and Phagius at Cambrydge, in the time of Quene Mary*. The subject matter of Golding's translation, the posthumous 'trial' of the German reformers Martin Bucer and Paul Phagius at Cambridge University in 1555, and the opposition there revealed of 'the fantasticall and tirannous dealynges of the Romische Church' to 'the godly ... regiment of the true Christian Church', delineate a text which is clearly part of a Reformist agenda.[32] As such, *A brief treatise* anticipates the doctrinal thrust of much of Golding's translative output, taken up with translating the texts of Calvin into English. In such a context, it seems hardly surprising that Golding's translation of the *Metamorphoses* would be marked by the express influence of the nascent Calvinist ideologies of the mid-sixteenth century.[33]

And yet there has been a reluctance to associate Golding's translation of Ovid with the religious and political climate of the reign of Elizabeth I. Thomas Nashe seems to be the only sixteenth-century writer to comment on Golding's religious involvements (Golding, 1937: 205). Not till the late nineteenth century do we find the link being made explicitly, and then it was matter of surprise; in 1897, W.J. Courthope found it 'remarkable that the first English translator of the *Metamorphoses* should have been a man strongly imbued with the rising spirit of Puritanism' (1897: 140). On the whole, this response to Golding's *Metamorphoses* has failed to make much mark on critical treatments of the text.

Recent studies of Golding's translation by Gordon Braden and Raphael Lyne, for example, have rightly sought to locate it within a contemporary political context. Nevertheless, both are tentative in their discussions of the religious nature of Golding's translation. Braden, for instance, has written that whilst 'Golding does do some small-time Christianising the poem is not being recast in any detail or rigor as a Christian allegory, but simply being moved to England' (1978: 12–13). He constructs Golding as a translator of Calvin and a Puritan, commenting that

> Golding's connection with Ovid is often considered a matter
> for surprise and something of a puzzle ... ca. 1567 Elizabethan
> society showed only early signs of its later cleavage, and one could
> hold together honourably possibilities that in time would insist on
> a choice (8–9).

Braden, then, is reading Golding's translation as a somewhat arbitrary
elision of the pagan and the Christian: all this despite the fact that the
first two editions of Archbishop Parker's Bible (1568 and 1572) made
use of a series of pictorial initials by Arnold Nicolai originally designed
for an edition of the *Metamorphoses*.[34] Braden gives numerous examples
of the manner in which Golding has domesticated Ovid's text:

> 'sacerdotes' ([*Met.*] VIII.707) are Chapleynes (VIII.889); 'inpietas'
> (iv.4) equals 'heresie' (IV.4); 'Sainct *Minerva*' ('Pallas ... dea,' iv.38)
> appears at IV.47; and Envy's 'murmura parua' (ii.788) becomes the
> 'Divels Paternoster' (II.984). (1978: 12)

Although Braden has emphasised moments in the text which clearly
signal its religious dimension, he does not develop his observations
further.

Lyne does go further: he suggests that the vocabulary employed by
Golding throughout his version of the *Metamorphoses* signifies a text
clearly engaged with mid-sixteenth-century issues. Beginning with the
use of dialect in Golding's translation, and concluding with words
that acquire special resonance in the context of contemporary religious
debate, Lyne concludes that Golding's translation 'displays how the
English language could forge its literary identity, define its own canon,
and assert its cultural independence, in the course of its translation of
Latin texts' (1996: 190).[35] For Lyne, Golding's translation has a 'markedly
Christian look' (190). Even so, he seems, like Braden, surprised that
Golding has a religious dimension to this text at all. This general critical reaction to Golding's Ovid becomes even more remarkable when
the history of the *Metamorphoses* in Christian Europe is considered.
Neither Braden nor Lyne, for instance, fully takes into account the details
of the text's production, its relationship with other translations from
Ovid published in the same decade or even the prefatory material offered
by Golding as an interpretative tool for the translation. That prefatory
material is, however, a very good place to begin.

Details from the dedication of *The Fyrst Fowre Bookes* show that Golding
began to translate Ovid at Cecil House, the home of William Cecil,
governor of the first Privy Council of Elizabeth I.[36] I have noted above

that Calvinism became a, if not the, normative Protestant doctrine for the subjects of Elizabethan England, but Calvinist doctrines were not immediately popular with Elizabeth herself. Calvin's dedication to Elizabeth of his *Commentaries upon Isaiah*, shortly after her accession, was poorly received, as she had blamed him for the printing of John Knox's *First Blast of the Trumpet against the Monstrous Regiment of Women* in Geneva in 1558. Aware of the political situation, Calvin wrote a letter to Cecil in 1559 denying any association with Knox. The question of Cecil's own particular religion has often been debated. Joel Hurstfield has stated, for example, that 'clearly he was not a Catholic; but equally clearly . . . he was not a Puritan' (1973: 81). Cecil's own ambiguous religious belief well illustrates the problems faced by authority at this time in trying to establish a Protestant religion that was distinct from Catholicism. It is significant, however, that Cecil called upon Calvinist doctrines in an attempt to unite the nation state. In 1561, he wrote to Nicholas Throgmorton that 'now is the time for Calvin and all such noble men . . . to impugn and suppress the tyranny of the papists' (cited in Hurstfield, 1973: 81). It was in this particular political context, then, that Golding's Ovid was undertaken. The entire translation was completed before the publication of his translation of Calvin's *Offences* (1567). Golding's *Metamorphoses* is therefore positioned strikingly in his translative canon between religious translations, the earlier *Treatise concerning . . . Bucer* and the later *Offences* of Calvin, and provides an early example of a Calvinist text in English designed, I want to argue, to strengthen Protestant identity. This makes for a distinct development from the (equally) Protestant but not overtly Calvinistic translation of *The Fable of Ovid Treting of Narcissus,* as also from Peend's didactic version of the myth of the hermaphrodite.

There is an important intertextual relationship between Calvin and Ovid, moreover, that significantly aids our understanding of Golding's decision to render Ovid into an English Protestant frame and that, so far, has been neglected in critical analyses of Golding's Ovid.[37] In the *Institutes,* Calvin employs two direct quotations from the *Metamorphoses.* In Book I , he takes a line from Book I of the *Metamorphoses* in order to discuss 'God's image and likeness in man'[38]:

> man was created in God's image [Gen. 1.27]. For although God's glory shines forth in the outer man, yet there is no doubt that the proper seat of his image is in the soul . . . And if anyone wishes to include under 'image of God' the fact that, 'while all other living things being bent over look earthward, man has been given a face

uplifted, bidden to gaze heavenward and to raise his countenance to the stars,' I shall not contend too strongly – provided it be regarded as a settled principle that the image of God, which is seen or glows in these outward marks, is spiritual. (I.xv.iii)[39]

There is no condemnation of Ovid here, which makes for a striking contrast with Calvin's comments on Lucretius, the author of the Epicurean *De Rerum Natura*, whom he describes as a 'filthy dog'.[40] But maybe this is not too surprising. In Lucretius, there is a freedom from an idea of an essential self totally at odds with Calvin's dogma. For Calvin, part of the appeal of Ovid is that many of the mythological figures of the *Metamorphoses* change their surface identity whilst remaining substantially unchanged.[41] This approach to the inner self can be accommodated by the Calvinist doctrine of predestination which states that humankind is inherently sinful from the outset of the Fall; there is no escape from this notion of the self. By way of *Metamorphoses* I,84–6, Calvin explains the relationship between God and man. The upright body is the way in which humankind identifies with God and distinguishes itself from others, and yet 'although God's glory shines forth in the outer man, there is no doubt that the proper seat of his image is in the soul' (*Institutes*, I.xv.iii). Calvin thus sets up a system of binarisms which characterises the Protestant view of the relationship with God, most notably the opposition between external/flesh and internal/spirit. And it is through this system of oppositions that the Protestant subject oscillates, in a continual attempt to overcome the affects and effects of corporeal desire, as witnessed above in the translations of the myths of Narcissus and the hermaphrodite. Indeed, Calvin's use of Ovid's *Metamorphoses*, a text whose association with desire we have already noted in Quintilian's *Institutio oratoria*, suggests that his own use of Ovid in itself is an attempt to overcome desire: to thwart the pleasures of the text by placing it within a Christian frame, much as, in the twelfth century, Alan of Lille had done in his *De Planctu Naturae*.[42] It is this use of Ovid that the reader encounters on the title-page of Golding's translation.

The fact that Golding's Ovid is dedicated to the Earl of Leicester demonstrates the political affiliations and considerations of this text.[43] Although the translation of the *Metamorphoses* was published at an early stage in Leicester's political career, Leicester had already achieved popularity with Elizabeth and had been rewarded with the Earldom in 1564 (Rosenberg, 1955: 219). Beneath the title of Golding's translation appears the statement that it is a 'worke very pleasunt and delectable'. This phrase, echoing the title of Peend's translation, contains no indication that

Golding's translation will be morally didactic in any way. A difference is thus witnessed in Golding's treatment of the *Metamorphoses* by comparison with the moralised Ovids of the Middle Ages. There is a further important caveat, however: Golding warns the reader to proceed into the *Metamorphoses* 'with skill, heede, and judgement . . . for else to the Reader it standes in small stead'.[44] Golding offers his prefatory material to the 1567 edition to guide the reader's 'skill, heede and judgement': a guide, quite simply, for affirming the status of the Protestant subject.

According to T.H. Parker, the sixteenth century was 'acutely conscious of the past' and 'the Christian renaissance entered into the Hebrew world of the Old Testament, the Greek world of the New, and of the Church fathers' in order to establish the authenticity of Reformed religion (1966: 61). God's word, the Bible, was the touchstone (King, 1982: 17). The structure of Ovid's narrative, dealing with the creation of the world and the development of human history down to our own present, as we shall see, is readily adaptable to the overall agenda of Protestantism. Golding introduces his Christian appropriation of the *Metamorphoses* quite gradually, speaking of the 'Goddes' euhemeristically as 'heathen men' in line 19, and then, before aligning Ovid's text explicitly with the Bible, dealing with the Pythagorean philosophy found in Book XIII of the *Metamorphoses*, 'disswading men from feare/ Of death' (24–5). This latter material does not affirm or deny the transmigration of the soul that Pythagoras speaks of; it speaks of Pythagoras simply in the context of the latter's attempted differentiation of the souls of animals from the souls of man. This early reference to the soul, however, does serve to guide the reader toward the contemplation of an interior, Protestant subjectivity. Moreover, this introductory reference to the soul at the outset of the translation reinforces the Calvinist belief that the 'proper place of man's image is in the soul'. It is also at this point in the preface that Golding describes the implied reader of his translation:

> Of this I am right well assurde there is no Christen wyght
> That can by fondnesse be so farre seducéd from the ryght
> And finally hee dooth procede in shewing that not all
> That beare the name of men (how strong, feerce, stout, bold,
>   hardy, tall,
> How wyse, fayre, rych, or hyghly borne, how much renowned
>   by fame,
> So ere they bee, although on earth of Goddes they beare the
>   name)
> Are for too be accounted men: but such as under awe
> Of reasons rule continually doo live in vertues law. (53–60)

From considering the place of the soul as argued for in Pythagorean thought, Golding has now moved on to a consideration of desire's excess. For it is the doctrine of living in 'reasons rule' and 'vertues law' that will fashion the Protestant subject of his text. The denial of corporeal desire features in much Christian theology from Augustine onwards. But in this particular historical context, which seeks to remove the image of Christ's body from the external scene of worship, and to replace it with the act of reading the word of God, the treatment of body and text in Golding's prefatory material takes on a greater contemporary significance.

As the Prefatory Epistle continues, Golding makes the textual relationship between the *Metamorphoses* and the Bible much clearer:

> What man is he that would suppose the author of this booke
> The first foundation of his woorke from Moyses writings
>   tooke?
> Not only in effect he dooth with Genesis agree,
> But also in the order of creation, save that hee
> Makes no distinction of the dayes . . . (343–7)

As William Bouwsma (1988) has argued, the treatises of Calvin were concerned with the restoration of order, on many different levels. The *Metamorphoses*, similarly, focuses on the creation of order out of chaos and moves from the depiction of Chaos in Book I, where heaven and earth are not divided, to the foundation of Rome and on, as earlier noted, to the apotheosis of Caesar in Book XV: in this conclusion, secular and religious order intertwine. Ovid's text also deals crucially with the disassembling/disordering effects of desire, offering figures whose identities are altered by the agencies of their own, and other people's, desires. Unlike Luther, Calvin had little to say about freedom and much to say about the servitude of a Christian. And according to Bouwsma, Calvin

> praised religion because it prohibited 'wandering freely'; godliness 'keeps itself within proper limits.' Christianity, he thought, acts to 'restrain and bridle' the mind and 'make it captive'. (1988: 88)

So Golding's mission to present order and cohesion is apparent from the opening lines of the Epistle:

> At length my chariot wheele about the mark hath found the way,
> And at their weery races end, my breathlesse horses stay.
> The woork is brought too end by which the author did
>   account

(And rightly) with eternall fame above the starres to mount,
For whatsoever hath bene writ of auncient tyme in greeke
By sundry men dispersedly, and in the latin eeke,
Of this same dark Philosophie of turned shapes, the same
Hath Ovid into one whole masse in this boke brought in
   frame. (1–8)

Control is emphasised here and will be reiterated throughout the 838 lines of prefatory material. By drawing attention to both the form and the content of the *Metamorphoses*, Golding depicts Ovid as a writer who has managed to synthesise 'into one whole masse' a variety of Greek and Latin texts by 'sundry men dispersedly'. Whilst Ovid's achievements as a translator are acknowledged, however, Golding signifi-cantly positions himself, as the driver of the Ovidian chariot, as the one in ultimate control over the *Metamorphoses* in English, and the translative exercise whose first fruits he published in 1565.

Notions of order and control are developed in greater detail in the Epistle to Leicester. Here Golding provides the moral interpretations of over sixty tales. These move from the spiritual to the social; from issues of corporeality to questions of class. This movement is reflected in the way that Golding has constructed his prefatory material hier-archically, producing a preface for his dedicatee and one for the ordinary reader. Turning first to the Epistle to Leicester, it is certainly possible to read Golding's text as helping to shore up the Earl's public identity. In 1567, the year when Golding's translation was published, Leicester was being regarded with suspicion because of the sudden death of his wife and his continued relationship with Elizabeth.[45] Named in the Epistle as 'ancient Nestor' (609), famous among the Greeks for his wisdom and eloquence, or 'Tithonussis' (610, Golding's spelling of Ovid's 'Tithonus'), who was granted eternal life, Leicester, declared as patron and thus implied as patriot and Protestant, is not explicitly or personally charged with corporeal desire. Thus Golding, like Calvin, is not only concerned with the spiritual aspects of the reformed Christian religion; the socio-political dimensions of Protestantism are also thrown into relief.

Like the ideal tutor described in Erasmus' *The Instruction of a Christian Prince*, Golding uses examples from the myths to describe his ideal nobleman. Theseus, for example, is defined as 'a spurre to prowesse, and a glass / How princes sonnes and noblemen their youthfull yeares should passe' (156–7). How to conduct affairs of state is also signified in the story of Jason and Medea: 'men should never hastely give eare

too fugitives / Or into handes of sorcerers commit their state or lyves'
(151–2). Ultimately,

> Augustus and a few
> Of other noble princes sonnes the author there dooth shew
> That noblemen and gentlemen shoulde stryve to passe the
>   fame
> And vertues of their aunceters, or else too match the same.
>   (294–7)

Noblemen, nevertheless, are still subject to desire, if only in that they
should 'stryve' to surpass the virtuous deeds of their ancestors. It is
also significant that the Ovidian figures Golding goes on to employ in
this preface are defined in terms of the hierarchical binary oppositions
of virtue and vice; a definition which depends on their relationship to
corporeal desire. From Daphne, 'a myrror of virginitie' (67) in Book I,
to the 'turning to a blazing starre of Julius Cesar' in Book XV, which
shows that 'fame and immortalitie of [*tr.* from] vertuous doing growes'
(292–3), Golding's prescriptive readings enforce the notion that desire
turns the subject from virtue to vice. Golding's text, moreover, reveals
a translator who is mindful in his Epistle not only of the dangerous
possibilities of excess in his own voice, but also of the need to maintain
control over the text itself. Golding's reluctance to 'add ... over
curiously the meening of them all [the narratives]' (300) significantly
signals a difference between the moralised Ovids of the Catholic church
and the religious ideologies of his own text. As Calvin famously asserted,
'allegories ought to be carried no further than Scripture expressly sanc-
tions' (*Institutes*, II.v.ix). This change in hermeneutic practice meant, as
noted above, that the word became of prime significance and that external
images became sites of mistrust. This critical practice is emphasised in
the reading strategy that Golding advises for his translation of the
Metamorphoses:

> Behold, by sent of reason and by perfect sight I fynd
> A Panther heere, whose peinted cote with yellow spots like
>   gold
> And pleasant smell allure myne eyes and senses to behold.
> But well I know his face is grim and feerce, which he doth
>   hyde
> To this intent, that whyle I thus stand gazing on his hyde,
> He may devour me unbewares. Ne let them more offend
> At vices in this present woork in lyvely colours pend ...

> For sure theis fables are not put in wryghtyng to thentent
> Too further or allure too vyce: but rather this is ment,
> That men beholding what they bee when vyce dooth reigne in
>   stead
> Of vertue, should not let their lewd affections have the head
>   . . . (552–66)

In the first six lines of this quotation, Golding presents himself as the subject who is able to overcome the specular sensuality of the fabricated image of the panther.[46] The reader, introduced in line 557, however, is not free from the dangers of the 'wanton woord' (547), and hermeneutic responsibility is placed firmly upon those who engage with the textual excesses of the *Metamorphoses*.

It is clear from this discussion of Golding's prefatory text that the control of desire and its excesses is continually advocated in the Epistle to Leicester. The *Metamorphoses* itself is framed by tales in which chariots race out of control,[47] and Golding, too, frames his Epistle with this image, an image which, we have seen, he uses to explain his own translative strategy. Further on in the Epistle, Golding uses the trope of the chariot again in order to instruct the reader:

> The use of this same booke therfore is this: that every man
> (Endeavouring for to know himself as neerly as he can,
> As though he in a chariot sate well ordered,) should direct
> His mynd by reason in the way of vertue, and correct
> His feerce affections with the bit of temprance, lest perchaunce
> They . . . headlong carie him to every filthy pit
> Of vyce, and drinking of the same defyle his soule with it:
> Or else doo headlong harrie him uppon the rockes of sin,
> And over throwing forcibly the chariot he sits in,
> Doo teare him worse than ever was Hippolytus . . . (569–79)

Here, the violent outcome of 'feerce affections' is made clear. In the search to know the self, and therefore to know God, the subject should restrain the self and steer a course away from sin and vice.

A somewhat different mode of address is employed by Golding when he turns from the Epistle to Leicester to the preface 'Too the Reader':

> For why this lumpe of flesh and bones, this bodie is not wee:
> Wee are a thing which earthly eyes denyed are too see. (101–2)

Golding does not employ the intellectual understandings of Pythagorean philosophy in order to articulate his argument. The body is completely denied as a 'lumpe of flesh', and Golding concentrates on the opposition between the visible and the invisible which keeps the force of desire at bay. In terms of offering a strategy of reading, Golding supplies two methods which uphold the opposition between the inner spirituality and outer display:

> Then take theis woorkes as fragrant flowers most full of
>   pleasant juce
> The which the Bee conveying home may put too wholesome
>   use
> And which the spyder sucking on too poyson may convert,
> Through venym spred in all her limbes and native in hir hart.
> For too the pure and Godly mynd, are all things pure and
>   clene (163–7)

The bee metaphor, common in conventional apologies for poetry,[48] suggests the inward ingestion of the 'wholesome' meaning of the text. By contrast, in the Old Testament (for example, in Isaiah 59.2–5 and Job 8.13–14), spiders are associated with iniquity. For Golding, then, the figure of the spider, a creature capable of producing a web of error, signifies a sinful interpretation of Ovid's text. It is telling, therefore, that in the preface 'Too the Reader', Golding actually inscribes readers into the *Metamorphoses* itself by casting them in the role of Ulysses:

> If any stomacke be so weake as that it cannot brooke,
> The lively setting forth of things described in this booke,
> I give him counsell too absteine untill he bee more strong,
> And for to use Ulysses feat ageinst the Meremayds song.
>   (215–8)

Following the edicts of Renaissance humanists, Golding had written in Leicester's Epistle that 'Ulysses dooth expresse / The image of discretion, wit, and great advisédnesse' (248–9). From ancient times, as John Freccero has explained, Ulysses' journey was generally understood as the

> spatial allegorization of circular human time; Ulysses' return to his homeland served as an admirable vehicle for Platonic and gnostic allegories about the soul's . . . gradual refinement back to its pristine spirituality. (1976: 102)[49]

The reader, like Ulysses, is placed in Golding's translation as the hero and enters into the realm of Ovid's text, thwarting desire and triumphantly returning to the safety of the Protestant homeland. Otherwise, as the final lines of the preface state, the reader must 'hold himself content with that [*tr.* what] too his fault is due' (222). Responsibility is thus handed over to the reader to interpret the written word in the correct fashion, for, as Golding has already informed us at the outset, no 'Christen person could be so far seduced from the right'.

From the prefatory material, then, it is evident that Golding attempts to control the reader's interpretative practice, by way of Calvinist doctrine, through repeated expression of the dangers of desire symbolised by the various figures and tropes to be encountered later in the text itself. In my discussion of the anonymous translation of Narcissus, a figure caught in the material world of signs, I suggested that the instability of the sixteenth-century subject becomes visible in the text's own linguistic confusion. It is significant, then, that the figure Golding chooses to cite in the preface is that of Ulysses, 'the antithesis of, or rather the taking over from, Narcissus on the journey of his transformation into speculative internality' (Kristeva, 1987: 109). Whereas the demise of Narcissus occurs because of desire, Ulysses is celebrated because of his effacement of desire. It is useful, therefore, to examine Golding's treatment of Narcissus, which will show an interesting development in the treatment of this Ovidian figure.

Comparison with the 1560 version of Narcissus shows that the metre favoured by Golding renders more coherent Ovid's text. Golding's translation describes how Narcissus,

> . . . as he dranke, he chaunst to spie the Image of his face,
> The which he did immediately with fervent love embrace.
> He feedes a hope without cause why. For like a foolish
> noddie
> He thinke the shadow that he sees to be a lively boddie.
> (III.518–21)

The metre used by Golding, the so-called 'fourteener', allows for a more expansive treatment of the text: Golding's version of the *Metamorphoses* is 2500 lines longer than Ovid's Latin verse (Braden, 1978: 26). In a discussion of Golding's treatment of the Narcissus myth, Braden suggests that a combination of the metre and vocabulary produces a 'spirit which is closer to Nashe than to Calvin'. According to Braden, moreover, the text 'shows a very secular combination of impatience and amusement' (14). The foolishness of Narcissus is certainly brought to the fore in the couplet rhyming 'noddie' with 'boddie', but if we read these lines in isolation we miss the subtle inclusion of Protestant ideology in Golding's text. When the reader reaches the part of the myth where the goddess secures Narcissus' fate, Golding's text states that the goddess '(who doth wreake on wicked people take) / Assented to his just request for ruth and pities sake' (III. 507–8). Although the authorial intrusion has been placed in parenthesis, it serves to situate Golding's rendition of the myth within a Christian frame. Wrath and vengeance are aligned with a pagan god, but the reader is also to understand from the parenthetical inter-ruption that sin is punished. And in a translative move which takes up the 'wickedness' of the deluded youth and situates it in a context bearing traces of contemporary debates over the images favoured by Catholicism, the narrative voice addresses God directly: 'O Lord how often did he kisse that false deceitfull thing' (III. 537). This particular apostrophe is not, of course, in Ovid and it draws attention to the relationship between the subject and God.[50]

Unlike Narcissus, who has been deemed sinful because of desire for the self, a desire which keeps him away from God, this translator of the *Metamorphoses* is mindful to bring in God, the One to whom the reader should be subject, the One beyond any image, and a textual manoeuvre takes the reader out of the narcissistic scene. Instead of the confused 'I am I see' of the 1560 translation, Golding has rendered the line in a much more measured fashion: 'It is my selfe I well perceyve, it is mine Image sure, / That in this sort deluding me, this furie doth procure' (III. 582–3). Ovid's text portrays the 'furie' as a result of Narcissus' confusion. Yet in Golding's translation, the effect of the metre is to render a text in which the disassembling nature of desire is effaced. The reader, it seems, is to understand that the subject will not be confused if his eyes are turned upward to God instead of to his own material self. Golding here thus operates to alter the reading subject's perception of the visible world.

Golding's treatment of the Hermaphroditus myth also offers a didactic narrative, emphasising the sinfulness of the confused, divided subject. In the prefatory material to Leicester, Golding interprets the myth as follows:

> Hermaphroditus and Salmacis declare that idlenesse
> Is cheefest nurce and cherisher of all volupteousnesse,
> And that voluptuous lyfe breedes sin: which linking toogither
> Make men too bee effeminate, unweeldy, weake and lither.
>   (113–6)

The figure of the hermaphrodite as presented above involves more than just corporeal desire. Defined in terms such as 'unweeldy' and 'lither', the biform figure is perceived as excessive. It goes beyond the bound-aries of control. However, Golding ultimately offers a different treatment of Ovid's myth to the one presented by Peend. For Peend, the divided masculine subject is open to interrogation. Golding, by contrast, presents the hermaphrodite as a fabricated 'toy/ Of double shape' (IV.468–9). As with the myth of Narcissus, Golding, more confidently than his predecessor, negotiates the existence of the divided subject, acknowledging the possibility of its existence in his address to Leicester whilst negating the split subject at the end of the myth.

In terms of establishing the 'true religion' of Protestantism, the opening decades of Elizabethan rule were unstable. As Eamon Duffy writes, 'the accession of Anne Boleyn's daughter . . . launched the parishes of Tudor England on the third major religious transformation in a dozen years' (1992: 565). The extent to which England can be termed Protestant when Elizabeth became monarch in November 1558 was thus debatable, and the efforts to remove the traces of England's religious past were evidently problematic. The general situation caused De Feria, the Spanish Ambassador, to comment to Philip II, soon after Elizabeth's succession, 'things are in such hurly-burly and confusion that fathers do not know their own children' (quoted in Doran, 1994: 1). From Narcissus to the hermaphrodite to Golding, Ovid is employed in the 1560s both to articulate the confusion of the English subject and to attempt to dictate a particular ideology.[51] At the beginning of the 1560s the translator of Narcissus shows the annihilating agency of desire in the very way that the text is rendered. Five years later, Peend articulates further anxieties in his attempt to identify desire as woman. Golding's text, however, produced within a Calvinist frame, has no difficulty in presenting desire to his readers. In his discussion of Golding's Ovid, Jonathan Bate has argued that 'Ovidian fluidity is replaced by the stability of Christian faith' (1993: 47). But Calvinist doctrine emphasises the corruption of humankind since the Fall, focusing on 'a universe divided in deep and perpetual strife' (Sinfield, 1983: 9). In the earlier-noted terms of Calvinist theology, 'a perpetual disorder and excess is apparent in all our actions,' and the human race thus exists in a state of perpetual desire. Significantly, Golding states in the Epistle to Leicester that

> Wee may perceyve in Dedalus how every man by kynd
> Desyres to bee at libertie, and with an earnest mynd
> Dooth seeke too see his native soyle, and how that straight distresse
> Dooth make men wyse, and sharpes their wits to fynd their owne redress. (173–6)

Through Daedalus, the figure who constructed the labyrinth to encase the Minotaur and who was himself confined on the island of Crete, the reader learns of the 'desyre too bee at libertie' and of how this 'straight distresse' can make men 'wyse'.[52] The affects and effects of desire that divide the English-speaking subject in the translations of the *Metamorphoses* preceding Golding's version of Ovid, a translation dependent on Calvinist policy and polity, becomes the very agency that defines the 'wyse' – English, Protestant, masculine – subject of Golding's text.

Notes

1. In the 'Introduction' to *Rethinking Translation*, Lawrence Venuti argues for a 'translation hermeneutic' which 'assumes a notion of agency that allows for the full complexity of the translator's work ... [treating] the translating subject as discursively constructed in self-presentations, theoretical statements, legal codes, the very process of developing a translation strategy, of selecting and arranging signifiers' (1992: 11).
2. In 1536 Tyndale was strangled and burned at the stake in Antwerp for heretical Bible translations. Dolet was hanged and burned at the stake in France in 1546 for a translation of Plato that was deemed heretical.
3. Other translations of Ovid published in this decade were Thomas Underdowne's *Theseus and Ariadne* (1566), Thomas Howell's *Cephalus and Procris* (c. 1568) and William Hubbard's *Ceyx and Alcione* (1569) (Alexander, 1968: 9). See also Pearcy, 1984.
4. Primarily, my project is a comparison of the English versions of the *Metamorphoses*. On the occasions when I consider Ovid's Latin text itself, and in the absence of any clearly established source for Golding's translation of the *Metamorphoses* among the many versions of Ovid's text on which he might have based his work (cf. Steiner, 1950, Oakley-Brown, 1999: 42 n. 39), I cite Frank Justice Miller's prose translation, revised by G.P. Goold, while bearing in mind that these translations are as much part of their period of production as the other translations discussed here. Line numbers for Miller's translations are given in the body of the text by Book and line number for the corresponding lines in the Latin.
5. For Karl Galinsky, 'the *Metamorphoses* cannot be properly understood without the realisation that they were meant to be Ovid's answer to Vergil's *Aeneid*' (1975: 15). See further the excellent analysis by Stephen Hinds, in his chapter 'Repetition and Change' (Hinds, 1998), of the shifting relationship between the *Aeneid* and the *Metamorphoses*. Writers have often viewed Ovid as the subordinate term in this classical binarism; Hinds's 'mid-90's spin on this [relation] would be that Ovid is engaged in a tendentious poetic appropriation of his predecessor ... Rather than construct himself as an epigonal reader of the *Aeneid*, Ovid is constructing Virgil as a hesitant precursor of the *Metamorphoses*' (1998: 106).
6. The last six books of the *Metamorphoses* clearly support this view of the whole work. As Leonard Barkan explains, 'the apotheosis of Hercules in Book IX prefigures a sequence of similar events in Books XIV and XV, the apotheosis of Aeneas, Romulus and Julius Caesar, who were often identified with Hercules. The culminating figure is Augustus, whose apotheosis (XV.869–70) is inevitable but outside the poem's time span' (1986: 83).

7. *Inst. Orat.* IV.i,77. I quote Quintilian in the Loeb translation by Butler (1920–2).
8. See further Olmsted, 1996 for comment on ways in which the *Metamorphoses* negotiates borders, boundaries and, more generally, cultural difference. For general comment on the question of 'borders, boundaries and frames', see Henderson, 1985.
9. Calchas interprets the omen of the snakes and birds at Aulis (XII,19ff.). Mopsus is presented as the killer of Hodites, but he is also known as a seer (VIII,316ff.).
10. Alison G. Elliott also makes the point that 'Ovid tells many tales of failure of communication' and lists Io, Callisto, Pyramus and Thisbe, Acteon, Philomena, Arachne and Orpheus as examples (1985: 17).
11. Callisto is changed into a bear and 'with constant moanings she shows her grief, stretches up such hands as are left her to the heavens' (II,484–7). Ocyrhoë is transformed into a horse; as she changes, 'the last part of her complaint became scarce understood and her words were all confused' (II,665–6).
12. The tongue was an important emblem in the early modern period. A striking example is Thomas Tomkis' play *Lingua* (1607); equally striking are Shakespeare's representation of Rumour 'painted full of tongues' in the Induction to *II Henry IV*, and George Wither's emblem, in his *Collection of Emblems*, featuring 'the tongues unruly motion' (1635: 42); see also Parker, 1989 for a stimulating account of the treatise by Erasmus 'On the Use and Abuse of the Tongue' (1525).
13. I draw here on Fradenburg, 1989, which includes a discussion of the image of the severed tongue in the twelfth-century *Sefer Zekirah [The Book of Remembrance]*: 'The eloquent tongue . . . is at once mutilated and reduced to embodiment, denied those physical movements that make the tongue something to speak with as well as to eat with, that make the tongue itself capable of the symbolic, the fictive, the creative . . ., a subtle and shifting borderline between the body and its meanings' (1989: 80).
14. Susan Bassnett notes that 'translation came to be used as a weapon in both dogmatic and political conflicts as nation states began to emerge and the centralisation of the church began to weaken' (1991: 57).
15. Patrick Collinson argues: 'Culturally speaking, the Reformation was beyond all question a watershed of truly mountainous proportions. On the far, late mediaeval side of the range. . . [r]eligion was "intensely visual". Seeing was believing, more than hearing and much more than the privatized mental discipline of absorbing information from a written text. On this side of the divide we confront the invisible, abstract and didactic word: primarily the word of the printed page, on which depended the spoken words of sermon and catechism. In crossing this range we are making a journey from a culture of orality and image to one of print: from one mental and imaginative "set" to another' (1995: 37). In the early years of the Reformation, however, as Collinson argues, this divide is not easy to determine.
16. Arguably, these processes were already in place by the time of the Wycliffite Bible in the closing years of the fourteenth century, as the previous essay in this volume has suggested. For further comment on the Wycliffites, see Aston, 1988 and Hudson, 1988; and, for comment on developments in the first half of the sixteenth century, Cummings, 1999. My concern here, however, is to locate the argument specifically within the socio-political climate(s) of the sixteenth century.

17. Although the Great Bible (1540) and the Bishops' Bible (1568) were designed for official use, the Geneva Bible, the first vernacular Bible for use by the laity, contained a Calvinist commentary in the first edition, to which two Calvinist catechisms were added in 1568 and 1570. See Lloyd E. Berry's introduction to the facsimile of the Geneva Bible, 1969: 14ff. and Fox 1997: 62.

18. The full title of this text is *The Institution of Christian Religion, Wrytten in Latine by Maister Jhon Calvin, and Translated into Englysh According to the Authors Last Edition. Seen and Allowed According to the Order Appointed in the Quenes Maiesties Instructions.* It is generally abbreviated *Institutes* (and so throughout this essay).

19. Quotation from the *Institutes* is from Ford Lewis Battle's translation.

20. As William Keach has explained, '*lascivia* is the word which Quintilian uses [in *Institutio oratoria* V.i,7 and X.i,88, 93] to characterise the art of Ovid ... *Lascivia* means primarily "sportiveness", "playfulness" but also "wantonness", "lewdness"' (1977: 235).

21. Ghisalberti is writing about medieval *accessus* to the *Metamorphoses*. For fuller comment on traditions of medieval commentary on classical texts, including the *accessus ad auctores*, see Elliott, 1980, Minnis, 1988a, 1988b.

22. All quotations from this text are taken from the 1560 edition, and cited by line number alone: see bibliography under the entry 'Anon. 1560'.

23. In an essay discussing Ovid's Narcissus and Shakespeare's *Richard II*, A.D. Nuttall has stated that 'in older civilisations material which we address directly in psychological language was explored – often with an astonishing though uncontrolled subtlety – through myth. The latent analogy between much mythological narrative and some psychological explanations became explicit when Freud began freely to borrow from Greek sources: Oedipus, Electra and – of course – Narcissus' (1988: 139).

24. Nuttall identifies Thomas Howell as the translator of this text (1988: 140); no translator is named on the title-page. Alexander states that the myth of Narcissus was the first vernacular translation of Ovid to be printed (1968: 1). According to Ralph Hexter, the first episode from the *Metamorphoses* translated into English in this period is 'T. Hedley's broadside *Midas* of 1552' ('Ovid in medieval translation', in *Ubersetzung. Translation. Traduction. An International Encyclopedia of Translation Studies*, eds A.P. Frank *et al.* [Berlin: De Gruyter], forthcoming). I would like to thank Professor Hexter for allowing me to consult this article.

25. For a clear discussion of the relevant Lacanian material, see Easthope and McGowan (1992: 68).

26. Both the translator of this text and Arthur Golding give Narcissus' age as 16.

27. On the problematic textuality of the sign, cf. the following comment by Saint Jerome, from his *Letter to Pammachius* (cited in Copeland, 1991: 48): 'until one flees the tedium of writing, one weaves a web of errors'.

28. This myth has an interesting translation history in the early modern English period. Francis Beaumont produced a version in 1602; Edward Sherburne another in 1651; Joseph Addison a third in 1693. For fuller comment on Beaumont and Addison see Oakley-Brown, 1994.

29. All quotations from Peend's text are from a facsimile of the 1565 edition held in the Bodleian Library at Oxford, and are identified by line numbers alone in the body of the article.

30. Other couples include Echo and Narcissus, Medea and Jason, Phyllis and Damon, Sappho and Phaon, Romeo and Juliet, and Helen and Paris.

31. Golding published *The Fyrst Fowre Bookes of the 'Metamorphosis'* in 1565. Editions of his translation of the *Metamorphoses* were published in 1567, 1575, 1576, 1584, 1587, 1593, 1603, 1612 and 1675: which readily shows the importance of his work.

32. Louis Thorn Golding explains: 'In 1549, when exiled from Strasbourg, Martin Bucer and Paul Phagius accepted the invitation of Cranmer to come to England ... Bucer became a leading figure in the religious debates of the period ... Bucer died in 1551, but as result of his attacks upon the church of Rome, his body was disinterred in the "purge" of Cambridge and burnt at the stake February 6, 1555' (1937: 18).

33. Other translations by Golding not so far noted in this paper include *Caesar's Commentaries* (1565); *John Calvin, his Treatise Concerning Offences* (1567); *The Psalmes of David and Others, with M. John Calvin's Commentaries* (1571); *A Booke of Christian Questions and Answers by Theodore Beza* (1572); *Sermons of M. John Calvin upon the Epistle of Saincte Paul to the Galations* (1574); *Sermons of M. John Calvine upon the Booke of Job* (1574); *A Catholike Exposition Upon the Revelation of Sainct John* (1574); *The Sermons of M. John Calvin upon the Epistle to the Ephesians* (1577); *The Sermons of M. John Calvin upon ... Deuteronomie* (1583).

34. The Book of St Matthew, for example, opened with a letter T that figured Neptune rising from the sea, whilst the word 'God', which began the Epistle to the Hebrews, depicted a semi-clad Leda being ravished by the swan. By 1575 the image of Leda had been removed; the Neptune initial, however, was re-used for the King James Bible (1611) (Aston, 1995: 197, 216).

35. Golding's practices 'range ... in scale from brief conspicuous phrases, as when Envy mumbles a "Divils Paternoster" [II,983–5] to herself, to Christianized characters and settings'. A further example, of Perseus' fight with Phineus and his men at Perseus' wedding (V,120–9), shows how 'Golding's translation emphasises the religious setting and Christianizes certain aspects' (Lyne, 1996: 190). According to Lyne, Golding's Christianising incorporates objects with specifically Christian connotations, such as 'miter' (V,133), and 'Church' (VIII,879). Moreover, Golding's use of the term 'holiday' (IV,5) engages with contemporary debate over 'Protestant reforms [which] had eroded traditional forms of popular celebration' (1996: 195).

36. On the relationship between Cecil and Golding, see Golding, 1937: 60ff.

37. In a notable exception to this generalisation, Jonathan Bate has said that 'the Elizabethan translation movement in which Golding was prominent was a significant part of a post-Reformation project to establish England as a Protestant nation with its own high culture' (1993: 30). Bate also states that Golding 'thus contrived to make Ovid sound at least a little like the other major author whom he translated into English: John Calvin' (49), but does not examine this debt to Calvin further.

38. I was alerted to the use of Ovid in Calvin by the extensive index to Battle's translation of the *Institutes*. William J. Bouwsma notes that Calvin 'more than once cited the familiar lines of Ovid' describing the 'erect stature of human beings that enables them to look up' (1988: 73).

39. In Book II of the *Institutes*, entitled 'Knowledge of God the Redeemer in Christ, First disclosed to the Fathers Under the Law . . .', Calvin also makes use of Medea's dilemma from Book VII. 20ff. of Ovid's text.
40. *Institutes* I.v.v. See also K. Sara Myers for comment on the complex intertextual relationship between the *Metamorphoses* and *De Rerum Natura* (1994: 6ff.), and Homi Bhaba for comment on the contrast between Ovid and Lucretius (1994: 224).
41. For example, Lycaon, Io, Daphne, Clytie, Philemon and Baucis and Myrrha (Galinsky, 1975: 44). This aspect of Ovid can be found in twelfth-century *accessus*: for example, that of Arnulf of Orléans (Ghisalberti, 1946: 18).
42. On the role of desire in the *De Planctu Naturae*, see Sheridan, 1980: 147ff. The Dreamer asks Nature to provide a description of desire, and the text uses many narratives from the *Metamorphoses* to answer the question. In particular, Book IX, the central book of the *De Planctu*, uses the myths of Melicerta (IV,512–42), Antaeus (IX,183), and Byblis (IX,454–665).
43. Apart from the two editions of the *Metamorphoses*, Golding also dedicated to Leicester a translation of a work by Bullinger, *A Confutation of the Popes Bull Against Elizabeth* (1572), *Sermons of Master John Calvin upon the Book of Job* (1574), and a translation of a work by de Mornay, *A Woorke Concerning the Trewness of the Christian Religion* (1587) (Rosenberg, 1955: 355–562).
44. All quotations from Golding's text are from the facsimile of the 1567 edition, and are identified by line numbers alone (for the prefatory material) and Book and line numbers alone (for material from the actual translation) in the body of the article.
45. See Rosenberg, 1955: 9ff. for details of Leicester's early career.
46. In the *Institutes* Calvin states that 'many are so delighted with marble, gold and pictures they become marble, they turn, as it were, into metals and are like painted pictures' (III.x.iii).
47. In *Met.* II,1 Phaeton fails to control the spirited horses of Phoebus' chariot. In order to save the Earth from destruction, Phaeton is eventually destroyed by Jupiter's thunderbolt. In XV, 517ff. Hippolytus is thrown from his chariot and torn apart.
48. For fuller discussion of this point, see Chance, 1990: 3–46.
49. Saint Basil also used the myth of Odysseus and the Sirens to illustrate how young men should flee from all that is base in poetry (Heinrichs, 1990: 29).
50. In Ovid, the text reads 'O fondly foolish boy, why vainly seek to clasp a fleeting image' (III, 430ff.).
51. It is hardly accidental, therefore, that terms for labyrinth, *labyrinthum* and *ambages*, occur frequently in Calvin's texts. On this point, see Lewalski, 1986: 293 and Bouwsma, 1988: 45.
52. The episode is narrated in *Met.* VIII, 155ff.; Ovid also writes of Daedalus' ingenuity in IX, 742ff.

Chapter 3
Women Translators, Gender and the Cultural Context of the Scientific Revolution

CHRISTA KNELLWOLF

The seventeenth century experienced a confluence of changes in political, religious and social outlook that, broadly speaking, were all part of a systematic questioning of the modes of representing knowledge. As a result, revisions of factual knowledge were taking place against the background of a radical critique of the ways and means of acquiring knowledge. This period, in fact, experienced a transition from a largely unreflecting acceptance of current scientific orthodoxies to a theoretical investigation of the premises of knowing, as it was articulated at the outset in Francis Bacon's methodological programme. Any historiography of science that seeks to account for the formative role played by culture in scientific developments needs, in particular, to explore the extent to which concrete formulations of knowledge draw upon gender and nationalistic stereotypes.

We are by now familiar with the criticisms that have been levelled at the simple equation of science and progress. Recent approaches, therefore, prefer to emphasise the ways in which such narratives of scientific progress are employed. The attempt to understand how the early modern period expressed new ideas about self, nature and knowledge requires us to understand the processes by which its goals and objectives were turned into a coherent narrative. At issue are acts of translation that eradicate the incongruous elements contained in disparate ideas. But much more importantly, when new ideas are being circulated, they undergo multiple reformulations that ensure that they meet the different needs of different audiences: which means, in turn, that our task is to investigate the manner by which texts devise strategies to grasp the attention of their targeted readership. Of course, explicit or implicit censorship played a role, too.[1] More important for the purposes of this essay, though, the new science continually came up against its own conceptual boundaries, and self-consciously experimented with those modes of representation that empiricism had found to be lacking in objectivity.

If, as it was often perceived to be, the language of natural philosophy was encumbered by metaphor, and unsatisfactory for the description of observed facts, it could appeal more strongly to an amateur audience. So we find Francesco Algarotti, one of the major figures to be studied in this chapter, disregarding Bacon's warnings about the subjective nature of sensory experience and advertising his popularisation of Newton's theories as follows: 'I have endeavoured to set truth, accompanied with all that is necessary to demonstrate it, in a pleasing light, and to render it agreeable to that sex, which had rather perceive than understand' (1739: vi). For his simplified account of Newton's theories, first produced in 1737, Algarotti made use of discursive conventions that had been invented by Bernard le Bovier de Fontenelle, the other major figure in this study, who popularised Descartes' cosmic theories in his own *Entretiens sur la pluralité des mondes habités* (1686). Writing some fifty years after Fontenelle, Algarotti defines the implicit intentions which motivate his work, and thus confirms that Fontenelle had invented a new textual category or genre: the scientific romance. When Fontenelle superimposed the generic conventions of the romance on a scientific treatise, he represented the abstract desire for knowledge as a spectacle replete with erotic tensions. In both Algarotti's and Fontenelle's works, the female interlocutor serves as a dramatic means to problematise the conventional narrative pattern, according to which a male scientist investigates a female nature. A detailed analysis of the texts, however, will reveal that these scientific romances resist an easy categorisation of gender (cf. Douglas, 1994).

Fontenelle's *Entretiens* was received with enormous enthusiasm, and three English translations appeared within the next two years, among which Aphra Behn's (1688), used for quotation in this chapter, stands out as the most elegant[2]; the famous female scholar Elizabeth Carter translated Algarotti (1739). The fact that these works had considerable appeal for a female audience, however, does not mean that women interested in science merely concentrated on those aspects which appealed to the senses. Since a current stereotype of femininity defined women as creatures of the senses, the female protagonist is expressive of a certain role and must not be confused with contemporary scientifically-minded women. Gendered metaphors for knowledge, moreover, are present in highly complex treatises of scientific analysis as much as in populist accounts. By studying the genre of popularisations of science, this chapter examines the role of the audience in scientific publication and asks in what ways gender figures as an element that facilitates (or hinders) the transmission of knowledge.

Studying these popularisations through their translations, and attempting to unravel their frequently tangled relationships, adds a further dimension to the discussion, of considerable importance for the interests of the present volume: that is, it allows us to see differently gendered and nationalist conceptions of knowledge competing for supremacy. The seventeenth century saw an increasing competition between the Cartesians and the Newtonians, which, because of political and economic conflicts between England and France, turned into a nationalistic rivalry between its major thinkers. Far from being differentiated only according to dress and customs, English and French thinkers were differentiated at the deepest level, in respect of their different modes of knowing.[3] By celebrating Newton's discoveries as a product of English culture, as we shall see, the Italian Algarotti further contributed to the apotheosis of the English scientific hero while he also threw down a challenge to the French followers of Descartes.[4] Analysing the convoluted relationships between gender, nation and knowledge, this chapter argues that translation is a forum in which stereotypes and prejudices are both challenged and confirmed.

Fontenelle's Scientific Romance

Descartes' theories were comparatively easy to follow. This had the effect of making female participation in philosophical debates much easier. Erica Harth explains that 'because Descartes offered a philosophy that was accessible to women in a way that none other had been before, women in significant numbers began to venture into an arena that had previously been reserved for men' (1990: 151; cf. Harth, 1992, Goodman, 1994). In the French context, the active involvement of women in the production and propagation of philosophical ideas was dependent on the existence of a salon culture. In such a setting, women had the role of hostesses to an intellectual circle of both genders. It can be argued that women had a purely subsidiary role, and were present at the meetings of the salon only so as to enable the male intellectuals to deliver sparkling arguments. Though a few women may have managed to achieve recognition for their own intellectual abilities, it is probable that most were primarily listeners. Nevertheless, their role required at least sufficient general knowledge to allow them to ask the right questions and so to act as prompts for the discussion.

In the later years of the century, science was becoming increasingly institutionalised (Stewart, 1992): the foundation of the English Royal Society in 1660 had been followed by the French Académie Royal des Sciences in 1666. Harth may be overstating her case when she says that the state institutionalised the 'new philosophy' (1990: 152); at this historical moment, the success of science was still doubtful. But, then, it was all the more important to advertise the study of science as a morally and culturally rewarding project; since the economic profitability of abstract investigations had not yet demonstrated itself, it was necessary to conceptualise new knowledge and new intellectual gains as advantageous to an individual's (and society's) self-understanding. That science was deemed immensely relevant to state and society explains why Fontenelle, the future secretary of the French Académie Royal des Sciences, felt called upon to negotiate between the beau monde and the 'serious' practitioners of natural philosophy. By participating in the contemporary debate over the extent and quality of women's education, he demonstrated how strongly questions about women's proper behaviour were grounded in general concerns about social self-definition. In his work, therefore, the dialogue of the male savant with the female interlocutor dramatises the significance of science for contemporary culture and society as much as it problematises the role of women in science.

One of Fontenelle's major concerns, Harth argues, was to define the boundaries between scientific investigation and religious enthusiasm, magic and amateurish dabbling. An important background text can be seen in the third *entretiens* of the Abbé de Gérard's *Philosophie des gens du cour* (1680) in which a learned marchioness who serves as philosophical muse appears alongside another 'learned lady, a witch who spends night after night on her rooftop peering at the moon through a telescope' (Harth, 1990: 150–1). By contrast, Fontenelle's marchioness expresses her amazement at the idea of the world's continuous and rapid movement, but she is by no means given to enthusiastic protestations.[5] Although 'the astronomy lessons take place in her garden, she speaks to her teacher, as it were, from the depths of the salon, as a worldly-wise but unschooled woman' (Harth, 1990: 156). She expresses admiration for the new theory of the cosmos but her responses are guided by reason and not by emotion.

But then, Fontenelle's text also includes an important subtext that sketches an erotic attraction between the marchioness and the philosopher and that reports their nightly conversations using the generic conventions of romance – rather than those of a scientific treatise – without attempting to exploit the romantic potential of the scene. The moon is deprived of its poetic resonances, and any emotional responses to the objects of empirical observation are firmly held in check. The potential sexual attraction between the marchioness and the philosopher, moreover, is played out in very stylised formulas. It appears to be a mere reflex of convention that the philosopher remarks that 'the Presence of a Person of her Wit and Beauty hindered me [the philosopher] from giving up my Thoughts intirely to the Moon and Stars' (Behn, 1688: 93).

The nightly encounters between the marchioness and the philosopher, however, are by no means devoid of passionate tensions. While engaged in a highly conventional comparison of the respective merits of night and day, they toy with the *doubles entendres* which define the ritual of gallantry:

> Do not you believe, Madam, said I, that the clearness of this Night exceeds the Glory of the brightest day? I confess, said she, the Day must yield to such a Night; the day which resembles a fair Beauty ... is not so charming as one of a brown Complexion, who is a true Emblem of the Night. You are very generous, Madam, said I, to give the advantage to the brown, you who are so admirably fair your self: Yet without dispute, day is the most beautiful thing in Nature; and most of the Heroines in Romances ... are generally described to be fair. But, said she, Beauty is insipid, if it want the pleasure and power of charming; and you must acknowledge that the brightest day that ever you saw could never have engaged you in so agreeable an Ecstasie, as you were just now like to have faln into by the powerful attractions of the Night. (Behn, 1688: 93–4)[6]

Enumerating the comparative merits of night and day appears to be a rhetorical exercise by which the marchioness and the philosopher demonstrate their skills of argumentation: they respond smoothly to each other's statements and cautiously propound their reasons for being more interested in the secrets of the dark than in the, apparently more easily accessible, features of the day. This passage incorporates the discursive convention of the apology, but, while it gives some explanation for what is being talked about and why, it is also evasive and expends more energy stimulating interest in the characters than appealing to the intellect of its readers. Both marchioness and philosopher state their preference for the night but, by reading the night in anthropomorphic terms, by way of criteria applied to female beauty, they confirm their fascination with natural philosophy by appeal to the conventions of romance.

This linking of different genres makes us wonder whether the gestural apology refers to the subject matter or the formal structure of the *Entretiens*. Even while it is not presented as an explicit apology, it also serves the purpose of attracting its readers' attention. Far from explicitly stating the benefits and rational advantages of astronomical enquiries, it tackles the issue from the perspective of sketching how pleasurable such activities are. Fontenelle's work, therefore, argues for the suitability of natural philosophy for fashionable conversation. By mingling an exposition of the Cartesian system with the conventions of romance, he adds a special edge to a potentially dry subject. Apart from that, he also demonstrates the dependence of scientific arguments on codes of linguistic representation. Dressing the new science in the guise of romance is a strategy by which Fontenelle whets the appetite of his readers and makes them inclined to grant it moral as well as financial support.

Far from trying to ignore the distorting effects of linguistic representation, Fontenelle implies that the demise of an illusory congruence between form and content opens a vast potential for reconceptualising knowledge. By bringing knowledge into relation with desire, he confirms the legitimacy of conducting a scientific argument under the guise of romance, a genre explicitly invoked in the comment that 'most of the Heroines in Romances, which are modelled after the most perfect *Idea* fancy can represent by the most ingenious of mankind, are generally described to be fair'. When the dialogue concludes that the heroines of romance lack charm or sexual seductiveness, and are generally insipid, it does not simply dismiss romance as a superficial generic category, but instead calls for a more sophisticated method of presenting the findings of science in a way that allows for the operation of desire.

Fontenelle sketches an alternative romance, which yields to the passion for the unknown and cheerfully exploits the tensions between social conventions and the act of expanding the boundaries of knowledge. That the scientific is also a social drama is by no means accidental. The generic form produced by linking an abstract desire for knowledge with sexual desire may be called the scientific romance, a term which indicates that knowledge is not only sexualised but that sexual interest is itself represented as a desire for knowledge. This understanding helps to explain the uncomfortably cerebral conception of sexuality in the work, one which prevents the potential attraction between the marchioness and the philosopher from following through to its logical conclusion, after the pattern of, for instance, the Heloise and Abelard narrative.[7] The sterile relationship between

Fontenelle's figures, however, follows on from the way the story presents itself as a romance. It can be argued that Fontenelle made an effort to suppress the potential attractions between the two figures because this would have undermined his wish to gain approval for the new science. This is not the whole story, though. By reconfiguring the attractions between a male teacher and a female disciple as the 'powerful attractions of the Night', Fontenelle reintroduces as a literary element the mystery which he sought to dispel through his rational approach to cosmology. The scientific romance, therefore, is an attempt to negotiate between the scientist's endeavour to bring the mysteries of the cosmos within the rigid grid of scientific analysis and the writer's wish to preserve a sense of wonder *vis-à-vis* countless possible worlds far out in space.[8]

The Emergence of Scientific Popularisation

Erica Harth argues that Cyrano de Bergerac wrote the first scientific popularisation. She describes him as follows: 'Cyrano was not a man of science, nor was he particularly learned. But his work served the invaluable purpose of presenting in fanciful and eminently readable form scientific and philosophical ideas of the day' (1970: 4). She draws the portrait of someone, midway between the scientist and an uninformed lay audience, who offers to interpret the former to the latter. Living in the twentieth century, we are familiar with a situation in which abundant specialisation in each discipline confronts us with a mass of knowledge that no single individual can master; so we take for granted that there should be scientific journalists who explain in simple terms the meanings of new discoveries. When we talk about the first writers of scientific popularisation, however, we need to investigate in more detail what historical conditions called them into existence; in other words, what aspects of the organisation of knowledge called forth such a mediatory role.

The choice of dialogue form was familiar, most famously, from Plato's depiction of the Socratic method of reasoning. Fontenelle had used the convention in *Nouveaux Dialogues des morts* (1683), a work that stages an imaginary exposure to the philosophy of the ancients on the part of a 'mind seeking its bearings', as E.D. James describes it (1987: 133). Aspiring to philosophical depth, this work is labelled a 'dialogue'; by contrast, the *Entretiens*, a work which in its own manner deals similarly with a mind seeking to find its bearings, suppresses its generic affiliation with philosophical dialogue. Fontenelle retains the conversational setting of the dialogue convention, but reconfigures it as a mere 'conversation' or an exchange of views.[9] The emphasis on the informality of the exchange may be a means by which he seeks to guard himself against the imputation of philosophising in a frivolous vein. By focusing his interest on the social context in which knowledge is passed on, however, he raises the issue of the cultural relevance of the new ideas about nature.

What is new in the late seventeenth century is the significant spread of literacy, which created a rising demand to be up-to-date with new ideas without having to engage with science at the level of abstract arguments and mathematical formulas. What has changed is the relationship between the scientific investigator and society at large. But then, it is important to remember that the concepts of 'vulgarisation' or 'popularisation' did not yet exist, the former being an early eighteenth-century, the latter a late eighteenth-century, coinage.[10] The idea that highly complex arguments need an interpreter, however, draws on a communitarian ideology that reflects a twentieth-century perspective and is incompatible with the élitist bent of seventeenth-century culture. Nevertheless, the need for a mediation between a lay public, no matter how select, and the specialist, indicates that boundaries were being negotiated. A mediation between different groups, all defined by their possession of different kinds of knowledge, involved the accommodation of different modes of expression to one another. As a result, the question whether such a translation was possible, or whether the transformation from one representational mode to another produced an altogether different message, became an urgent issue.

Translation denotes an explanation of unfamiliar ground, but Fontenelle's explicit reference to translation also functions as a self-conscious gesture by which to problematise his relationship with his audience. He begins his explanation of the rationale behind his work by noting that Cicero introduced the practice of philosophising into the Latin language. Cicero not only translated philosphy but also created a new cultural and linguistic context for a discipline which had hitherto been practised only in Greek. The precedent of Cicero draws attention to the complex relationship between subject matter and form: not only does it refer to the choice of language in the conventional sense (French, rather than Latin, in Fontenelle's case) but it also points to a stylistic shift in terms of Fontenelle's formal framework for the discussion of the new science. Fontenelle begins:

> I find myself reduced almost to the same Condition in which *Cicero* was, when he undertook to put Matters of Philosophy into Latin; which, till that time, had never been treated of, but in Greek. He

tells us . . . [that] those who loved Philosophy, having already taken the pains to find it in Greek, would neglect, after that, to read it again in Latin (that not being the Original;) and that those who did not care for Philosophy, would not seek it, either in the Latin, or the Greek. But . . . those who were not Philosophers would be tempted to the Reading of it, by the Facility they Would find in its being in the Latin Tongue; and . . . those who were Philosophers would be curious enough to see how well it had been turned from the Greek to the Latin. (Behn, 1688: 87)

Fontenelle uses Cicero as a precedent for his own stylistic experiments. In Cicero's case, the act of translation is not a word-for-word rendition but an attempt to make philosophical language compatible with the conventions of a different culture. As Cicero had already recognised, and as twentieth-century critical theory has argued more fully, language largely determines what can be said and how ideas can be expressed.[11] Fontenelle picks up on Cicero's implicit claim that philosophy is a language and that, like a national language, it can be translated, at least, to a certain extent. He mentions the objection voiced against Cicero's project, that Greek is the original language of philosophy. By using Cicero's argument in favour of translatability, he implicitly refutes the idea that there is such a thing as an 'original language of philosophy'. Since there is no original, or neutral, mode of representing facts, and since facts have to conform to the structural potential of language *per se*, linguistic transitions are legitimate, whether they are from one language to another, or from the discourse of the scientists to that of drawing-room culture.

While this argument justifies Fontenelle's project, it also subverts the truth claims implied in his own work. If there is no absolute truth – that is, if there is no practical access to a non-mediated truth – Fontenelle needs to come to terms with the language of his own culture. If the idea of an original and unbiased representation of fact is abandoned, the socially defined perimeters of a language acquire new prominence. If, that is, translation is a loose approximation rather than an exact rendition, the choice of formal conventions for the representation of ideas becomes a self-conscious act that demands the negotiation of conventional definitions of form and problematises the relationship between writer, reader and text.

In the second paragraph of his preface, Fontenelle explains his stylistic choices as follows: 'for I would treat of Philosophy in a manner altogether unphilosophical, and have endeavoured to bring it to a Point not too rough and harsh for the Capacity of the *Numbers* nor too light and trivial for the *Learned*' (Behn, 1688: 87). His stated goal is to reach the specialist as well as the non-specialist audience. Why he should want to reach the learned becomes more clear if we recall his remark that 'those who were Philosophers would be curious enough to see how well it had been turned from the Greek to the Latin'. In the context, 'it' grammatically refers back to 'Philosophy'; the structural looseness of the passage, however, underlines the problems of conceptualising the object of philosophising. If we assume that 'it' stands for 'Philosophy', the sentence means that philosophers are curious about how easily their object of study, philosophy, can be lifted out of one set of conventions and integrated into another. By focusing his interest on a comparison between different languages, rather than on the abstract representation of knowledge in language, Fontenelle proposes, as appropriate object of philosophy, a comparative study of different languages or modes of expression. Self-consciousness, then, not only concerns the philosophers' attitude to their object of study, but also involves a whole complex of questions about the relation of form to content, as also of abstract concepts to their concrete expression within particularised conventions.

It is also important to remember that knowledge functioned like property: as with property, it was not merely requisite to own knowledge, it was necessary to display it (Woodmansee, 1994; Johns, 1998). In an age in which hereditary nobility was being replaced by an economically defined social hierarchy, abstract notions of property came to justify social status; after all, money and investment are ultimately fictional entities. This is not the place to discuss in detail the relationship between the rise of capitalism and a changing understanding of the role of scientific knowledge: it is enough, here, to state that at the time when money, rather than inherited land, came to define social status, intellectual property grew increasingly important. As Steven Shapin (1994) has shown, how one represented oneself in public, therefore, was more important than who and what one was as such. In a world that attached extreme importance to how one presented oneself in society, knowledge was going to be more in demand than ever. The central role played by wit in social relations indicates that knowledge, and awareness of how to represent oneself in fashionable society, were the keys that opened the doors to more material gains.

In a cultural context that prized a talent for representation almost above everything else, imagination is a central concept. A precondition for the representation of the self, imagination set limits to personal development. That the success story of the parvenu, colourfully described in the picaresque genre, was so central an element in the contemporary imagination indicates that the question of how to fashion oneself was symbolically central. Since a large number of changes depended on whether, and how far, it was possible to abstract oneself from one's concrete situation, the power to imagine different social constellations, or a different role for the self within the existing constellation, was a potentially subversive activity. Moreover, although the Copernican theory of the cosmos was generally accepted, the violent suppression of its earlier supporters, Giordano Bruno and Galileo, was a recent memory. It no longer required courage to discuss and develop the theory in public; now its potential subversiveness lay elsewhere.[12]

E. D. James observes:

> how controlled is the imagination of Fontenelle, how closely attached to experience and to the evidence of scientific observation. It is only because of the extraordinary modes of behaviour revealed by scientific investigation of animal and insect life, that Fontenelle considers himself entitled to allow his imagination to entertain thoughts of exotic forms of life on the planets. His method of speculation is a form of reasoning from experience by way of imaginative analogy. (1990: 143–4)

It is true that the text makes huge efforts to control the imaginative potential of its material, but we must not overlook the fact that it boldly enters the new terrain by joining together fact and fiction. But then, as James concludes, it is obvious that Fontenelle had an ambivalent attitude towards imagination (140). Even while *Entretiens* claims to be an accurate account of Descartes' theories, its title serves as a sort of disclaimer, implying that, since it is objectionable to allow the imagination to intrude into science proper, this work presents itself as something different. And in implying that its place in the literary domain is indisputable, it argues that literature, or imaginative writing, is the proper domain for discussion of the relevance and implications of new discoveries. The informal tone of a literary work subverts any serious claims it might make. An awareness of this tug-of-war, between the privileging of imaginative engagements with new ideas and their rejection for lacking scientific seriousness and objectivity, adds an additional dimension to *Entretiens*. It is precisely this tension between the work's abandonment to the potential of fiction and continuous attempt at control, then, that demonstrates that this first experiment in the genre of scientific popularisation is the product of a major intellectual reorientation, and not simply a translation of scientific knowledge across intellectual boundaries.

Representing the Copernican Cosmos

The contests and conflicts generated by the transition from the Ptolemaic to the Copernican theory of the universe chiefly concerned the question of what it meant for contemporary epistemology if a static and determined model of the universe gave way to a dynamic one. The major threat of the new theory, related to the dissolution of a single perspective, and the subsequent impossibility of imagining a universe with the earth as its centre and rationale, however, went hand-in-hand with changes in social order, affecting, among other things, the perception of women's role in the propagation of knowledge.

Evocative attempts to describe, explain and *imagine* the exact nature of the far-off and alien territories which had been brought closer by the help of mathematical computations, and by the technical assistance of the telescope, were made, above all, by Kepler and Galileo. Even while enclosed in the narrative framework of a dream, Kepler's *Somnium* offers a scientifically accurate account of the surface of the moon, describing its topography as he had learnt it from Michael Maestlin and Tycho Brahe.[13] For all its imaginative novelty in allowing its readers to set foot, as it were, on alien territory, Kepler's *Somnium* presents a nightmare scenario rather than a sympathetic description of a site that has always stimulated the imagination. In so doing, he was following in the footsteps of Galileo's *Sidereus Nuncius* (1610), which had not only described a variety of new planets, moons and stars, but also confronted its readers with such a vast conception of space that Marjorie Nicolson (1956) describes it as the single publication that triggered off one of the most significant intellectual reorientations of the scientific revolution.

The potentially disorienting and gloomy outlook that resulted when science found itself face-to-face with the threat of infinity, one that was to be consolidated in Newton's theories, is almost absent in Fontenelle. During the first night, the marchioness repeatedly expresses her concern that, as she imagines, she is 'inhabiting such a little Humming-Top' (Behn, 1688: 107). The all-wise philosopher, however, gently gets her used to the idea and gradually dispels her fears, so that she can finally declare, 'I feel I have Courage sufficient to turn round' (107). The *entretiens*, therefore, not only enlighten her but also abate her fears; in other words, Fontenelle uses the narrative framework in which a manly philosopher calms the fears of a female interlocutor so as to render harmless what Blaise Pascal famously described as the abyss of infinity. Interestingly enough, it is precisely the comic dimension of *Entretiens* that functions as a means for Fontenelle, as he hopes, to regain control over spatial imagination.

Cyrano de Bergerac's *Histoire comique des Etat et Empire de la Lune* is one of the most significant points of reference for Fontenelle: not only is it a scientific popularisation in comic mode, but it is also one of the first works to make use of the vernacular. The period under discussion was fascinated by imaginary worlds that appeared exactly to reverse the customs and laws of nature on earth, and in Bergerac's 'Monde renversé', human behaviour is explicitly labelled 'burlesque' (1961: 76).[14] Contrast this with Richard Brome's play *The Antipodes* (1640), which uses the idea of a world upside-down to throw a critical light on existing customs: Bergerac tarts up his description by engaging speculatively with the idea that animals might have reason, plants instinct, and metals feelings.[15] Bergerac begins his story by telling us that he let himself be carried away into imagining the moon to be a world like the earth. But then, in a blend of satire and utopian speculation, he sketches his ideas of what this other world might be like. Bergerac's narrative technique appears to have influenced Fontenelle in two respects: on the one hand, it taught Fontenelle how to weave human foibles, in the shape of the relationship between the marchioness and the philosopher, into the fabric of his work; on the other, it was a model against which he had to set his face. While, therefore, Fontenelle made use of the carnivalesque to sharpen his readers' narrative appetites, his awareness of the ways in which Bergerac's use of comic elements challenged the very possibility of a stable meaning taught him of the need to keep laughter under control so as to preserve that stable meaning. Within the linguistic realm, of course, laughter is the element that brings about the transition from a static and stable to an unpredictable and dynamic system. What Bakhtin (1981) calls a dialogic discourse, consisting of ironic parallel voices which question and subvert linguistic meaning, therefore, would be a most suitable tool for representing Copernican theory. This idea must have hit Fontenelle so powerfully that he concentrated his energy on fighting against it.

Paula Findlen points out that, as secretary of one of the leading scientific societies, Fontenelle was strictly opposed to 'ludic accounts of nature, relegating them to more popular publications such as his well-known *Conversations on the Plurality of Worlds*' (1998: 266). That he tried hard to exclude the attitude of wonder from the practice of science can also be observed in his *Entretiens*.[16] The comic, or ludic, element is no doubt prevalent in this work; but it also deprives the playful narrative form that he derived from Bergerac of its subversive potential or, rather, reduces it to humorous details which provide pleasing moments in an otherwise sober account. The philosopher, for instance, refers to the

Copernican cosmos as if Copernicus had been its architect, rather than the one who discovered its logical principles; so Fontenelle uses this technique as a means, as it were, to reconstruct the theory, and, by allowing the marchioness (and his readers) to watch its development, he leads her, and them, to accept it gradually and gradually to trust its rationality and therefore its necessity:

> Know then, that a certain German, named *Copernicus*, does at one blow cut off these different Circles, and the Christalline Spheres, invented by the Antients; destroying the one, and breaks the other in pieces; and . . . takes the Earth, and hangs it at a vast distance from the Centre of the World, and sets the Sun in its place . . . (Behn, 1688: 102)

This passage toys with the idea that, instead of merely overturning a false scientific theory, Copernicus faced the Ptolemaic world as a material reality. Imagining him to be rearranging the orreries and cosmic models as if they were the cosmos itself, Fontenelle not only makes the idea funny, but also gives an evocative account of the psychological reverberations of the transition from the old to the new theory. At the same time, his account also ridicules those who fail to differentiate between theory and reality, and thus creates a tacit complicity between the philosopher and the marchioness, or between Fontenelle and those among his readers who think they are capable of understanding that a model (or a representation) differs radically from the thing represented.

When Fontenelle's narrator reports news from the moon, he sketches a literary scenario according to which such an idea can be imagined without problems. The marchioness is curious about the nature of such communication, and the philosopher replies that this news is 'such as are brought us every Day by the Learned, who travel daily thither by the help of long Telescopes: They tell us, they have discover'd vast Countries, Seas, Lakes, high Mountains, and deep Valleys' (Behn, 1688: 117). This is another instance where the imagination appears to be given free rein, but only to be curbed more harshly afterwards. The act of looking through a telescope is metaphorically described as making a journey to the far-off regions espied by the glass. Immediately after, though, we note that the news is not *from* the moon or *from* its inhabitants but *about* the moon. The formulation, furthermore, almost literally quotes Galileo's title *Sidereus Nuncius* [message from the stars], and thus places Fontenelle on a par with the principal authority in astronomy. The age-old desire to communicate with beings who are utterly different is thereby suppressed, in favour of a discourse of discovery that names and integrates into the conventional cognitive boundaries whatever might at first have been felt to exceed them.

It is the hallmark of Fontenelle's methodology to introduce new ideas circuitously; so his narrator camouflages the new theory of the cosmos as if it were a flight of the imagination. E.D. James (1990: 143) claims that, when he draws 'imaginative analogies' between the earth and the moon, Fontenelle reconceptualises imagination itself. In what follows, I want to argue that the imagination not only plays a vital part in determining the mode of representing new and daring theories but also, above all, is required as a tool to enable the self to position itself in a world that has become radically unfamiliar. The narrator first broaches the issue of whether there are other worlds apart from the earth:

> I am sorry that I must confess I have imagined to my self, that every Star may perchance be another World, yet I would not swear that it is so; but I will believe it to be true, because that Opinion is so pleasant to me . . . (Behn, 1688: 95)

Why is such an 'Opinion . . . so pleasant'? A simple answer is that it has sprung out of the 'world' of his imagination, and is his own. At issue, therefore, is an attempt to extend the accepted boundaries of the observer's self-identity. If we understand discovery, or the imaginative projection of an idea, as an instance of intellectual proprietorship, we can conclude that the reasons why this 'Opinion is so pleasant' are to be found in the fact that the speaker is conscious of his extraordinarily powerful imagination. He is pleased, therefore, not so much by the idea itself, or the product of his imagination, as by the self-conscious experience of his own mind. In this sense, his own creating mind takes over the role of the biblical God, who is not otherwise mentioned in the work. This celebration of the superiority of his intellectual and imaginative capacities, therefore, re-establishes man, or the male mind, represented by the figure of the philosopher, in the hub of the universe from which the Copernican theory had expelled him.

The significance of the imagination is futher emphasised in a metaphorical comparison between the cosmos and the theatre:

> I fansy still to my self that Nature is a great Scene, or Representation, much like one of our *Opera*'s; for, from the place where you sit to behold the *Opera*, you do not see the Stage, as really it is . . . [T]he Ropes, Pullies, Wheels and Weights, which give motion to the different Scenes represented to us by Nature, are so well hid both from our sight and understanding, that it was a long time before mankind could so much as guess at the Causes that moved the vast Frame of the Universe. (Behn, 1688: 96–7)

When the narrator says that he fancies to himself that nature is a 'Representation', he again allows himself a great deal of liberty to experiment with hypotheses: if nature is described as a theatrical representation, we might indeed wonder who the implied playwright is. When the narrator claims to reveal the 'Ropes, Pullies, Wheels and Weights' required for a dramatic representation, he creates them rather than merely pointing out their location. Not only do these instruments have specific associations with make-believe and deception, they are also needed for the projection of a particular point of view rather than for the simple representation of truth. In spite of its mechanical nature, the theatre cannot produce a strict correspondence between its own meanings and the 'meanings' it purports to represent. Hence, in presenting nature as a theatrical set, Fontenelle indicates that an understanding of how representations, or theories, work is more important than a knowledge of the true nature of things (were such a knowledge, of course, possible). When, therefore, a brief history of natural philosophical enquiry begins with the narrator's remark that he 'need only draw the Curtain, and shew you the world' (Behn, 1688: 98), he is legitimating his own perspective rather than offering a conclusive theory about the nature of the universe.

Fontenelle's work originally consisted of five *Entretiens* but, one year after it was published, he added a sixth (1687). In this last fictional encounter, the philosopher's tone has changed: no longer playfully patronising, he is clearly demonstrating his superior authority. While the work had previously finished with a tribute to the marchioness's extraordinary beauty, it now concludes:

> Really I am more and more of opinion that Europe is in possession of a degree of genius which has never extended to any other part of the globe ... [S]ome invincible fatality prescribes to it narrow bounds. Let us then make use of it ... and let us rejoice that it is not confined to science and dry speculations, but equally extended to objects of taste, in which I doubt whether any people can equal us. Such madam, are the things that should engage your attention and constitute your philosophy. (Fontenelle, 1803: 150)

It is not accidental that a celebration of Europe, the supposed cradle of the Enlightenment, excludes women from participation in science proper, even as it denigrates any form of non-European learning. Even though only a short time had elapsed between the two versions, the boost to Fontenelle's self-confidence as a scientist in the interim is clearly reflected in his unwillingness to acknowledge the subversive potential contained in the theories about the cosmos and in his refusal to allow gently-born women a place in his scheme as advocates of the new science. In the words of Erica Harth, he no longer speaks *with* the ladies but *to* them (1992: 148), thus allowing himself to assign a greater role to the male philosopher, who gets to study the nature of the universe, and a lesser one to the lady, who must now content herself with matters of taste and morality.

At the end of a book that discusses with sympathy the idea that other planets and stars may be inhabited, it is disappointing to observe how jealously Fontenelle guards the preserves of science, and concludes his description of a cosmos peopled by a huge variety of different inhabitants with a confirmation of his own Eurocentric perspective. An intellectual journey that exposes how strongly knowledge depends on its social context, of course, has questioned the very possibility of a single stable representation of truth. While this recognition implies that the most ethical solution is to practise tolerance towards different people and different views, it also makes clear that existing prerogatives cannot be maintained unless they are defended – if necessary, by force. So Fontenelle's preaching of tolerance is subtly undermined by his desire both to legitimate the violence required to defend European prerogatives and to maintain the illusion that the learned men with their long telescopes are discovering the truth, and not simply one possible perspective on truth.

And there is more to observe here. Even though the act of gendering science as masculine was detrimental to women, woman was not simply a figure for ignorance, any more than man was simply a figure for knowledge. Women occupied an ambivalent mediating role, and consequently were not entirely powerless. That Fontenelle felt the need to add a sixth *entretien*, in which he seeks to persuade women not to step out of their secondary role and engage directly in scientific study with their male counterparts, is a sign that his female contemporaries indeed wanted to do so. His pontificating tone may sound off-putting enough; noticing, though, that he felt called upon to define the boundaries between male and female intellectual occupations, we cannot help but conclude that female readers interpreted the figure of the marchioness in much more positive terms than he had originally done. Categories were fluid at the historical moment when lay and specialist audiences were being differentiated from each other, and the indeterminate nature of the situation offered women an opportunity to redefine their social role.

For French women, especially for those coming from an aristocratic background and familiar with the female-centred salon culture,

Fontenelle's patronising representation of the marchioness was at best a slight on the traditional participation of women in the production of knowledge. For those who had never belonged to such circles, even the moderate level of learning displayed by the marchioness suggested that women could have a stake in science and philosophy. It was the unexpected ambivalence of his message, I suggest, that induced Fontenelle to spell out with emphasis his views about the gendered distribution of knowledge in his sixth *entretien*.

Aphra Behn's Translation of Fontenelle

Aphra Behn's translation includes only the original five *Entretiens*, even though she could just about have known about the additional section. If she did know about the latter, she must have decided to maintain the work's original shape as first published. We do not know what attracted her to engage upon the translation. Her prefatory 'Essay on Translated Prose' suggests that she wished to present herself as a serious intellectual with the skill and moral integrity to read the new scientific theories through the lens of biblical exegesis. It seems likely that, in so arguing for the compatibility of the Copernican and Cartesian theories with the scriptural account of the world, she was attempting to shed the reputation of flippancy and immorality that she had gained as a writer of numerous, highly popular, Restoration comedies. Her insistence that the Bible should be read for its spiritual rather than its literal message, though, prepares us for a certain degree of freethinking on her part.

Careful though it is, Behn's translation demonstrates her wish to make changes and, among other things, to shift the philosopher's casual tone into a slightly more serious register. In her preface she remarks, 'I have endeavoured to give you the true meaning of the Author, and have kept as near his Words as was possible; I was necessitated to add a little in some places, otherwise the book could not have been understood' (1688: 76); she ends the preface by saying, 'And I resolv'd either to give you the *French* Book into *English*, or to give you the subject quite changed and made my own; but having neither health nor leisure for the last I offer you the first such as it is' (86). In the dedicatory epistle to William, Earl of Dumlangrig, Behn says no more than that this book 'pleased me in the *French*' (72); her preface explains her reasons at greater length:

> The General Applause this little Book of the Plurality of Worlds has met with, both in *France* and in *England* in the Original, made me attempt to translate it into English. The Reputation of the Author,

> . . . the Novelty of the Subject in vulgar Languages, and the Authors introducing a Woman as one of the speakers in these five Discourses were further Motives for me to undertake this little work; for I thought an *English* woman might adventure to translate any thing, a *French* woman may be supposed to have spoken . . . (73)

Arguably, Behn was attracted to Fontenelle's book, in part, because she was uncomfortable with it. She found the translation more difficult than she had at first assumed ('I found the task not so easy as I believed at first', she writes, (73)), for several reasons: the different sound and flow of English and French; the problems of translating technical vocabulary; and the implications of the new theory about the cosmos for other fields of scientific study. Behn further singles out the absence of religious argument as a problem for the translator. Fontenelle's failure to say one 'Word of God Almighty, from the Beginning to the End' (77) denotes a loss of the authority that guarantees the stability of the world and of meaning as such; in drawing attention to this failure, Behn exposes the fears that had already motivated Fontenelle's argument.

Behn's essay discusses translation as a theoretical issue, and not only for the practical questions her own translation involved, or the difficulties she encountered while working on it – say, the problem of finding a corresponding English term for the Cartesian 'tourbillion' (76). That she is as worried about Fontenelle's *Entretiens* as she is attracted to the work comes out most strongly in the following passage:

> I know that a Character of the Book will be expected from me . . . but I wish with all my heart I could forbear it; for I have that Value for the ingenious *French* Author, that I am sorry I must write what some may understand to be a Satyr against him. The Design of the Author is to treat of this part a Natural Philosophy in a more familiar Way than any other hath done, and to make every body understand him . . . But if you would know before-hand my Thoughts, I must tell you freely, he hath failed in his Design; for endeavouring to render this part of Natural Philosophy familiar, he hath turned it into Ridicule; he hath pushed his wild notion of the *Plurality of Worlds* to that heighth of Extravagancy, that he most certainly will confound those Readers, who have not Judgment and Wit to distinguish between what is truly solid (or, at least, probable) and what is trifling and airy . . . (76–7)

Behn's disapproval of Fontenelle's imaginative 'Extravagancy' led her to play down the implications of a title which literally translates as

'Conversations on the plurality of worlds', or, more freely, 'sociable get-togethers for the purpose of discussing the idea of a plurality of possible worlds'; her title, 'A Discovery of New Worlds', suppresses both the conversational quality of the text and its uncomfortably provocative idea about the possible existence of many other worlds. Consequently, her title elicits expectations of a travelogue rather than a scientific treatise.

Behn claims that the purpose behind Fontenelle's *Entretiens* is to render natural philosophy familiar and to 'make every body understand' Fontenelle. She accuses him of failing in this objective, not merely because his work shows insufficient clarity but also because it lays the material open to misinterpretation. An élitist bias, we may conjecture, would not have disturbed her as much as does her understanding that complex ideas have been simplified at the expense of their truth claims. Hence, she attacks him for including discussion of the laws of nature in what is essentially sensationalist writing. In her claim that 'for endeavouring to render this part of Natural Philosophy familiar, he hath turned it into Ridicule', she implies that his chief goal was to entertain, rather than to instruct, his audience. While she disapproves of the motive, she also appears to have been attracted by the satirical potential of *Entretiens*. Herself a resourceful satirist of social mores – in *The Emperor of the Moon: A Farce* (1687), she satirised the human aspirations to communicate with the inhabitants of the moon – she was well used to the powerful attractions of satire. What she appears to be saying here is that satire's proper place is in literature, and her anger is directed at a work that not only blurs the boundaries between comic and serious modes but also confuses philosophy and literature. When she accuses Fontenelle of treating the existence of plural worlds as if they were a fact, rather than a mere possibility, she takes issue with the question of publicising unproven scientific hypotheses that may lead ignorant readers seriously astray. Tackling the translation in spite of her stated reservations, however, allows her to assume the role of mediator. While the translation itself shows her to be tactfully staying in the background and letting the text, so to say, speak for itself, her reason for turning Fontenelle into English may well have been to curb, however slightly, the subversive potential of his meanings. This act allowed her to participate in a world of science from which, as a woman, she was otherwise excluded. In Janet Todd's words, 'translated prose provided an opportunity for a woman to enter into controversies on science, religion and philosophy which, as an unlearned female, she apparently had to eschew in her poetry' (Behn, 1688: 4).

To illustrate Behn's techniques as a translator, I propose to offer a comparative analysis of the passage from the French and English versions where Fontenelle's narrator introduces his explanation of the new theory of the world:

> Toute la philosophie, lui dis-je, n'est fondée que sur deux choses, sur ce qu'on a l'esprit curieux et les yeux mauvais; car si vous aviez les yeux meilleurs que vous ne les avez, vous verriez bien si les étoiles sont les soleils qui éclairent autant des mondes, ou si elles n'en sont pas; et si d'un autre côté vous étiez moins curieuse, vous ne vous sourcieriez pas de le savoir, ce qui reviendrait au même; mais on veut savoir plus qu'on ne voit, c'est la difficulté. Encore si ce qu'on voit, on le voyait bien, ce serait toujours autant de connu; mais on le voit tout autrement qu'il n'est. Ainsi les vrais philosophes passent leur vie à ne point croire ce qu'ils voient, et à tâcher de deviner ce qu'ils ne voient point . . . (Fontenelle, 1945: 48)

Behn translates this passage as follows:

> All philosophy is grounded on two Principles, that of a passionate thirst for knowledge of the Mind, and the weakness of the Organs of the Body; for if the Eye-sight were in perfection, you could as easily discern there were Worlds in the Stars, as that there are Stars: On the other hand, if you were less curious and desirous of know-ledge, you would be indifferent, whether it were so or not, which indeed comes all to the same purpose; but we would gladly know more than we see, and there's the difficulty: for if we should see well and truly what we see, we should know enough; but we see most Objects quite otherwise than they are; so that the true Philosophers spend their time in not believing what they see, and in endeavouring to guess at the knowledge of what they see not . . . (96)

Her stylistic choices suggest that she was highly aware of the major feature of this passage: the construction of the philosopher as a person who masters knowledge with nonchalance and polite (manly) vigour. Fontenelle's narrator is presenting himself as someone who has worked out the rationale of philosophy as a discipline, and who possesses both the intellectual insight and the rhetorical competence to express its essence in a single sentence without using any scientific jargon. As Behn argued in her translator's preface, though, Fontenelle went too far in his avowed purpose of avoiding difficult vocabulary. By translating 'Toute la philosophie . . . n'est fondée que sur deux choses' as 'All philosophy is grounded on two Principles', she adjusts the tone to a less flippant style of reasoning: first and foremost, she refuses to render 'deux choses' as 'two things', as Knight, a more overtly scientifically-minded translator of *Entretiens*, does (Fontenelle, 1687: 5). She thus makes clear that the drawing room has no problems with terms like 'principle'. When Fontenelle decided to use the word 'choses' instead of 'principes', she implies, he was unduly simplifying his subject matter and infantilising his audience. That the patronising formulations are addressed to a woman reveals Fontenelle's suspect gender politics, which Behn subtly tries to edit out. By intervening to modify his condescendingly simplistic formulations, she has the satisfaction of being able to teach the ambitious young scientist that he may understand natural philosophy but that he has still miscalculated the proper terms to use when addressing a cultivated lay audience.

Further instances of Behn's stylistic liberties, indicating deliberate intervention – and not merely solutions born of necessity – proliferate. For instance, Behn expands Fontenelle's pithy summary of the 'two things' that make up philosophy, 'ce qu'on a l'esprit curieux et les yeux mauvais', to 'a passionate thirst for knowledge of the Mind, and the weakness of the Organs of the Body'. Since it has its own parallelism, her formulation not only breaks (or refuses to reproduce) the precise rhetorical parallelism between an 'inquisitive mind' and 'bad eyes' but it provides us with more detail so that we are convinced by the argument, and do not merely succumb to the power of Fontenelle's rhetoric. Translating 'l'esprit curieux' as 'a passionate thirst for knowledge of the Mind' identifies such curiosity as both powerful and legitimate, because it is intellectual in origin and has nothing to do with prurient interest in forbidden matters.[17] Furthermore, expanding 'les yeux mauvais' to 'the weakness of the Organs of the Body' demonstrates familiarity with the philosophical arguments of Locke, among others, about the unreliability of sensory perception, and enables Behn to correct Fontenelle's reductive statement, and argue that the problem springs not only from weak eyesight but from the inevitably subjective nature of sensory perception as a whole. Even though Fontenelle's narrator begins by insisting that better eyesight would put an end to the problem, he cannot steer clear of the fact that 'we see most Objects quite otherwise than they are': which is to say that Behn's immediate insistence on the problem both indicates her knowledge of it and indicts Fontenelle for trying to sweep it under the carpet.

In her translator's preface, moreover, Behn emphasises her misgivings about Fontenelle's portrait of the marchioness: 'And as for his Lady Marquiese, he makes her say a great many very silly things, tho' sometimes she makes Observations so learned, that the greatest Philosophers in Europe could make no better' (77). Behn attacks Fontenelle not for inconsistencies of characterisation – after all, the marchioness is a figure for the cultivated woman – but for propagating the stereotype of a female intellectual who is liable to lapse into stupid remarks because her learning is superficial and ultimately incompatible with her femininity. In spite of her misgivings about Fontenelle's use of gender, or maybe because of them, Behn's stylistic changes show that she indeed wanted to rewrite Fontenelle's *Entretiens*. Even though she explicitly says that she had 'neither health nor leisure' to perform the task 'to give you the subject quite changed and made my own' (86), we should not conclude that she did not in fact make such an attempt. Or indeed, realising that rewriting it in a major way was beyond her capacities, Behn decided to intervene in the gender politics of the work by way of practising an almost imperceptible form of censorship.

The Newtonian Translator of Fontenelle

William Knight's translation of Fontenelle appeared one year after the French original, and translates the original five-part version. In the address to his patron, William Molyneux, Knight gives vent to his disapproval of the whole French cultural context involved in the dissemination of Cartesian theory. He brings his annoyance most clearly into focus in his dedicatory epistle, when he attacks the feminisation of a masculine science and blames Cartesianism and French culture for bringing about an effeminacy of mind. Knight's stated reason for translating Fontenelle, then, is an attempt to destroy what he takes to be the French plan of 'inlarging the French Monarchy beyond the Moon':

> concern'd for the Honour of our Nation, we have hitherto outdone the French by the Progress of our Arms in *this* World, why should we fall short of them in our Discovery of *others*, when a *Chimera* will do the business. I have therefore rectify'd his French Telescope the best I could for the use of an English Eye, and recommend it first to yours as the best Judge, that I know, of what may be perform'd by Opticks. I was once inclin'd (there being a Woman concern'd in the Discourse) to have address'd it to the Fair ones of that Sex; but when I consider'd that they themselves make up the glorious number of those Planets that influence and adorn our Globe, and that 'tis the greater Business of Mankind to discover their *Vortices*, I declin'd that thought, and concluded it a Work more proper for Men (Fontenelle, 1687: sig. A3ᵛ).

Objections to a supposed feminisation of science are closely linked to national prejudice. Knight indicts Fontenelle for fabricating the chimera of inhabited planets and stars as a means of extending the French empire; he implies that Fontenelle not only uses the imagination to aggrandise the French nation but indeed colonises imagination as such.

Knight's hostile attitude towards female philosophers is countered by William Molyneux's address to the bookseller, which follows immediately afterwards. In an attempt to qualify Knight's attitude, Molyneux flourishes his best manners so as to re-include those members of the 'Female Sex, that desire to become Philosophers', even though his tone is condescending and his motive is perceptibly to target female readers for their economic potential as purchasers of the book. He says that

> an ingenious Marchioness is introduced as chiefly ingaged in these Contemplations; which are deliver'd not with the severe Air of Philosophy, but so interspersed with pleasant Illustrations, and facetious instructive Remarks, that certainly he that once sets upon them, will hardly lay the Book aside till he has run quite through them, the whole is so very charming. (1687: sig. A5ᵛ)

Molyneux's protestation that the book 'is so very charming' stands in open contrast to Knight's call for a masculine science. The aggressive stance of the latter's dedicatory epistle is symptomatic of his fear that the study of nature might lose its masculine force and fail to realise its task of confirming the superiority of the male mind. Approaching Cartesianism with his own prejudices firmly in place, Knight accuses it of being an effeminate theory. Consequently, he is altogether unaware of the already-noted opposing tendency in Fontenelle, which would have suited his purposes much better: he attacks Cartesianism for empowering women to participate in philosophical disputes, and so fails to notice that Fontenelle's book functioned as a tool with which the male *philosophe* tried to claim the study of nature as a male prerogative. The effeminacy that Knight finds to blame in Cartesianism rests on the fact that Descartes' distinction between *res extensa* and *res cogitans* implicitly rejects a gendering of knowledge, which explains why Knight wants to return to a theory that defines the investigator as male, because such a theory assumes that knowledge is produced by a male mind that penetrates a female nature and forces her to yield her secrets to him.[18] To compare Knight's ill-bred attack on female learning with Molyneux's trite gallantry is to see that women who wanted to study natural philosophy were forced to position themselves between overt hostility and patronising gallantry.

Knight's implicit gendering of science as male also reinforces his view of science as English. Hence, his claim that he has 'rectify'd [the]

Telescope ... for the use of an English Eye' assigns national property rights to intellectual achievements. In rhetorical terms, he presents a scientific theory about the nature of the universe in parallel to the telescope. Describing the telescope as an object that has revealed the physical nature of the universe, he advances a specifically English method of reasoning as an analogous tool with which to rectify the errors of other nations. He not only enters into battle with the French theory, assuming that Newton got right what Descartes had got wrong, but also goes so far as to imply, in his use of the term 'Opticks', that Newton's theory of light has solved all problems relating to seeing and understanding. An 'English Eye', therefore, goes well beyond being a metonym for the English readership of Fontenelle's French book, and comes specifically to represent the English mind: because it was an Englishman who had explained the nature of light and who, as Knight implies, had done so for 'the Honour of [his own] Nation', the 'English Eye' excels that of every other nation. The fact that Knight evaluates scientific achievement in nationalistic terms is an instance of his time's changing attitude towards knowledge: no longer content merely to re-map and extend the boundaries of conventional knowledge; moving towards a situation in which claiming ownership of intellectual terrain was more important than proving the soundness of the argument.

Algarotti and the Conflict between the Cartesians and Newtonians

When Francesco Algarotti wrote *Il Newtonianismo per le dame* (1737), the expectations of the audience had changed significantly from what they had been when Fontenelle published his *Entretiens* some fifty years earlier. By now, polite readership was familiar with the generic convention of scientific popularisation. Addressing a female audience had also become a conventionally agreed way to reach a non-specialist readership who accepted a gendered distribution of knowledge: while science was increasingly successful in legitimating itself as a serious pursuit, scientific popularisation had consolidated a distinction between the proper scientist, defined in masculine terms, and a feminised polite readership, interested in, and limited to, imagining the implications of the new science. To set themselves off from the scientist proper, whose single-mindedness was used at the time as a popular topic of satire – so, for example, in Shadwell's play *The Virtuoso* (1676) – the drawing-room enthusiasts were identified with the ladies. The immensely popular *Entretiens* was not restricted to a female readership; it was certainly read by a large number of men, who, even if they read it only so as to acquire subject matter for polite conversations with women, formed a significant part of its readership.[19]

Unlike the motives behind the simplification of complex ideas in Fontenelle's *Entretiens*, Algarotti's project of simplifying Newton's ideas resulted quite straightforwardly from the considerable hostility he had met when trying to publicise more serious work on Newton in Italy. Notwithstanding their general support for Newtonian projects, even Voltaire and his partner Emilie du Châtelet, when Algarotti visited them in Cirey in 1735, opposed his plan to join Maupertius on his expedition to the Arctic Circle, where the latter wanted to prove some of Newton's claims about the earth's gravitational forces. Operating on the margins of science proper, Algarotti framed his scientific persona according to the stereotype of the masculine scientist as it had been adopted, among others, by Maupertius himself. Mary Terrall comments on the journal which the latter kept on his expedition to the Arctic Circle: 'First-person reports, whether oral or written, were instrumental in creating the public persona of the adventuring man of science' (1998: 237). Concerning its narrative status, she says that

> writing the book became as crucial to the success of the venture as the measurements themselves, and writing in the heroic vein was in part a play for the sympathy of women readers . . . To represent the validation of Newton's theory of gravity as a romance was to claim a significance and an audience for science that reached beyond the confines of the Academy, and this is surely what appealed to Voltaire about the expedition. (232–3)

It is to the challenging atmosphere of the discussions about Newtonian science between Voltaire, Emilie du Châtelet and Algarotti in that year that we owe Algarotti's work on Newton, by way of a striking reworking of the formal elements of Fontenelle's *Entretiens*.[20] Algarotti's marchioness and his philosopher are modelled on Fontenelle's characters, but the scientific lady is recognisably Emilie du Châtelet, and the philosopher Algarotti himself. His marchioness, however, is deprived of Emilie du Châtelet's extraordinary knowledge of science and philosophy. Du Châtelet was, for instance, about to embark on the task of translating Newton's *Principia*; similarly, by 1735, she had already begun to do calculus. In the trio's joint discussions of Newtonian science, her knowledge was equal to that of the two men.[21]

When he reworks this relationship in his fiction, Algarotti removes the second male figure and describes the marchioness as follows:

> To the charms of wit, and the most polite imagination she joined an
> uncommon strength of judgment, and to the most refined sentiments
> a learned curiosity. Superior to the rest of her sex, without being
> solicitous to appear to, she could talk of ornament and dress when-
> ever there was occasion for it, and ask proper questions upon more
> important subjects . . . She had beauty enough to gain her consort
> many friends, and judicious enough not to shew any one a partic-
> ular regard . . . (1739: 18–19)

By comparison with Fontenelle's very brief characterisation, which did
not go much beyond the narrator's assessment of the marchioness
as 'perfectly witty', Algarotti's description is an excellent instance of
baroque chit-chat. In complex clauses, Algarotti repeatedly sets alongside each other the marchioness's social aplomb and her intellectual
abilities. Her 'most polite imagination' and 'most refined sentiments'
demonstrate her excellent mastery of the conventions of her society,
while her 'uncommon strength of judgment' and 'learned curiosity' show
her to have skills well in excess of what her social position strictly
requires. Aware that these skills could potentially be considered negative qualities in a woman, Algarotti is careful to emphasise that their
possession does not diminish feminine charm and social success. The
importance of these latter he stresses when he remarks that her ability
to 'ask proper questions upon more important subjects' does not detract
from her supposedly more natural interest in dress and ornament. By
countering the contemporary argument that learned women are ugly
and masculine, he constructs a picture of femininity according to which
a certain mixture of beauty and intelligence enables a woman to promote
her husband's interests better. As long as learning is not the dominant
quality in a woman, but is used as a means of setting off to best effect
her physical attributes, Algarotti encourages it.

Cultivation and refinement are key concepts for Algarotti, and he
begins *Il Newtonianismo per le dame* with a polemical history of civilisation. Focusing on English cultural achievements in the arts and the
sciences, he implicitly berates Italian and other European nations for
their intellectual backwardness. The motive behind this attack can
undoubtedly be found in the hostility of Algarotti's own country to his
scientific ideas, but, by establishing a causal link between Newtonianism
and English culture, Algarotti actively promotes a rivalry conceived in
explicitly nationalistic terms. The book includes a dedicatory epistle to
Fontenelle and commendatory poems by Mary Wortley Montagu, Lord
Hervey, Summer and Stillingfleet; and to the first *dialogo* is also prefixed

a poem by Voltaire in praise of Newtonianism. The choice of intellectual authorities to commend this work is both defensive and aggressive:
in dedicating it to Fontenelle, Algarotti makes to secure the goodwill of
the eminent scientist who is still secretary of the French Académie des
Sciences, a post he would not resign till 1740. Aligning himself with
Fontenelle some fifty years after the publication of the latter's immensely
popular *Entretiens*, however, allows Algarotti to claim not only that
he follows in the footsteps of the master but also that he has the right
to explain the contemporary state of knowledge. Even though Algarotti
nowhere explicitly says that Cartesian theory has been superseded, his
emphatic praise of Newtonianism, and of the culture which provided
the soil in which it could develop, aggressively dismisses whatever stands
in the way of Newtonian science.

Algarotti indicts the Cartesian habit of reducing nature to mechanical
principles, and calls for a theory which provides space for irrational
phenomena, when he rejects Descartes' view of a machine at the heart
of all being, whether animal, mineral or vegetable: 'The marvellous, of
which the heart, always desirous of being affected, is so fond, happily
arises in true philosophy of itself, without the help of machines' (viii).
Cartesian theory eliminates wonder from our response to nature, and
explains the human mind itself by way of mechanical principles, impa-
tient with anything that cannot be analysed in strictly rational terms.
Algarotti emphasises that true philosophy needs to recognise that the
marvellous, or the irrational, is a vital aspect of natural phenomena, and
concludes that a methodology which tries to reduce these latter to rational
principles fails to understand the nature of nature. By asking that the
affective should be valorised in its own right, he not only refutes a utilit-
arian approach to science but argues for a reversal of the continuing
secularisation of nature; in other words, he seeks to bridge the Cartesian
gap between mind and matter.

By the 1730s the division between a specialist and a lay audience was
generally accepted. The concept of 'laity', of course, is itself borrowed from
a religious discourse which differentiates hierarchically between those who
handle or address the sacred directly and those who deal with more mundane matters. Identifying the sacred as the subject of natural philosophy,
Algarotti uses religious terminology to describe the boundary between the
scientist and the mere enthusiast: 'The sanctuary of the temple will always
be reserved for the priests and favourites of the Deity; but the entrance and
its other less retired parts will be open to the profane' (ix).

Realising how important for Algarotti are the 'affects of the heart'
helps us understand why his work begins with a passage in praise of

English culture. The link he finds between science, art and culture in the English scene is not only strategically useful as a means of attracting the attention of a polite readership, but also significant in its own right: art teaches us to cultivate our emotions. The links can be seen when the narrator's need to explain a complex metaphor leads him naturally to embark upon an exposition of the basic concepts of Newton's theories: art, that is, functions as the trigger, but not simply that, for scientific discourse. The marchioness has asked for an explanation of the phrase 'seven-fold light' (22). She has encountered this phrase in a poem that, as it turns out, Algarotti wrote himself. That the natural philosopher writes poems is no coincidence. As Algarotti is keen to emphasise, Newton's approach to nature inspires poetical sentiments. Or alternatively, engaging with Newtonian theory offers a kind of knowledge about nature that is akin to poetry.

Since Algarotti seeks to emphasise that Newtonian theory has far more cultural reverberations than any other scientific theory, his detailed descriptions of the setting in which the philosophical dialogue takes place imply that there is an analogy between the laws of nature and the laws of language: just as the desire to understand nature makes us aware of the limits of reason, so an engagement with the potentials of language makes us question the modes of representation. The close relationship between form and content, therefore, illustrates how, in Newtonian theory, reason and representation not only depend on each other but similarly confront us with their own limits.

In such a context, a poetic use of language can evoke a vivid understanding even of the nature of light, which explains why the marchioness has asked for enlightenment herself: 'Now we are speaking of epithets, is not *the seven-fold Light*, which I read some time ago . . . in an Ode made in honour of the philosophical lady of Bologna, some Chinese hieroglyphic?'[22] Her remark that the term 'seven-fold Light' is a 'Chinese hieroglyphic' shows her awareness that, far from being a mere metaphor, the phrase must refer to a complex theory that she cannot understand. The conjunction between 'Chinese' and 'hieroglyphic' underlines the sense of alienation experienced by anybody not familiar with the Newtonian concepts. It is at this moment, therefore, that Algarotti steps in as interpreter. His role is not only to translate and explain but also, by implication, to introduce a whole new mode of seeing and experiencing the world to his readers; he thus broadens their whole cultural perspective.

This important relationship between art and science, or experience and knowledge, is one to which the text continually returns. Emphasising their similarities, the text also argues that they are complementary and, therefore, should not compete for dominance with each other. As the narrator remarks, 'As our senses are not microscopical, so neither are our hearts philosophical. It would be very bad for us, if our pleasure was in the hands of philosophers, and if beauty, in order to prove its existence, must stand out against all the experiments of a naturalist' (59). Aesthetic considerations are extremely important as means of bridging the divide between empirical and aesthetic responses to nature. Regrettably, the scope of the present study does not permit further comment on Algarotti's conception of knowledge; it must suffice to note that his work divided his readers, not only because he hardened the battle lines between the Cartesians and the Newtonians, but also because he called for a revised understanding of the role of reason. So he sounds like a Romantic when he overthrows the rule of sober rationalism, and puts in its place a method of seeking knowledge that takes account of everything that exceeds neat categories and tidy methodological systems. Of course, reason plays quite a different role in the Cartesian and the Newtonian world-views, and Algarotti's work suggests that Newtonian science has not only vanquished older scientific theories but also shown the need for different epistemologies to conceptualise the changed relationship between mind and matter.[23] Since Newtonianism radically challenged previous modes of thinking, it naturally encountered a great deal of hostility. When Algarotti emphasised its importance for contemporary culture and society, the Cartesians understood his popularising account as a declaration of war.

France was the stronghold of the Cartesians, and it is no surprise that Algarotti's work was torn to shreds in the very French translation of it that appeared a year after its publication. In the preface to this shoddy and frequently inaccurate translation, the translator, Du Perron de Castera, points out that he translated Algarotti so as to have an opportunity to explain to a French audience how utterly wrong-headed was Newtonian theory. In his elaborate preface he clearly distances himself from Algarotti's arguments:

> Un Pueple, qui aime les Sciences & les beaux Arts, doit toujours de l'attention aux découvertes de les voisins, ou pour adopter leurs idées, ou pour les réfuter justement. Si d'autres Nations pensent mieux que nous, notre honneur & notre intérêt veulent que nous profitions de leur lumieres; si ces mêmes Nations sont dans l'erreur, mettons-nous en état de les éclairer; quelle gloire de triompher sous les drapeaux de la verité, aussibien que ceux de Mars! (1738: iii) [A people who loves the sciences and the arts always has to watch out

for the discoveries of its neighbours, either for the purpose of taking over their ideas or to be in the position of refuting them with just arguments. If other nations have ideas that are superior to ours, our honour and our interest demand that we should profit from their insights; if the same nations should be in error, let us assume the role of enlightening them; it is equally glorious to triumph under the banner of truth as well as under that of Mars! (my translation)]

Du Perron de Castera understands himself as his nation's guardian of intellectual purity. He positions himself as a mediator between the scientific and cultural achievements of his own country and those of foreign countries, and describes his task as the carrying out of an enlightened censorship: although Algarotti's rendition of Newtonian theory is not to be banned – it is even made more accessible through its translation into French – it is now being offered to French readers so as to invite them to give expression to their distaste. Reading Algarotti's argument as a slight on the French nation, on the one hand, is a polemical strategy by which du Perron de Castera seeks to enflame the spirits of his readers; on the other, it demonstrates that Algarotti's praise of England was indeed understood as belittling France. Du Perron de Castera's attack is directed neither at Algarotti nor at Newton. Since the competition between Cartesianism and Newtonianism has become a matter of national honour, it is England which must be attacked for wilfully persisting in error.[24]

While he legitimates himself with the remark that he has already published a detailed refutation of Newtonian theory – one, he emphasises, that was written in Latin – Du Perron de Castera tongue-lashes Algarotti for his lack of respect for French intellectual authority:

> Zelé partisan des Sçavans d'Angleterre, il n'en parle qu'avec vénération, & sans doute il n'a pas tort. Prévenu contre Descartes & contre tous nos Philosophes Français, il les traite de temps en temps avec un mépris souverain; ce sont, si l'on vent l'en croire, des esprits Romanesques, livrées à la temerité des conjecteurs, entrainés par la fureur de fabriquer des Systèmes, toujours exposés aux insultes des Observations & de l'Expérience. (vi) [Zealous advocate of the English intellectuals ['savants'], he only talks about them with admiration and he undoubtedly is not wrong. Predisposed against Descartes and all of our French philosophers, he occasionally treats them with haughty contempt; they possess, if we were to believe him, Romanesque minds that are given to the boldness of conjecture, carried away by a furious desire to construct systems and are always proved wrong by [the method which is based on] observations and experimentation. (my translation)]

The chief purpose of Du Perron de Castera's preface is to give a synopsis of his two major objections to Newton's theory, which, he argues, is based on 'cette qualité plus ténébreux que toutes les qualités occultes de l'ancienne Ecole' [this quality which is more shady than all the occult qualities of the old school] (xxxi). His most eloquent objections, as demonstrated in the passage quoted above, concern the English method of privileging observation and experience.[25] In his attempt to vindicate Descartes, he all but confirms the stereotype of French thinkers, which he lays at the charge of Algarotti, and lets himself be carried away so far as to say: 'Descartes fut le pere de la saine Philosophie . . .' [Descartes was the father of sane (rational) philosophy] (viii). The means by which he personalises ideas and equates them with their respective nations is indicative of an increasing tendency, as earlier noted, to treat knowledge as a national property.

When we compare the French with the English translation of Algarotti, we are, above all, struck by the fact that the English translator's name is nowhere mentioned: Elizabeth Carter gets no acknowledgement for her painstaking and well-written translation, which appeared in 1739. Another remarkable feature is the disappearance of the commendatory sections which precede the Italian text, though these were in English in the original and would not have needed to be translated. Even more strikingly, though it was included in later editions, the dedication to Fontenelle was also suppressed in the first English edition. When Algarotti's book makes its first appearance in the English cultural context, the text stands on its own, as if to assert that Newton's ideas, brought full circle to their country of origin, need neither recommendation nor embellishment. By the 1730s, of course, a proper cult had established itself around Newton, and Pope's famous couplet, 'Nature and nature's laws lay hid in night / God said, let Newton be and all was light', is only one among many tributes to a genius who was celebrated as a national hero.

The aggression displayed by the French translation shows that Newtonianism was more than a scientific theory with a strong impact on culture, as Algarotti had described it. As had already happened with Fontenelle's *Entretiens*, a recognition of the importance of the imagination for both scientific and cultural productions of meaning sparks off vitriolic contests over imagined and imaginary entities, like a nation's honour, or the appropriate social roles for men and women. When Newtonianism abandons the mechanical principles cherished by the Cartesians, and relegates the ultimate understanding of the laws of nature to the imagination, national pride over the possession of such bold ideas also encourages a kind of intellectual colonialism. The intellectual contesting of differences of nation and gender surfaces most strongly when the attempt is made to communicate across boundaries of nation and gender. The endeavour to make it possible for each side to understand the other, either by means of simplifying complex ideas or by translating them into another language, lays bare a host of contemporary preconceptions and stereotypes. The category of scientific popularisation, which I have discussed through the work of its two most famous early representatives, may sometimes come across as wanting to iron out conflicts and misunderstandings. If we analyse Fontenelle and Algarotti through the works of their translators, though – if, for that matter, we read Algarotti as a 'translator' of Fontenelle – we note that they are, subtly or openly, advocating views sometimes radically opposed to the drift of their originals.

The examples I have discussed in this chapter display a complex entanglement of national and gender interests. Addressed as they are to a broad, non-specialist audience, they are intensely preoccupied with the modalities of representing knowledge, and reveal an awareness that the definition of identity is largely determined by access to knowledge. In other words, the formulation of scientific ideas combines an attempt to communicate factual knowledge and an attempt to consolidate assumptions about gender and nation. When the translations discussed here seek to redress a perceived bias of the original, they certainly point to the biased nature of representation, but they primarily explore the scope for self-representation entailed by the impossibility of an objective representation. As such, they are at the forefront of contemporary disputes over the definition of identity, and they demonstrate that science was not only an instrument with which to explain the world but also (to change the metaphor) a container for culture's most sensitive concepts. Even though such a project was itself subject to the subjective nature of linguistic representation, the writers and translators involved in scientific, or pseudo-scientific, publication made every effort to use the aura of objectivity attaching to scientific discourse for the definition of such contested concepts as gender and national identity.[26]

Notes

1. For instance, Johannes Kepler's *Somnium* (1609) makes use of a literary form so as to express with impunity astronomical computations that went against the interests of an authoritarian government.
2. Aileen Douglas (1994: 2) notes that Fontenelle's *Entretiens* had appeared in seven different translations by 1803, principally because Fontenelle's work

sold so well that publishers were willing to commission new translations as a way of avoiding copyright problems with existing translations. That is, the high number of translations says more about the popularity of Fontenelle's *Entretiens* than about the wish of different translators to make this work their own. That translation, as such, self-consciously moves into the centre of interest, however, is an unavoidable side-effect.

3. Peter Dear (1990) argues that the use of narrative style was understood as a distinctively English practice, by contrast with the French recourse to, and dependence on, mathematical formulas.

4. Newton's theories were almost immediately circulated in fashionable society, which is to say that the contemporary culture did not need Algarotti to hear about Newton's spectacular discoveries; cf. Nicolson, 1946. Therefore, Algarotti's work did not primarily serve the purpose of familiarising its audience with the new ideas, but rather contributed towards an engagement with science for the sake of exploring the implications of the new ideas for contemporary culture; on this point, see Jacob, 1988.

5. The philosopher invokes the Indian myth according to which 'the Earth is supported by four Elephants', and playfully remarks, 'And I dare say, if these Indians thought the Earth in any danger of falling, they wou'd quickly double the number of Elephants ... And, Madam, we will add as many as you please to our System for this Night, and take them away by degrees, as you get more Assurance. Really, said she, I do not think they are needful at present; for I have Courage enough to turn round.' (Behn, 1688: 107)

6. Here, and throughout the chapter, all emphasis in quoted passages is original.

7. For an analysis of the Heloise and Abelard topos, see Kamuf, 1982; see also Radice's translation (1974) of their letters.

8. For a discussion of Fontenelle's engagement with the idea of possible worlds as a semantic concept, see Van den Abbeele, 1990. For a discussion of the role of wonder in the development of science, see Daston and Park, 1998.

9. For a discussion of the contemporary popularity of genres which drew attention to the conversational style in which they were written, cf. Kalverkämper, 1989.

10. The *OED* defines 'vulgarisation' as 'the action of making usual or common; the process of rendering familiar or popular; general dissemination', and 'to vulgarise' as 'to reduce to the level of something usual or ordinary'. The term 'popularisation', which became current only towards the end of the century, is defined as 'the adapting of ideas or theories to the level of an educated but non-specialist public; freq. with derogatory connotations, the oversimplifications of a subject to suit popular taste'. Both terms have negative connotations, indicating that the act of adapting the modalities of discursive prose to the needs of an audience provoked a great deal of suspicion.

11. So, for example, Derrida, 1978; for a discussion of translations of Cicero, see Copeland, 1991.

12. For a discussion of the death sentence passed on Giordano Bruno for proposing a possible plurality of inhabited worlds, see Yates, 1964; for a discussion of Galileo's background, Feldhay, 1995.

13. For an account of the background theories which informed Kepler's scientific story about the moon, see Patricia Frueh Kirkwood's introduction to *Kepler's Dream*.

14. In his introduction to Bergerac's *Histoire comique* (1961), Charles Nodier points out (xvi) that it is uncertain when Bergerac wrote this work: in particular, whether or not it predates the French translation, by la Montagne in 1653, of Wilkins' *The World in the Moon*.

15. The idea of comic inversion had established itself as a familiar category through carnivalesque customs; see, for example, Babcock, 1978.

16. For a discussion of his life-long endeavour to subject science to the order of reason, see Daston and Park, 1998: 324, 352.

17. For a thorough account of how the desire for knowledge was transformed from a reprehensible curiosity into a laudable intellectual occupation in the early modern period, see Daston and Park, 1998, esp. pp. 310–28.

18. For a historical analysis of the gendering of natural philosophical enquiry, see Keller, 1983.

19. So, in 1748, Lord Chesterfield urged his loutish son to read Fontenelle in order to occupy his mind with sober and useful ideas, a request repeated in 1751 (Meyer, 1955: 23).

20. Voltaire undertook the task of explaining Newton's theories in a more prosaic form: see the introduction by Walters and Barber to Voltaire's *Elements de la philosophie de Newton* (1738: 84).

21. I am grateful to Judith P. Zinsser for explaining to me the personal context of Algarotti's relationship with Voltaire and du Châtelet.

22. The 'learned lady', as the footnote to this passage explains, is 'Laura Maria Katherina Barsi, a learned lady in Italy, who in 1732, at 19 years old, held a philosophical disputation at Bologna, upon which she was admitted to the degree of doctor in that university' (1739: 22).

23. Immanuel Kant (1848) was the first to discuss the problems posed by Newtonian physics in a systematic manner.

24. For an explanation of why subsquent theories (primarily those of Locke and Hume) sought to revise and/or displace the Cartesian view, see Yolton, 1984.

25. For an analysis of the influence of cultural background on scientific method, see Shapin and Schaffer, 1985.

26. On Algarotti and Elizabeth Carter see also Agorni, 1994: 1–10, a paper which I discovered only when the prsent volume was at press.

Chapter 4

Hooked on Classics: Discourses of Allusion in the Mid-Victorian Novel[1]

HUGH OSBORNE

Sufficient critical attention has not been paid to the use of classical allusion, or indeed of allusion generally, in mid-Victorian fiction, certainly not to the extent that awareness of such allusion self-evidently informs our reading practice.[2] This situation is probably linked to a prevailing view of nineteenth-century fiction, one profoundly coloured by vaguely defined notions of 'realism', which assumes that fiction of the period necessarily shies away from self-reflexivity and deliberately intertextual narrative strategies.

In this chapter I seek to quantify the nature of classical allusion in the novels of Anthony Trollope in particular, a writer whose output has long and predominantly been thought of as 'realist'. Yet Trollope's textual practice problematises the narrative self-effacement upon which a representationalist aesthetic is predicated, through, among other things, the incorporation of classical allusion and quotation, both translated and untranslated, into the fabric of his narrative.

Specifically, this study examines Trollope's initial contribution to the *Cornhill Magazine*, *Framley Parsonage* (1860–1), so as to lay bare an implied discourse of Englishness to which, paradoxically, classical allusion contributes. It then tries to define more precisely the nature of this 'Englishness', and, through examining a number of writers contemporary with Trollope, uncovers a specifically male, public-school-derived 'discourse of remembrance'. Such a discourse inscribes memories of one's schooldays with a unilateral power to define and perpetuate a formative community of one's youth, an inclusive community which surrounds one even into adulthood, and which necessarily excludes those denied a public school education. Classical allusion here functions as a metonym for the 'discourse of remembrance', and replicates textually the exclusivity that a public school education was thought to confer. Finally, the study examines how classical allusion contributes to mid-Victorian notions of 'gentlemanliness', and details how the assumptions about class and gender inherent in such notions were both naturalised and challenged. Trollope's fiction reveals that classical allusions, and contemporary discussions of them, become textual spaces in which various class- and gender-based power struggles can be enacted. In short, the middle-class male subjectivity implied in Trollope's target readership is constructed not through a simple representationalism, but rather through his texts' generation of extra-textual cultural meanings.

Before we consider the various discursive functions of classical allusion, we need to clarify the terms of the discussion. Michael Wheeler offers a set of definitions:

> An adopted text is a work or part of a work from which material is borrowed in the act of quoting or referring, and an adoptive text is a work in which that material is placed. A quotation is an identifiable word, phrase or passage taken from an adopted text. A marked quotation is one whose nature is indicated by means of punctuation or typography, whereas an unmarked quotation is one whose nature is not thus indicated. A reference is a word, phrase or passage which directs attention to an adopted text but which does not share stylistic similarities with it. Allusion is the generic term for quotations and references, and for the act of quoting or referring. (Wheeler, 1979: 2–3)

This has the benefit of clarity, and I would concur with Wheeler's broad definition of allusion, which differs from that of Harold Bloom, and allows the term to include 'quotation' within its general meaning. For Bloom, to think of 'allusion' as including 'quotation' is simply inaccurate, though he concedes, reluctantly, that the range of the word's signification is diachronically unstable:

> the history of 'allusion' as an English word goes from an initial meaning of 'illusion' on to an early Renaissance use as meaning a pun, or word-play in general. But by the time of Bacon it meant any symbolic likening, whether in allegory, parable or metaphor . . . A fourth meaning, which is still the correct modern one . . . involves any implied, indirect or hidden reference. The fifth meaning . . . now equates allusion with direct, overt reference. (Bloom, quoted in Wheeler, 1979: 3)

Wheeler's response is admirably matter-of-fact: 'I use allusion in this generic sense for two reasons; first, it is now part of critical usage, and secondly, no other word, such as quotation or reference, will do.' More importantly, '[t]he old meanings of allusion (word-play or symbolic likening) are not finally eradicated as soon as its fourth (modern) meaning gives way to the fifth, as Bloom seems to suggest' (Wheeler, 1979: 3).

However, we might criticise Wheeler's overall definition, or, at least, complicate it slightly, for failing to take into account a whole range of allusions that do not fall under any of its categories. For instance, in Trollope's *The Belton Estate* (1865–6), Mrs Askerton talks to Clara Amedroz of '"the gentleman who always had the sword hanging over him by the horse's hair . . ."' (chap. XVIII).[3] She is undoubtedly making a classical allusion – to the sword of Damocles – but it is, in Wheeler's terms, neither 'quotation' ('marked' or 'unmarked') nor 'reference'. Rather, it belongs to a realm, outside any specific adopted text, that we might ineffectually denote by the term 'culture'; it is not therefore limited either to what its deployment in the adoptive text, or to what its original context within the adopted text, might signify. The absence of a readily identifiable source for the Damocles allusion prevents us from containing its meaning within the condition of an explanation, which would, in fact, ultimately and only constitute a set of bibliographic details: prevents us, in Bloom's elegantly contemptuous phrase, from being labelled as 'those carrion-eaters of scholarship, the source hunters' (Bloom, 1975: 17), scholars whose critical methodology directs attention away from what an allusion might signify performatively. In other words, the very act of alluding is probably more important, in terms of what it signifies culturally, than whatever might actually be alluded to, whatever the context in which the allusion appears. Discussing allusion is not merely a matter of undertaking an arid scholarship of identification, for a critical enquiry predicated solely on tracking down sources would render each adoptive text a seemingly unproblematic literary artefact that blandly accepts back, as being uniquely its own, whatever the scholar may decide to mine from it. It would be, in fact, an exercise in mutual flattery: the scholar finally tracks down that tantalisingly elusive allusion that has for so long been winking mischievously at him/her from the pages of an adopted text, and the text responds by conferring upon the scholar the privilege of being the first to elucidate the hitherto 'lost' meaning. Effectively, text and scholar both congratulate each other for displaying such extraordinary breadth of reference. Wheeler distances himself from such self-serving aridity by insisting that the significance of allusion lies just as much in how it is interpolated by the reader as in its existence as an allusion – a matter of what is read from a text as well as of what is said by a text:

[t]he reader's response to an allusion which he recognises as he reads, and whose context in its adopted text is familiar to him, is obviously more spontaneous, and generally stronger and more rewarding, than his response to an allusion located with the help of reference books or computers can ever be. (Wheeler, 1979: 6–7)

However, the problem here, one might argue, lies in defining the precise nature of what Wheeler terms this 'spontaneous' response. What are the cultural criteria that might allow such a 'stronger and more rewarding' response to appear 'spontaneous'? And how might one qualify these disarmingly vague concepts of 'strength' and 'reward'? The implicit claim to the obviousness, the self-evidence, of his critical vocabulary reveals a degree of complicity with the very discourse(s) that the act of allusion might constitute, to which it might contribute, and in which it might participate.

Returning to the invocation of Damocles in *The Belton Estate*, we can see that, through functioning as a sort of 'authorless' allusion, it eludes the restrictive critical terminology that Wheeler's set of definitions creates, and helps us focus our attention on the fact that allusion always reaches out beyond both adopted and adoptive texts; it helps us concentrate on its function, above and before all, as a cultural practice. It comes as no surprise that Wheeler argues that 'the most interesting and important' type of allusion acts 'as a plot pointer or thematic pointer in the adoptive text' (1979: 22). By stressing this function of a given allusion, Wheeler explicitly directs attention away from the allusive act as a discursive practice, in order to concentrate on how it might operate within a given text, apparently unproblematically, according to a critical methodology based predominantly upon a formalist aesthetics.

Before proceeding any further, however, it is necessary to clarify one further term used throughout this essay. In using the term 'tag' as referring to a short quotation, I give it a more specialised definition than is customary. The *OED* gives the following definition: 'A brief and usually familiar quotation added for special effect; a much used or trite quotation.' While we might broadly agree with this definition, it fails to take into account the possibility that a 'tag' – as opposed to a quotation – might have an explicitly connotative function; the 'brief and usually familiar quotation' might operate to activate recognition of its context within the adopted text. In *Can You Forgive Her?* (1864–5), for example, the novel's introductory description of Plantagenet Palliser describes the aftermath of his unsuccessful flirtation with Lady Dumbello, the narrative of which is related in the earlier *The Small House at Allington* (1862–4), in the following terms:

On the morning after the lady had frowned on him he had told
himself that he was very well out of that trouble. He knew that it
would never be for him to hang up on the walls of a temple a well-
worn lute as a votive offering when leaving the pursuits of love.
Idoneus puellis he never could have been. (chap. XXIV)

Palliser, in other words, is not suited by temperament to the young
man's pursuit of the opposite sex. He is not *idoneus puellis* [fit for young
women]. The allusion is to Horace, incorporating both a quotation and
translation from the third Book of the *Odes*.[4] Our chief concern here is
with the way in which the quotation is 'tagged', so that ultimately it
is not a quotation at all: two separate words are taken from the Horace
original and placed together, creating a phrase that seeks to activate
recognition of the adopted text from which it has been extracted. The
tag, rather than being simply a 'brief and usually familiar' or 'much used
or trite' quotation, might be more profitably defined as a specific deployment of an adopted text, that differs in kind from a quotation, translated
or untranslated, inasmuch as it functions as an instance of synechdochal
deixis and actively solicits recognition of its source text.

However, a classical tag, so defined, does not need to be re-inscribed
by the adoptive text in its original language in order to function. For
instance, in *The Roundabout Papers* (1863), Thackeray alludes to the same
Horace ode by means of a tag that combines both the Latin and an English
translation: 'Nuper – in former days – I too have militated; sometimes,
as I now think, unjustly; but always, I vow, without personal rancour'
(chap. VI). Here the ode is signified by *nuper* ('until recently', helpfully
rendered by Thackeray as 'in former days'), and 'I . . . have militated', a
translation of the original's perfect indicative active *militavi*. Similarly,
Trollope's *Doctor Thorne* (1858) recalls the same ode chiefly though the
use of the wholly translated tag *non sine gloria* [not without glory]:

Young ladies like Miss Dunstable . . . do not usually tell young
gentleman that they are very fond of them . . . Now Frank Gresham
regarded himself as one who had already fought his battles, and
fought them not without glory; he could not therefore endure to be
told by Miss Dunstable that she was very fond of him. (chap. XX)

In this latter example, the whole context of the adoptive text – Frank's
self-perception of being experienced in love's battles – might help
towards identifying the adopted text; however, it is the translated 'not
without glory' that presumably acts as the chief signifier of the Horace.

Whatever the method of its inscription, the tag resists being fully
subsumed by the adoptive text, reaching out from beyond the confines

of its narrative re-inscription. In effect, it functions simultaneously inside and outside its adoptive context, explicitly drawing attention to its status as part of a much larger network of cultural signification and practice. We can now begin our examination by turning to one of the more prominent Latin tags in Trollope's fiction, 'omnes omnia bona dicere',[5] the opening chapter title of *Framley Parsonage*, which Trollope was commissioned by Thackeray and George Smith to write as the centrepiece of the very first number of the new *Cornhill Magazine*. Undoubtedly, these words, from Terence's *Andria*, would seem to have a thematic function, and to solicit active recognition of the adopted text; not only does the tag stand as a chapter title, but the opening words of the novel itself are a close paraphrase of the Latin original:

> When young Mark Robarts was leaving college, his father might well declare that all men began to say all good things to him, and to extol his fortune in that he had a son blessed with so excellent a disposition. (chap. I)

In the *Andria*, these words, spoken by Simo, ironically presage his son Pamphilus' 'going to the bad', as Mark Robarts will in the course of the novel. But the comic structure of the *Andria* ensures that Pamphilus' 'fall' is temporary, and that a happy ending is inevitable. Thus the tag, as well as connoting the possibility of 'going to the bad', possibly points to the overarching comic structure of *Framley Parsonage*. This implicit invocation of the generic model within which Mark Robarts' troubles will be inscribed gives reassurance from the outset that Robarts' financial and social disgrace will be a temporary one.

The tag is a good instance of a quotation which had a wide cultural currency during the nineteenth century, but which, subsequently, has been collectively 'forgotten'; for, as David Skilton mischievously remarks, 'people trained . . . to exemplify this phenomenon [quoting, and recognising quotations, from the classics] are becoming rarer birds in the world today than a century ago' (1988: 42). Skilton points out that Terence's words would have been 'familiar not only to those who have studied . . . passages of Terence's *Andria* . . . but also to any schoolboy who . . . [would have] had to learn them off-by-heart . . . in such a textbook as the so-called *Eton Latin Grammar*' (49). Such familiarity cannot be presumed today, and a quick glance at the history of Trollope criticism and scholarship reveals how far 'omnes omnia bona dicere' has become relatively obscure. John W. Clark, for instance, in his discussion of Trollope's use of classical quotation, confesses that he has not been able to trace the tag, 'even with the assistance of the learned' (1975: 180); P.D. Edwards, in his 1980 World's

Classics edition of *Framley Parsonage*, mistakenly claims it is from the Vulgate: "'[Woe to you when] all men speak well of you." (Luke 6.26)' (Trollope, 1860–1: 583).

There were, of course, plenty of mid-Victorian readers who might have been blissfully ignorant of Latin, and who didn't know the source-context of 'omnes omnia bona dicere', but who were nevertheless dimly aware that, in certain contexts, it hinted at paternal pride or a young person's 'going to the bad'. And many other readers may not have known even that. These latter, nevertheless, we may assume, produced successful readings of *Framley Parsonage*. It was argued by at least one contemporary commentator, Henry Sidgwick, that

> for the general reader . . . classical knowledge does not do much more than save some trouble of referring to dictionaries and histories, and some ignorance of quotations which is rather conventionally than really inconvenient . . . [M]odern authors . . . contain numerous allusions to preceding and contemporary authors whom we do not think of reading . . . We content ourselves with the fragmentary lights of a casual commentator. I do not see that it would be so dreadful if classical allusions were apprehended by the general reader in the same twilight manner. (Sidgwick, in Farrar, 1868: 106)

Here, Sidgwick, arguing against the necessity for an education in the classics, acknowledges that successful readings can be produced of texts that deploy classical allusion without knowledge of the latter. More importantly, having recognised that 'ignorance of quotations . . . is rather conventionally than really inconvenient', he perceives that one should distinguish between the ability to recognise a given allusion as a necessary prerequisite to full comprehension of its adoptive text, and the cultural prestige conferred by an alleged knowledge of the classics:

> classical literature, in spite of its enormous prestige, has very little attraction for the mass even of cultivated persons at the present day. I wish statistics could be obtained of the amount of Latin and Greek read in any year (except for professional purposes), even by those who have gone through a complete classical curriculum . . . [S]uch statistics, when compared with the fervent admiration with which we all still speak of the classics, upon every opportunity, would be found rather startling. (Sidgwick, 1868: 102–3)

This, however, is precisely the point. Any and every possible intertextual significance of the tag's deployment probably counts for less than the mere fact of its presence in the text. The sheer prominence of the allusion, in the first number of the first novel in the first issue of the *Cornhill,* indicates something about the magazine's cultural expectations of its prospective readership; which, claims Skilton, is a good instance of the wider discursive function of quoting from the classics generally: '[a] bond of equality is established with a like-minded speaker, and a corresponding and no less important barrier is erected against those for whom the utterance seems less particularly intended' (1988: 39–40). When the Latin, translated or otherwise, is deployed, 'the meaning of what is said is, in one sense, scarcely impeded. A sense of belonging on the other hand may well be' (40). In other words, rather than trying to locate and prescribe the limits of signification of a given allusion, we should try to establish, if possible, whom Trollope's books construct as their readers, and whom they exclude.

The account of the inception of *Framley Parsonage* provided by Trollope's *An Autobiography* demonstrates how far successful participation within, and promulgation of, a discourse of middle-class Englishness, were deemed crucial to the *Cornhill's* success in the market place. Trollope, we are told, had initially suggested supplying Thackeray and Smith with *Castle Richmond* (1860). As, however, *Castle Richmond* tells the heart-warming tale of a mother and daughter competing for the same man, while all about them Irish peasants are dying of starvation because of the Great Famine, George Smith soon realised that this wasn't the novel to signify the middle-class Englishness that the *Cornhill* sought to embody and use as the basis of its appeal to its potential readership:

> when he [Smith] heard that *Castle Richmond* was an Irish story, he begged that I would endeavour to frame some other for his magazine. He was sure that an Irish story would not do for a commencement . . . He wanted an English tale, on English life, with a clerical flavour. On these orders I . . . framed . . . the plot of *Framley Parsonage.* (Trollope, 1883: chap. VIII)

An Autobiography clearly attributes the success of *Framley Parsonage* to its apparent encapsulation of the Englishness demanded by Smith:

> The story was thoroughly English. There was a little fox-hunting and a little tuft-hunting, some Christian virtue and some Christian cant. There was no heroism and no villainy. There was much Church, but more love-making . . . Consequently they in England who were living, or had lived, the same sort of life, liked *Framley Parsonage.* (chap. VIII)

Here, even as it claims that it was the novel's representational accuracy that guaranteed its success among those 'in England who were living, or had lived, the same sort of life' as that conveyed in its pages, *An Autobiography* reveals that the novel's 'Englishness' resides in the sort of virtues and values that it either espouses or takes for granted. After all, 'a little fox-hunting', for instance, or the absence of 'heroism' or 'villainy', may well refer to mere incidents of plot. By contrast, gaining the approbation of one's readership for such inclusions and exclusions, as the passage implies, relies on a shared set of cultural values, which presumably includes the language within which the novel is inscribed.

The *Cornhill's* deliberate undertaking to construct a certain sort of middle-class Englishness is also apparent in Thackeray's circular letter of November 1859 to potential contributors to the magazine, which demonstrates how unequivocal his and Smith's editorship was in soliciting both middle-class contributors and middle-class readers. Thackeray adopted the metaphor of hospitality, which the *Illustrated London News* had used facetiously to announce the forthcoming appearance of the magazine, to promote, as an ideal for the magazine, the image of the civilised dinner party at which contributors and readers alike are to be considered 'guests':[6]

> at our contributors' table, I do not ask or desire to shine especially myself, but . . . to invite pleasant and instructed gentlemen and ladies to contribute their share to the conversation . . . If we can only get people to tell what they know, pretty briefly and good-humouredly . . . what a pleasant ordinary we may have . . .! If our friends have good manners, a good education, and write in good English, the company, I am sure, will be all the better pleased . . . A professor ever so learned, a curate in his country retirement, an artisan after work-hours . . . may like to hear what the world is talking about . . . At our social table, we shall suppose the ladies and children always present . . . [W]e can promise competent fellow-labourers a welcome and a good wage; and hope a fair custom from the public for our stores at 'THE CORNHILL MAGAZINE.' (Thackeray, reprinted in Ray, 1945–6: 161)

The quintessentially upper middle-class metaphor of the dinner party Thackeray uses to describe his magazine, then, acts as a framework within which to contain, or, to pursue the metaphor, to entertain, a broad range of middle-class activities, occupations and professions ('a Foxhunter . . . a Geologist, Engineer, Manufacturer, Member of the House of Commons, Lawyer, Chemist'), so that, for instance, even the 'artisan after work-hours' who may care to peruse the *Cornhill* becomes middle-class by default, as it were, through his implicit and inevitable subscription to the bourgeois 'good manners' and mores radiating from the magazine's pages: welcome at the table, the artisan, in order to find pleasure and instruction from the *Cornhill*, will have to surrender to the tastes, preoccupations and modes of expression of its contributors.

Returning to the 'Englishness' of 'omnes omnia bona dicere', we may note that Thackeray's circular lays particular stress throughout on a good education as a necessary prerequisite for both contributor and reader. Thackeray establishes his own credentials and suitability for an editorial role by declaring that he has 'lived with educated people in many countries', and that there is hardly any subject readers won't want to hear about so long as it is 'from lettered and instructed men who are competent to speak on it' (Ray, 1945–6: 160). Similarly, in the extract quoted above, he solicits contributions from 'pleasant and instructed gentlemen and ladies', in whom he can hope for 'good manners, a good education, and . . . good [written] English'. As, at this stage in the nineteenth century, and certainly for Thackeray's contemporaries – or, more precisely, his social peers – a 'good education' invariably meant an education in the classics (see Clarke, 1959), one sees that Trollope's opening chapter title for *Framley Parsonage* complies readily with one of the main criteria for acceptance of commissions and submissions for publication by the *Cornhill*, as laid out in Thackeray's circular. Hence there is nothing obscurantist, at least for its target readership, in the fact that the first four words of Trollope's English tale of English life are in Latin. On the contrary, as Skilton has written,

> 'omnes omnia bona dicere' does not stand in the way of the novel . . . but is a gesture of class recognition – a sign that the narrator is, like the novelist, 'One of us' . . . Having established their social credentials, the reader and narrator can now proceed on a friendly basis. (Skilton, 1988: 49)

In other words, in this instance the allusion not only functions thematically, it also functions discursively, to produce and reinforce a sense of upper middle-class Englishness that defines both the magazine and its readership.

Thackeray's conception that his ideal contributors to, and readers of, the *Cornhill* will have received a 'good education' helps to clarify the question whether one can define more precisely the nature of what I have termed 'upper middle-class Englishness'; and, having done so, whether one can chart more accurately its relationship to the use of classical allusion. We might begin such an inquiry by recalling that such allusions apparently functioned, in part, through their contribution to and perpetuation of a specifically masculine, public-school-related discourse, which flourished throughout the Victorian period, and which I have labelled a discourse of remembrance. This discourse of remembrance tries to inscribe as overpoweringly emotional the very act of recalling one's schooldays. It thus operates in two ways at once. By inscribing such recollections as the property of narrator and reader, it excludes automatically those who have not received a classical education: those who, by extension, have not come from the 'right' social background, or have been born the 'wrong' sex. At the same time, it legitimates such exclusivity by presenting such recollections as subject to a higher power outside the recollector's control (in the following extract, for example, when the headmaster of Rugby School is addressing the boys in the school chapel):

> What was it that moved and held us, . . . reckless, childish boys, who feared the Doctor with all our hearts, and very little besides in heaven or earth; who thought more of our sets in the School than of the Church of Christ, and put the traditions of Rugby and the public opinion of boys in our daily life above the laws of God? (Hughes, 1857: Book 1, chap. VII)

Here, the narrator of Thomas Hughes's *Tom Brown's Schooldays* breaks off from his narrative to ponder the nature of the mystique that encouraged Rugbeians to find organised religion less important, for purposes of instruction, than the organised division of boys into 'sets'; allegiance to the laws of God subordinate to allegiance to the laws of the School; and worship and fear of the headmaster the chief emotions experienced by the pupils during the headmaster's sermon (since the boys were made to 'believe first in him, and then in his Master' (Book 1, chap. VII)). Such extreme positions are legitimated rhetorically by the narrator's use of the interrogative, which allows him to assert as ontologically secure the very existence of this strange, all-pervading Rugbeian influence, without having to actually demonstrate its existence. The mysterious bonds between the boys and Rugby, and the indefinable spell cast by the headmaster's voice as he addresses the school, can be wondered at but never qualified, recalled but never explained.

This neat rhetorical procedure, of course, can easily be called upon to provide, whenever necessary, at least partial resistance to any outside investigation or interference. By acting as vouchee to the impenetrability of Rugby's Eleusinian rituals to all but past, present and future public school initiates – those for whom, according to the 'Preface' to the second edition, the work has been produced – Hughes's narrator implies that readers not so initiated will possess only an imperfect comprehension of the subject under discussion, and will be denied meaningful access to it. From this particular distant prospect of Rugby School, then, Hughes's narrator draws a meaning precisely opposite to that in Thomas Gray's 'Ode on a distant prospect of Eton College': where wisdom is bliss, 'tis folly to be ignorant. The social exclusivity conferred upon the lucky few is thus simultaneously constructed and preserved.

Writing in 1865 on 'Public Schools' for the *Fortnightly Review*, in the aftermath of the Clarendon Commissioners' report of 1861, Trollope uses precisely the same rhetorical trick as Hughes's narrator, both to acknowledge the speaker's own place within a closed community, and – more practically – to question the propriety of tampering with the English education system, in the name of 'reform'. By so doing he clearly demonstrates how any affirmation of the elusive qualities conferred by education at a public school operates within the realm of cultural politics. Before this, however, he testifies nostalgically to the social benefits of an education at Harrow and Winchester:

> Whilst there we made our friendships. There we learned to be honest, true and brave . . . to disregard the softnesses of luxury, and to love the hardihood and dangers of violent exercise. There we became men . . . after such a fashion that we are feared or loved, as may be, but always respected, – even . . . in spite of our ignorance. (Trollope, 1865: 479–80)

Trollope's account here is wholly different from that given in *An Autobiography*: the terms of affection expressed here bear little resemblance to the latter's narrative of the remorseless indignities endured by Trollope-the-social-outcast at Harrow and Winchester. Presumably this difference can be attributed to the different generic demands of the discourses within which Trollope is inscribing his experiences. In *An Autobiography*, the twin demands of the self-help narrative and the *Bildungsroman* virtually necessitate the inscription of an unhappy childhood, in order to make Trollope's subsequent successes all the more impressive. In the passage quoted above, by contrast, Trollope is concerned to lament the changes to the existing system, and appears the more qualified to speak on the benefits of the old system the more he is able to demonstrate that he is part of that community, with first-hand experience of its benefits, all summmed up in the one word 'nobility'. Defining this 'nobility', however, requires him to resort to the same evasiveness deployed by Hughes's narrator:

> Who can define the nobility that has attached itself to Englishmen as the result of their public schools . . .? But its presence is so thoroughly acknowledged, that few among us do not feel that it has

more than compensated for that lack of real instruction of which we
all complain. Is this nobility to be lost through our reforms? . . . In
our thoughts on so dear a subject the conservative element becomes
so strong within us, as almost to overcome the reforming element.
(Trollope, 1865: 480)

In terms strikingly similar to the passage quoted from *Tom Brown's
Schooldays*, Trollope at first questions rhetorically the precise nature of
the nobility gained by his education, then takes for granted that such
questioning is redundant because '[the] presence [of nobility] is so thoroughly acknowledged'. Indeed, he suggests implicitly that the defining
feature of 'nobility', paradoxically, is its very indefinability. In both cases,
of course, the love of one's school is inscribed as an emotional response
so overwhelming as to be wholly beyond the control of the sufferer; it
therefore becomes neither susceptible to, nor susceptive of, outside interference. To ensure that the love of one's school is ineffable is to ensure
that it can't be, as it were, effed about with.

The main similarity between the two passages, however, lies in the
fact that both appear as reminiscences in the texts in which they occur.
Hughes's narrator feels justified in interrupting his narrative with an act
of remembrance about his own schooldays; so, too, does Trollope the
essayist. Both, equally significantly, use the first person plural to inscribe
their memories, so that 'we' are able to look back together from a shared
present to a shared past. In other words, both construct a collective
history; both articulate a sociocultural position in the present so apparently unproblematical that it can be safely universalised through use of
the first person plural, thereby constructing and appealing to an entire
community of like-minded readers who are exhorted, as it were, to
remember in unison. Thus the consequent act of exclusion, the necessary obverse of these rhetorical acts of inclusion, becomes all the more
powerful, as it can present itself as operating both synchronically and
diachronically; once excluded, always excluded. In other words, the
temporal straitjacket that ensures that the present is defined, and thus
contained, by the past, also ensures that those for whom the experience
of attending public school is an alien phenomenon are effectively
excluded from the genetically determined concept of history that the
discourse of remembrance engenders.

If the discourse of remembrance functions to exclude those sociocultural groups denied a public school education, it accomplishes this, in
part, by invoking the notion of a fully-functioning autonomous community, which not only surrounds and defines one in one's youth, but also

and inevitably surrounds and defines one ever after. This discourse can thus legitimate itself by presenting the exclusionary acts, which must inevitably follow from the act of defining the boundaries of this notional community, as wholly beyond the control of those who construct themselves as members of it. In this way, the discourse is able to defend itself from potential critique: the bonds that link one to one's fellows, both in the past and in the present, are inscribed as so powerful as to prevent those who belong from ever escaping their parameters. Consequently, the overriding rhetorical effect of Hughes's and Trollope's digressions is the pretence that they are not rhetorical digressions at all, and consequently not subject to analysis of their discursive properties. Rather, they are natural phenomena which pre-exist their very inscription. Their manifestation might facilitate the claim that the texts in which they appear have been conceived organically, rather than determined linguistically.

It follows that the autonomy accorded by the discourse of remembrance to the individual acts of memory that it tries to articulate bestows upon them the power to regulate efficiently those individuals for whom they occur. Memories become, in other words, unanswerable agents of social control. The concluding paragraphs of *Tom Brown's Schooldays*, for instance, reveal the regulatory function of these self-generating acts of remembrance. Tom, now an Oxford undergraduate, revisits the school chapel upon hearing of the headmaster's death, and becomes subject to the moral guidance forced upon him by his memories of school, as he tries, unsuccessfully, to indulge his grief alone. The passage is too long, regrettably, to quote in its entirety, but it shows Tom engaging in one last struggle to assert an individuality that selfishly denies the possibility of a precedent formative community. His egocentric attempts to grieve alone over the Doctor's death, we are to infer, are self-indulgent and – because of their initial ignoring of the community of which he is inevitably a part – necessarily doomed to failure. Guidance and redemption are at hand, however, in the form of school-time memories which 'rush ... back again' and chastise him for his selfishness, and which are so powerful they are inscribed as appearing physically before Tom, in a quasi-militaristic display of regimental might and moral superiority: 'form after form of boys, nobler, and braver, and purer than he, rose up and seemed to rebuke him'. It is only when Tom relinquishes his individuality, and voluntarily lets himself be embraced by the community, from which he can never escape, by beginning to share his grief with others, that his actions can be vindicated: his grief becomes 'gentle and holy', and he kneels at the chapel altar 'humbly and hopefully', in the knowledge that his own grieving experience is part of an entire network of similar grieving experiences; he shares, that is, in 'a burden which had proved itself too heavy for him to bear in his own strength', and which is synechdochally indicative of 'the bond which links all living souls together in one brotherhood'. Tom's memories, in short, regulate his conduct, through their provision of moral guidance, and their acting unilaterally to prevent him from ever forgetting that his sense of self is preconditioned by, and forever contained within, a specific community. The novel then concludes by stressing the importance of Tom's recognition of the social network that precedes and defines him, at the same time as it tries to excuse his worship of the Doctor:

> And let us not be hard on him, if at that moment his soul is fuller of the tomb and of him who lies there, than of the altar and Him of whom it speaks ... [A]ll young and brave souls ... must win their way through hero-worship, to the worship of Him who is the King and Lord of heroes. (Hughes, 1857: Book 2, chap. IX)

The theological ambivalence that the novel has hitherto constructed is finally clarified with the narrator's insistence that the 'mysterious human relationships', of which the Rugbeian community is but one instance, not only have divine authority, but actually function as agents of revelation. 'Hero-worship', not only of the Doctor, but of all human relationships, is not heretical; rather, it operates as a metonym for the worship of God, a practice that one can legitimately follow in this world precisely because it is revelatory of the existence of the next. Hence the importance of acknowledging, and submitting to, one's memories of this formative community: enjoying, so to say, divine sanction, their regulatory function has a power not just socially, but also (and fundamentally) spiritually redemptive. Tom's submission to his memories becomes submission to God.

If this is the case, then it is no accident that the final image confronting the reader of *Tom Brown's Schooldays* is of Tom kneeling at the altar of Rugby School chapel; indeed, as the narrator admits, 'where better could we leave him?' After all, if submission to one's memories constitutes a double recognition, of one's allegiance and duty not just to the institutionalised community of Rugby School, but also to God, then the altar of the school's chapel is a fitting signifier of both the institution and the God of whom the institution is revelatory.

However, this final image of Tom kneeling at the altar serves another function. It can be interpreted as a confirmation of the self-gendering masculinity of the discourse. Tom's alliance with the memory of his dead headmaster operates as nothing less than a symbolic marriage, a ritual of union that confirms both Tom's maturity and his masculinity. The consequent exclusion of the female that such a union represents is then confirmed rhetorically by the narrator, through his construction of three sets of binary oppositions that divide and contrast the sexes in terms of their social roles: mothers/fathers, sisters/brothers and, crucially, wives/teachers:

> it is only through our mysterious human relationships, – through the love and tenderness and purity of mothers, and sisters, and wives, – through the strength and courage and wisdom of fathers, and brothers, and teachers, – that we can come to the knowledge of Him, in whom alone the love, and the tenderness, and the purity, and the strength, and the courage, and the wisdom of all these dwell for ever and ever in perfect fullness. (Hughes, 1857: Book 2, chap. IX)

Tom's 'marriage' to the Doctor's memory, therefore, necessarily excludes the female, as one of the main social functions that a woman can fulfil, that of being a wife, is judged, by the narrator, intrinsically antonymic to one of the main social functions that a man can perform, that of being a teacher; union with the one automatically precludes union with the other. There is consequently no space for the female subject in this particular discursive ordering of the social roles that men and women might perform. Both Tom and the reader, the latter clearly implicated by the narrator's lapse into the first person plural, can only define themselves, and their respective masculine subjectivities, against the gendered alterities of mother, father, sister, brother, wife and teacher: social categories transcendentalised by the narrator as 'our mysterious human relationships'. That these last two categories are constructed as opposites, and that there is no place in these three sets of binaries for an extra category, 'husband', indicates that one of the chief effects of the discourse of remembrance is its necessary privileging of male experience, through its equally necessary exclusion of female experience: we are all, as it were, husbands. In short, in *Tom Brown's Schooldays* the discourse of remembrance functions as a space where only male subject positions can be articulated.

One of the main functions of classical literature, in the mid-Victorian period, is to act simultaneously to invoke and to perpetuate this discourse of remembrance; classical literature, that is, is repeatedly inscribed as a stimulus to profound emotional experience, and a never-ending source of comfort and mental stability. For instance, Frederick Temple uses the cultural phenomenon of youthful reminiscence as a metaphor to argue for and explain the contemporary appeal of studying the classics:

> The inspiration which is drawn by the man from the memory of those whom he loved and admired in the spring-time of his life, is drawn by the world now from the study of Greece and Rome. The world goes back to its youth in hopes to become young again, and delights to dwell on the feats achieved by the companions of those days. (Temple, 1860: 28)

Temple draws an explicit parallel between the 'inspiration' drawn from remembering one's youth and the study of the classics. Using his metaphor of world-as-man to facilitate comparison between the various ages of (middle-class, classically-educated) mankind and the different periods of world history, he thus pursues a number of circularly inter-dependent rhetorical strategies. First, he is able to stake a claim for the innate supremacy of his own subject-position, by claiming that the history of the world naturally mimics the progress through life of, say, an old Etonian. Inversely, he is able to validate the cultural practice of remembering one's past companions, because such remembering is as self-evidently natural as the global act of remembrance otherwise known as 'history'. Studying the classics thus becomes not socioculturally contingent, but as natural as remembering the companions of one's youth, which is, of course, as natural as the history of the world itself.

Disentangling oneself from Temple's metaphors, one can see that the main purpose of this passage is to render recourse to the classics an automatic activity. If one cannot help recalling one's youth, equally one cannot help using the classics to facilitate such recollection. Temple, of course, is speaking generally; however, contemporary claims abound for the solace of the classics for the old as they look back on times past. For instance, Trollope's posthumously published novel *An Old Man's Love* (1884) stresses, throughout, the power of classical literature to provoke emotion and, crucially, to provide solace:

> He took to his classics for consolation, and read the philosophy of Cicero, and the history of Livy, and the war chronicles of Caesar. They did him good, – in the same way that the making of many shoes would have done him good had he been a shoemaker . . . Gradually he returned to a gentle cheerfulness of life . . . (chap. II)

In this passage, the narrator describes how William Whittlestaff, the 'old man' of the title, comforts himself in times of emotional stress. Throughout the novel, the unhappy and lonely Whittlestaff, with whom the reader's sympathies are clearly meant to lie, is depicted as relying on his favourite Latin authors for emotional support. The reader is encouraged to feel compassion for the predicament in which Whittlestaff finds himself, as an old man in love; and his devotion to the classical authors is a key indicator of his need for companionship. It is the same companionship to be found in old age from books that motivates the Duke of Omnium's advice to his wayward son Lord Gerald in *The Duke's Children* (1879–80):

> 'Cicero and Ovid have told us that to literature only could they look for consolation in their banishment. But then they speak of a remedy for sorrow, not of a source of joy. No young man should dare to neglect literature. At some period of his life he will surely need consolation. And he may be certain that should he live to be an old man, there will be none other, – except religion.' (chap. XXV)

Here again classical literature provides solace, and operates as a sub-stitute for community. Significantly, the duke's equation of the classics with religion invests the former with the same spiritual quality associ-ated with memories of school in the already-noted closing pages of *Tom Brown's Schooldays*. In this way, both of Trollope's narratives can be readily assimilated into the discourse of remembrance, even though schooldays are not mentioned once in either of the passages quoted. The recollections provided by classic literature form the same link, between the present and the formative community of the past, that is central to the discursive power of remembering one's schooldays.

In the extract from *An Old Man's Love*, moreover, Trollope's narrator suggests that such recourse is paradoxically both culturally constructed and natural for a member of the gentlemanly class. The statement that the classics do Whittlestaff good 'in the same way that the making of many shoes would have done him good had he been a shoemaker', introduces a whiff of trade into the description, as though reading the classics for pleasure and comfort is, and, implicitly, should be, Whittlestaff's professional and primary occupation. Trollope is thus able to have it both ways. The passage may well recognise that the reassur-ance to be derived from reading the classics is, in one sense, a class-based cultural construction; even so, it implies, for members of the gentlemanly class, recourse to the classics becomes, as it is for Temple, the 'natural' thing to do. Very possibly the whole tenor of this passage is governed by another classical allusion, though one barely hinted at: the narrator's invocation of the shoemaker, to indicate without question the social distinction between the gentleman and the artisan, recalls the Latin tag most often used in Victorian literature to promote 'sticking to what you know', *ne sutor ultra crepidam*, the conventional rendering of Pliny the

Elder's 'Ne supra crepidam iudicaret [sutor]' (*Natural History*, XXXV, 36(10)), itself conventionally rendered 'let the cobbler stick to his last'.

In short, the act of recalling the classics repeats and strengthens the major project of the discourse of remembrance, to assert the presence of a formative community to which one is in thrall, and which renders one's place within that community unproblematical, because its status as a precondition of one's own subject-position means one is freely absolved from questioning the assumptions upon which it is founded. In this way, deployment of the classics becomes an automatic reaffirmation of one's sense of belonging to a fully-formed precedent social network that makes possible a sense of self. However, this sense of belonging can be reaffirmed not just through reading the classics, but also through quoting them. For instance, here are selected stanzas from Lionel Johnson's poem of 1889, *Winchester*, a paean to his schooldays:

> A place of friends! a place of books!
>   A place of good things olden!
> With these delights, the years were golden . . .
> A place of friends indeed! And age
>   Such friendship only mellows:
> And, as our autumn slowly yellows,
>   Defies the wintry rage . . .
> The best of all good fellows! . . .
> There would we roam, and haply quote
>   Some old, well-proven poet:
>   Plain truth, as Horace loves to show it,
>   Or Virgil's holier note . . . (Johnson, 1917: 268, 277)

Here one clearly sees simultaneously: the construction of a collective memory giving way to nostalgia ('With these delights the years were golden'); the related assumption of a communal bond strengthened by time ('A place of friends indeed! And age / Such friendship only mellows'); approval for the values of such a community (Wykhamists are 'best of all good fellows'); ultimately, an indication of the sort of cultural practice that forms a part of the foundation for all of the above ('There would we roam, and haply quote . . . Horace . . . [or] Virgil'). Quoting from the classics is one of the occupations from the past that, Johnson alleges, formed a central and habitual part of the Wykhamist community; hence his juxtaposed exclamations 'A place of friends! a place of books!' It would also seem that one of the features of the discourse of remembrance is the inscription of a huge temporal distance between the present and the past. Johnson's description of the ageing process clearly indicates that, where once 'life wore sunny looks', he and the community of which he is a part are now so thoroughly in the 'autumn' of their life that they use their collective friendship to defy 'the wintry rage'. When he wrote this poem, Johnson had reached the advanced age of twenty-two. In the same way, the 'old memories' of Tom Brown's 'old schoolfellows', which appear in such abundance at the end of *Tom Brown's Schooldays*, imply a schooltime long past, even though Tom is only in the summer vacation of his first year as an Oxford undergraduate.

If quoting from the classics is an activity of youth, so too is it an activity that repeatedly and inevitably forces itself upon men during their progress through life. Thus, Edward Bulwer Lytton, in introducing his own 1869 translation of Horace's *Odes and Epodes*, makes the following claim:

> It is an era in the life of the schoolboy when he first commences his acquaintance with Horace. He gets favourite passages by heart with a pleasure which ... [almost] no other ancient poet inspires. Throughout life the lines so learnt remain on his memory ... applying themselves to varieties of incident and circumstance with the felicitous suppleness of proverbs ... [A]s men advance in years they again return to Horace ... That the charm of Horace is thus general and thus imperishable, is a proposition which needs no proof. (Lytton, 1869: I,viii)

Lytton here ascribes almost the same powers to Horace's texts as we have seen Hughes, and Temple, ascribe to their memories of youth. Like one's memories, Horace's texts recall the community of youth; are capable of acting unilaterally ('applying themselves'); have an unquestionable appeal 'as men advance in years'; and thus have the same regulatory power as does memory, dictating appropriate responses to every given situation. Just as importantly, Lytton's account of Horace performs a neat rhetorical trick, which begins by acknowledging that one's knowledge of the poet is dependent on the educational environment in which one is raised, but concludes by asserting that 'the charm of Horace is thus general and thus imperishable, ... a proposition which needs no proof'. Lytton's declaration of the apparent universality of Horace's appeal and appropriateness ensures that the cultural practice of classical quotation becomes naturalised, at the expense of any recognition that it might operate discursively.

The regulatory power of acting unilaterally that Lytton ascribes to classical quotations is endorsed by John Henry Newman in his *Grammar of Assent* (1870):

Passages, which to a boy are but rhetorical commonplaces ... at length come home to him, when long years have passed ... and pierce him as if he had never before known them, with their sad earnestness and vivid exactness.

Then he comes to understand how it is that lines ... have lasted generation after generation, for thousands of years; with a power over the mind, and a charm, which the current literature of his own day ... is utterly unable to rival. (Newman, quoted in Locker, 1879: 14)

For Newman, the chief benefit of a classical education lies in the way it traps the former schoolboy, 'when long years have passed', into a position of enforced susceptibility to the 'power over the mind' wielded by classical literature. Here again, classical quotations are imbued with the power of acting unilaterally to enforce their emotiveness and innate truthfulness ('their sad earnestness and vivid exactness'); here again, too, this apparent power is deemed to universalise their application, to render obvious the fact that they 'have lasted generation after generation, for thousands of years'. This universality then ensures that when one recalls the classics, one sees the world through the eyes not only of one's youth, but also of the classical authors, whose wisdom, because universal, is readily assimilable to present-day circumstance. Confirmation of this apparent universality is easily found: the frequency with which Latin tags are deployed as chapter headings in Victorian fiction, as captions to Punch cartoons, and as epigraphs to Victorian poetry, indicates how readily such apophthegms were seen as revelatory of universal truth and wisdom. Indeed, the mere fact of their application demonstrates the apparently self-evident appositeness to contemporary circumstances and texts that they are deemed to possess.

The use of Latin to denote the important class-based emotional ties engendered by a classical education is a recurring trope of Victorian literature, not least when inscribing farewells. The Latin acts as a shorthand to signify the departure from the formative community that surrounds the departing figure, and is therefore designed to be hugely sentimental. Probably the most famous instance of this is the last chapter (LXXX) of Thackeray's *The Newcomes* (1853–5), 'In Which The Colonel Says "Adsum" When His Name Is Called':

At the usual evening hour the chapel bell began to toll, and Thomas Newcome's hands outside the bed feebly beat a-time. And just as the last bell struck ... he lifted up his head a little, and quickly said 'Adsum!' and fell back. It was the word we used at school, when names were called; and lo, he, whose heart was as that of a little child, had answered to his name, and stood in the presence of The Master.

It is not merely the fact of the spoken Latin, but also its appeal to an implied collective memory, that gives this passage its emotional force: so much so, indeed, that Trollope could find it 'perhaps as fine as anything that Thackeray ever did' (Trollope, 1879: 120), and George Saintsbury could claim that 'except Lear's there is no death to surpass it in literature' (Thackeray, 1853–5: x). Pendennis, Thackeray's narrator, ensures that we are aware that both he and Colonel Newcome hail from the same sociocultural background, and solicits the participation of like-minded readers, even as he provides an explanatory gloss for those excluded from the community. Moreover, just as Hughes, at the end of *Tom Brown's Schooldays*, describes hero-worship of the Doctor as a metonym for the worship of God, Thackeray inscribes heaven itself as a public school: 'he, whose heart was that of a little child, had answered to his name, and stood in the presence of The Master'. Colonel Newcome has gone simultaneously to heaven and back to school, as he finds himself before the supreme schoolmaster, God himself. The implicit claim is that the public school is nothing less than a heaven on earth, while heaven itself is nothing more than a public school transcendentalised.

The sentimentality of Colonel Newcome's final, Latinate acknowledgement of his school, and of the social network he is about to leave for its celestial counterpart, recalls Trollope's *An Old Man's Love*. Here, as we have already seen, a substantial contribution to the reader's understanding of William Whittlestaff's loneliness is made by the latter's fondness for the classics, which, as it were, act as a substitute community of culturally suitable companions. Classical allusion in a novel thus becomes a means of conveying to the reader the profundity of the emotions therein described.

This practice is mocked in Trollope's *Ayala's Angel* (1880–1), in which one of the novel's many young male lovers, Frank Houston, playfully fantasises to his lover Imogene about writing a three-volume novel to exorcise his doubts about marrying her:

'the novel['s] hero would be a very namby-pamby sort of a fellow, whereas the heroine would be too perfect for human nature. The hero would be always repeating to himself a certain line out of a Latin poet, which of all lines, is the most heart-breaking: –
   The better course I see and know; –
   The worser one is where I go.
But then in novels the most indifferent hero comes out right at last . . .' (chap. XXXVIII)

Frank here alludes to one of Trollope's favourite Latin quotations, 'video meliora proboque deteriora sequor' [I see and approve the better path, but follow the worse], from Ovid's *Metamorphoses* (VII,20). Frank's bathetic verse translation of the Ovid quotation is presumably intended to be comic, as is his light-hearted contempt for contemporary novel-istic convention. Even so, his flippant comments indicate how the twin practices of quotation and allusion were designed, at least in part, to reveal the depth of a particular character's emotional state; Trollope's novels generally seem to affirm with a deadly earnestness Frank's facetious remark that, 'of all lines', this particular Ovid quotation is 'the most heart-breaking'. Significantly for the present argument, allusion to the Ovid tends to appear in Trollope's fiction whenever the narrative describes a character undergoing, normally self-imposed, exile from one social milieu to another, and to suggest the heart-rending poignancy of leaving one's preferred community.

In *The Small House at Allington* (1862–4), for example, Adolphus Crosbie reflects bitterly on his decision to jilt Lily Dale, and thus to forego the rural idyll that was the Allington community, in favour of marriage to the frigid Lady Alexandrina De Courcy. As Crosbie leaves with his new bride for Folkestone, on the first leg of their honeymoon, the narrator tells us:

> It was in this that Crosbie's failure had been so grievous – he had seen and approved the better course, but had chosen for himself to walk in that which was worse. During that week at Courcy Castle . . . he had deliberately made up his mind that he was more fit for the bad course than for the good one. The course was now before him, and he had no choice but to walk it. (chap. XLV)

In the context of the passage from which this extract is taken, the allusion is clearly to the non-existent love-life to which Crosbie has consigned him-self. Even so, as the novel stresses repeatedly, his marriage primarily entails exile from two separate communities: Allington, and the London world of the gentlemen's clubs in which for so long he has been a leading light.

Similarly, in *John Caldigate* (1878–9), the eponymous hero, having lived a dissolute early manhood, takes one final look, in chap. II, at the Oxford college where, as an undergraduate, he had dearly hoped for a fellow-ship, before emigrating to Australia:

> He . . . looked into the old hall for the last time . . . [H]e could see the fellows up at the high table. Three years ago it had been his fixed resolve to earn for himself the right to sit upon that dais . . .

> He had certainly made a failure of his life so far . . . He had not
> hitherto chosen the better part, and now something of regret . . .
> came upon him.

The Ovid quotation is recalled by a mere seven words of a paraphrased
translation ('[h]e had not . . . chosen the better part'); even so, it is reason-
able to infer that the recalled Ovid is designed to augment, for the
classically-educated reader, the profundity of John's despair, as he
constructs a nostalgic, value-laden image of a past, formative community of which he is no longer a member. Significantly, John is outside
the 'old hall', looking in.

If John Caldigate alludes to the Ovid quotation through a mere translated paraphrase of a few words, *Phineas Finn* (1867–9) accomplishes the
same, in chap. VII, by a mere three-word English phrase, 'the better
way':

> 'I have made up my mind against taking the chambers, and am now
> off to the Inn to say that I shall not want them . . . If, after a trial of
> one or two sessions, I should fail in that which I am attempting, it
> will not even then be too late to go back to the better way.'

Here again we see a phrase that may recall the Ovid deployed in a
context that signifies leaving one community for another; in this case,
Phineas is explaining why he is leaving Lincoln's Inn for a parliamentary
career. If, as is probable, the Ovid is being recalled, it would lend, for
its target reader, the requisite momentousness that the quotation acquires
in both *John Caldigate* and *The Small House at Allington*. Certainly, by the
time the above passage occurs in *Phineas Finn*, the eponymous hero
has already found recourse to the classics a panacea for the worries
attendant on pondering the risks of his future career:

> He expected to be blown into fragments, – to sheep-skinning in
> Australia, or packing preserved meats on the plains of Paraguay; but
> when the blowing into atoms should come, he was resolved that
> courage to bear the ruin should not be wanting. Then he quoted a line
> or two of a Latin poet, and felt himself to be comfortable. (chap. IX)[7]

It is significant that Phineas's conception of annihilation, of being 'blown
into fragments', involves being exiled, through economic necessity, to
Australasia (shades of John Caldigate) and South America. In other
words, he equates political and social failure with banishment from the
community. Quoting 'a line or two of a Latin poet', by contrast,
can stave off nightmares of failing in his chosen career. In this way, the

threat of self-banishment and reliance on the classics for putative emotional support have both been associated with Phineas's worries about his political future. It is thus at least likely that 'the better way' is meant to be taken as a naturalised translation of *meliora*, re-awakening for the classically-educated reader the depth of Phineas's worries, and his instinctive way of curtailing them.

To draw these observations to a close, let us recall David Skilton's earlier-quoted comment that the tag 'is a gesture of class recognition' enabling reader and writer to establish their shared 'social credentials'. Arguably, as the previous analysis has shown, the tag represents something more profound than a 'gesture'. Talk of the tag's establishing 'social credentials', as though it were a mere textual equivalent of a carte-de-visite, might actually play down its power to act performatively. Its mere presence at the start of *Framley Parsonage* might do several things at once for its target readership. It might, for instance: aspire to the condition of an actual memory of the past; serve as a reinforcement of a precedent formative community that still exists in the present; possess an emotive power, through its awakening of the joys of youth, and correlated provision of solace for the old; reaffirm and naturalise gender roles; more importantly, as Skilton argues, function as a social ritual. Even so, as we have seen repeatedly, tag gains such discursive power as it enjoys by appearing to be, oxymoronically, a natural ritual, rather than a culturally constructed phenomenon.

Classical allusion does not merely contribute to a discourse of remembrance, whose use confirms and reveals a formative and definitional community of the past. It also signifies belonging to a community of the present, the community of the 'gentleman' – a community just as pervasive, just as seemingly self-evident, just as exclusive and, crucially, just as difficult to define, as the following passage from *Lady Anna* (1873–4) makes plain:

> 'I think that a girl who is a lady, should never marry a man who is not a gentleman. You know the story of the rich man who could not get to Abraham's bosom because there was a gulf fixed. That is how it should be: – just as there is with royal people as to marrying royalty. Otherwise everything would get mingled, and there would soon be no difference. If there are to be differences, there should be differences. That is the meaning of being a gentleman, – or a lady.' (chap. XXII)

The inability of so many Victorians to define the very terms by which they sought to categorise themselves proves fundamental to a maintenance of the existence of those terms; a strategic refusal to admit the possibility of a definition is an effective way to prevent its appropriation. Hence, in the above quotation, although Alice Bluestone appears to offer definitions of both 'gentleman' and 'lady' to curb the potentially transgressive Lady Anna, who is determined to marry the tailor, Daniel Thwaite, she actually does no such thing. Despite rhetorical appeals to the authority of scripture and the example of royalty, Alice's justificatory articulation is ultimately – and strategically – imprecise: 'If there are to be differences, there should be differences'. This proto-Saussurean declaration locates the concepts of both 'gentleman' and 'lady' within a network of differences without positive terms, and thus defines both in terms of what they are not.

Alice's non-definition is not unique; as Robin Gilmour's book on the idea of the Victorian gentleman has shown, the term 'gentleman' strikingly and repeatedly resists definition:

> the Victorians themselves were, if not confused, then at least much more uncertain than their grandfathers had been about what constituted a gentleman, and . . . this uncertainty, which made definition difficult, was an important part of the appeal which gentlemanly status held for outsiders hoping to attain it . . . [There was a] universal assumption that gentlemanliness was important and that its importance transcended rank because it was a moral and not just a social category. (1981: 3)[8]

Gilmour rightly notes the difficulty the Victorians had in defining the term adequately, and his book is a mine of contemporary quotations that amply back up this point;[9] he may also be correct in his assertion that this difficulty underlay the allure of the category for those who aspired to be contained within it. However, he does not consider that it is precisely this difficulty of definition that gives the very concept of the gentleman its discursive power. We might reformulate his comment that gentlemanliness 'transcended rank because it was a moral and not just a social category', and say that the discursive power of gentlemanliness lies in its ability to shift constantly between being either a moral or a social category; between being either behavioural (hence learnable and attainable) or innate (hence unattainable and exclusive). This discursive fluidity has a direct bearing on the mid-Victorian debate about the value of a classical education, because, of course, one of the alleged benefits of such an education was its capacity to civilise:

> [I]f [the son of the house] repeats a bit of Latin verse at home . . . his father . . . sees that he has a real pleasure in what he is reading . . . His mother finds a piece of poetry in his drawer . . . very original or

in some way exalted. Her husband tells her that it is after the manner of what the boy is reading, in Latin or Greek; . . . he really is getting an education. They become aware, also, of a general growth and substantial quality in his mind and conversation . . . [He] surprises them with a sort of insight, sensible and bright conclusions . . . which make them think him cleverer than they used to suppose him. They see now that it is true that the thorough study of those grand old languages and their literature does operate as they have been told, – in creating an accurate habit of thought, and admitting the mind to such a discrimination of shades of meaning as is not to be had by any other means . . . (Martineau, 1864a: 415)

Harriet Martineau, in vindicating classical education, here stakes a claim for the ethical and personal benefits to be gained from study of the classics. Her exemplary schoolboy finds himself, 'under some impulse', quoting Latin to his parents, secretly writing poetry, expressing himself with a new-found 'richness or eloquence', seeming 'cleverer' than formerly, and generally setting his parents' minds at rest that the money they are spending on school fees is not being squandered; 'he really is getting an education'. In short, the schoolboy is being civilised through prolonged exposure to classical literature: his education, whether he knows it or not, is helping him to construct himself within some predefined modes of expression and codes of conduct that he will carry with him through later life.

The knotty question still remains, however, whether exposure to the classics in itself can help to make one a gentleman. *Tom Brown's Schooldays*, for instance, repeatedly emphasises that Tom's 'real' education has nothing to do with being drilled in the classics, and the narrator complains of the lack of attention paid to the smooth running of the community during Tom's sojourn at a private school, before his admission into the Elysian Fields of Rugby College:

The object of all schools is not to ram Latin and Greek into boys, but to make them good English boys, good future citizens . . . To leave it, therefore, in the hands of inferior men, is just giving up the highest and hardest part of the work of education. Were I a private school-master, I should say, let who will hear the boys their lessons, but let me live with them when they are at play and rest. The two ushers at Tom's first school were not gentlemen, and very poorly educated . . . (Hughes, 1857: Book 1, chap. III)

Hughes's narrator demonstrates precisely the sort of sliding between categories outlined above: he argues that provision of classical education should be secondary to the manufacturing of 'good English boys, good future citizens', but then claims that the two ushers at Tom's private school fail in this respect because 'they were not gentlemen, and very poorly educated'. It seems at least arguable that the mere fact of the sub-clause lets the 'and' rhetorically convey causality. Grant as much, and the passage then relies on such discursive fluidity to advance its argument: one should not be receiving instructions primarily in the classics, but in the social skills that will help one function as a good citizen in later life. Tom's lack of proper instruction in these skills, however, is due to the 'ungentlemanlike' ushers in charge, whose 'ungentlemanlike' behaviour is in turn linked to their lack of a good education, which of course would have consisted of an education in the classics. However, one should not be instructed in the classics, but in the social skills that will help one function as a good citizen in later life. 'Education' and 'gentlemanliness', then, are not discrete categories. On the contrary, the circularity of the passage's argument is facilitated by the ambiguity of the signifier 'education', which retains its discursive potency through its ability to signify, either simultaneously or alternately, 'instruction in the classics' and 'cultivation of gentlemanly behaviour'.

Similarly, in the passages from 'Public Schools' already quoted, Trollope is able to resist calls for educational reform, in part, by implying that such calls are inherently fallacious. Those who think that school-days are merely a time when one is subject to a curriculum of dubious educational value ignore the fact that the ethico-social advantages (to paraphrase Trollope's term 'nobility') of education so self-evidently outweigh any pedagogic benefits that 'few among us do not feel that it has more than compensated for that lack of real instruction of which we all complain'. In making his case, and in preserving the discursive fluidity of his term 'nobility', Trollope finds himself in the logical difficulty of resisting – or at least, accepting grudgingly – reform of educational provision on the grounds that it will jeopardise the 'nobility' of the public schools, while simultaneously arguing that such 'nobility' has nothing to do with educational provision in the first place (Trollope, 1865: 480).

Nevertheless, a display of learning does become important in demonstrating that one has been exposed to the civilising influence of classical literature, and that, consequently, one is a gentleman.[10] Even Trollope's *An Autobiography*, which contains one of the most notorious Victorian refusals to acknowledge the ingredients of gentlemanliness, implicitly concedes that one of these ingredients, and a chief indication by which the gentleman can be recognised, is an outward manifestation of one's education:

> There are places in life which can hardly be well filled except by
> 'gentlemen' ... A man in public life ... would be defied to define
> the term [gentleman], – and would fail should he attempt to do so.
> But he would know what he meant, and so very probably would
> they who defied him. It may be that the son of the butcher in the
> village shall become as well fitted for employments requiring gentle
> culture as the son of the parson ... – but the chances are greatly in
> favour of the parson's son. (Trollope, 1883: chap. III)

An Autobiography is as tactically evasive in defining a 'gentleman', then,
as 'Public Schools' is in defining 'nobility': both are instinctively known
and defined through their very indefinability. Nevertheless, despite this
evasiveness, where *An Autobiography* tries to account in social terms for
the difference between the butcher's son and the parson's son, it does
so by stressing that 'gentle culture' is harder for one to attain than for
the other, thereby implicitly acknowledging that one potential index of
gentlemanliness is the evidence of such exposure to 'gentle culture'. The
ability to quote from the classics, by extension, might then function as
the sort of index that one has received such an education, and, in consequence, that one is a gentleman:

> It is as the proper and recognised education of the governing classes,
> the honourable accomplishment of all aristocracy, that the classical
> teaching endures so firmly ... For as soon as it became the qualifi-
> cation of a Gentleman to read and write at all, it was Latin that he
> read and wrote ... For centuries ... all gentle literature was mimetic
> of the ancient standards. All else, tongue and word, the vehicle and
> substance of native speech, were common, of the people – vulgar.
> (Houghton, in Farrar, 1868: 373)

In the above extract, Lord Houghton is unequivocal in equating the
ability to speak and read Latin with a display of social superiority.
Although the tenor of his essay is critical of the arbitrary nature of this
equation, he nevertheless acknowledges that the sheer weight of historical precedent is sufficient to guarantee the perpetuation of Latin as the
dominant mode of address for the governing classes, even up to the
present day. For Houghton, one of the key determinants of 'gentlemanliness' is a classical education.

Evidently, such a discourse of gentlemanliness functions exclusively,
and not simply in class terms; it also functions to exclude women. As
Kate Flint has written, the politics of defining gender roles in the nineteenth and early twentieth centuries can clearly be seen in authors'
choices of texts for literary allusions:

to employ a literary reference is to assert one's place within the cultural assumptions of that society. Quotations could thus be a means for women to claim . . . their right to be considered on equal terms with other, male writers. Alternatively, women writers could offer . . . quotations taken from a different set of texts from those . . . cited by men, suggesting, for example, women's readier familiarity with romantic poets and Shakespeare rather than with . . . Greek and Roman writings . . . (1993: 257–8)

Accordingly, one finds in the literature of the mid- to late Victorian period repeated instances of knowledge of the classics as a specifically male preserve. *An Autobiography*, for instance, stressing for the would-be novelist the necessity of acquiring a harmonious prose style, teaches its lesson thus:

[t]he boy, for instance, who learns with accuracy the prosody of a Sapphic stanza, and has received through his intelligence a know-ledge of its parts, will soon tell by his ear whether a Sapphic stanza be or be not correct. Take a girl, endowed with gifts of music, . . . and read to her such a stanza with two words transposed, as for instance [the first stanza of Horace, *Odes* III, xi] –
　　Mercuri, nam te docilis magistro
　　Movit Amphion canendo lapides,
　　Tuque testudo resonare septem
　　Callida nervis –
and she will find no halt in the rhythm. But a schoolboy . . . who has, however, become familiar with the metres of the poet, will at once discover the fault. And so will the writer become familiar with what is harmonious in prose. (1883: chap. XII)

Clearly, *An Autobiography* takes for granted separate educational and cultural spheres that men and women, 'the boy' and 'a girl', will inhabit; and while the above extract makes clear its awareness that the different 'acquirements' that men and women may possess are precisely that – acquired rather than innate, taught rather than natural – nevertheless, the overall implication of the passage is that writing itself (more precisely, the knack of appreciating 'linguistic harmony') is an occupation for which the educated male is better suited than the female. Consequently, one can see how Trollope's bland acceptance that a mere accident of social formation gives men access to the classics, while restricting women to 'musical acquirements', signifies the link between knowledge of the clas-sics and possession of a greater facility for linguistic expression. Trollope implicitly claims, in other words, that the very act of writing prose is an activity for which the male is, in general, better suited than the female.

Possessing a knowledge of the classics, then, becomes a way of maintaining, exemplifying and legitimating an assumed moral and social superiority. Consequently, classical allusion in Trollope's fiction serves, *inter alia*, to place the male protagonists in positions of moral superiority over women. In *Dr Wortle's School* (1881), for instance, the upright and conscientious Dr Wortle is twice characterised by means of an allusion to Seneca that contrasts him favourably with the vicious Mrs Stantiloup:

> There had been moments in which it seemed that the victory would be on the other side, that the forces congregated against him were too many for him, and that *not being able to bend he would have to be broken*; but in every case he had fought it out, and in every case he had conquered. (chap. I; my emphasis)
> 'She has often tried to do me an injury, but she has never succeeded yet. At any rate *she will not bend me. Though my school be broken up tomorrow*, which I do not think probable, I should still have enough to live upon . . .' (chap. XII; my emphasis)[11]

The reader is left in no doubt over which of the two characters is to be viewed sympathetically. The inscription of the allusion in the above quotations not only reinforces the moral authority of Dr Wortle; it also highlights his superiority over Mrs Stantiloup. Thus, the discursive power that the Seneca allusion in itself possesses is gendered, in that it not only appeals to a male readership, but also carries an implicit endorsement of the higher morality that classical literature was constructed as possessing, and which was designed to be accessible only for the male. Denying women access to this higher morality is thus one way of simultaneously constructing and perpetuating their social inferiority.

This use of the classics to buttress a position of male superiority is a common one in Trollope's writings, and Trollope's heroes often employ classical allusions precisely to instruct their female counterparts, so that the subservience of the latter to the former manifests itself metaphorically as a pupil-teacher relationship. In *An Old Man's Love*, for instance, in condemning to Mary Lawrie the loquacity of the local rector, William Whittlestaff solemnly intones a quotation from Horace, remarking to his ward 'I've taught you Latin enough to understand that . . .' (Trollope, 1884: chap. XIV).[12] Similarly, in *The Claverings* (1867), Lady Ongar, who has married for money, confesses her weakness to her true love Harry Clavering in the following terms:

'Do you remember how you used to teach me that terribly conceited bit of Latin, – *Nil conscire sibi*? Do you suppose that I can boast that I never grow pale as I think of my own fault?' (Chap. XLIII)

Lady Ongar admits her moral inferiority, and, by implication, Harry's superiority, when she reveals that her knowledge of this line, from Horace's *Epistles*, derives from Harry's repeated teaching of it in the past.[13] So thorough has his instruction been, indeed, that she constructs her failings within a vocabulary derived entirely from the quotation and the lesson it apparently contains. Her recourse to constructing her own subjectivity through direct reference to the Latin text indicates that her subject-position has been successfully legislated for, and created by, a masculine discourse that self-evidently proclaims its own moral authority even as it confirms her own failings.

Trollope's construction in his writings of two separate and gendered cultural spheres is in itself part of a discourse of exclusion that an education in the classics apparently constituted. As Harriet Martineau argues vigorously, an essential part of the struggle for women determined to enter the cultural space occupied and defined by accomplishment in the classics was a strenuous rejection of the contemporary myth, promulgated by such texts as Trollope's, that women were indeed ignorant of the classics. This, she contends, is far from being the case:

> some girls of the middle class were allowed to learn Latin and Greek . . . It was not only a solitary young creature, here and there, like Mrs Somerville, who desired it for special reasons . . . It must have been above sixty years since that little Mary, afterwards Mrs Somerville, said something to Professor Playfair . . . 'Did he think there was any harm in a girl learning Latin?'. . . [S]he wanted to study Newton's *Principia* . . . [I]t took only a few months to make her mistress of both the language and the book . . . [O]ut of that generation of pupils those ladies were to arise who have established Preparatory Schools for boys . . . some of the best schools in the country . . . [whose] mistresses grounded the boys . . . well in Latin and Greek grammar. (Martineau, 1864b: 552)[14]

Martineau recognises the way in which access for women to the classics poses a threat to male dominance in both domestic and professional spheres. Professor Playfair has to police Mary Fairfax's determination to learn Latin, and only endorses her request having assured himself that study of Newton 'could [not] hurt her'.

The picture is reinforced by a mini-narrative (not quoted here) of a 'timid young daughter' asking for a classical education. This narrative is inscribed in terms of a power struggle between the daughter and a paterfamilias 'accustomed to lead in his own little social world'. The fictional patriarch not only refuses his daughter's request, but chastises her for her presumption by reminding her of her social inferiority, and, implicitly, of her lowly status within the domestic hierarchy. Nevertheless, Martineau is at pains to point out that such overt patriarchal governance as characterises Trollope's deployment of the classics was not only comparatively exceptional, but also old-fashioned. By setting her little story 'fifty years ago', she implicitly criticises the current patriarchal strategy of denial as hopelessly outdated. Her claim for the right of women to study the classics thus parallels her claim for their right to be acknowledged as possessing familiarity with the classics. Denial of such acknowledgement is, for Martineau, an important part of the discursive regulating of female subjectivity. Consequently, her essay in itself acts performatively to signal two things. First, many women can read Latin: 'the movement of forty or fifty years ago', she writes, 'spread through family connections, through neighbourhoods, and from one grammar-school town to another, till it had quite ceased to be a remarkable thing that a girl read the Latin classics for pleasure' (Martineau, 1864b: 553). Second, women should no longer tolerate being constructed as unable to read Latin.

Martineau assists the staking of her claim by strategically constructing herself as belonging to an alternative cultural tradition spanning some sixty years, a female tradition that desires, in the face of male opposition, an education in the classics. She was not alone in her perception that female acquisition of a classical education signified a blow against male domination. George Eliot, in *Middlemarch* (1872), makes Dorothea's desire to learn the classics the central focus of her struggle with her husband:

> 'Could I not be preparing myself now to be more useful?' said Dorothea to him [Casaubon] . . .; 'could I not learn to read Latin and Greek aloud to you, as Milton's daughters did to their father . . .?'
> 'I fear that would be wearisome to you,' said Mr Casaubon, smiling;
> '. . . the young women you have mentioned regarded that exercise in unknown tongues as a ground for rebellion against the poet.' (I.vii)

Mr Casaubon is clearly aware of the dangers of the provision of such an education for women, and demonstrates his unease at giving Dorothea access to a source of what he perceives to be an emancipatory power. Sure enough, the narrator later tells us, it was not entirely out of devotion to her future husband that she wished to know Latin and Greek. Those provinces of masculine knowledge seemed to her a standing ground from which all truth could be seen more clearly. (I.vii)

The incipient rupture between Casaubon and Dorothea manifests itself in terms of the power relations within their marriage, and the site of their struggle is an exchange on an education in the classics.

The denial in Trollope's writings that such struggles even existed might be a silent yet salient feature of the discursive regulation of the sexes to which possession of a classical education contributed; moreover, classical allusion in the novels might operate not just to educate Trollope's female characters, but also to impart wisdom to his female readers. Even so, his determined reticence about how far women might actually have possessed such knowledge reveals the inherent fragility of this discursive mode of expression, which created and preserved 'gentlemanliness'. That such a studied falsification is even necessary, in other words, indicates the vulnerability of the classics to their appropriation by a non-gentlemanly Other. So how might the true Victorian gentleman defend himself from such impostors? More pertinently, how could the gentleman demonstrate that he himself was not an impostor, but the genuine article? One cultural response to this dilemma was the practice of a particular form of translation, which indicated performatively that one possessed more than a superficial knowledge of classical languages and literature.

Lawrence Venuti, in a recent and influential history of translation, argues that the history of translation in Anglo-American culture is the history of a domestication of cultural alterity, which domestication he calls an act of linguistic 'violence':

> The aim of translation is to bring back a cultural other as the same, the recognizable, even the familiar; and this aim always risks a wholesale domestication of the foreign text, often in highly self-conscious projects, where translation serves an appropriation of foreign cultures for domestic agendas, cultural, economic, political. (1995: 18)

For Venuti, the dominant discursive function of translation, historically, has been the eradication and consequent assimilation of foreign texts by the target language. This process can only achieve success, however, by the translator's aspiring to the condition of 'invisibility', through a rhetorical illusionism that claims that the translation is not a translation at all, but the original foreign text:

> By producing the illusion of transparency, a fluent translation masquerades as true semantic equivalence when it in fact inscribes the foreign text with a partial interpretation, partial to English-language values, reducing if not simply excluding the very difference that translation is called on to convey. (21)

Venuti sees the history of translation as a perpetual tug-of-war between these fluent, invisible, 'domesticating' translations on the one hand, and what he calls 'foreignizing' translation on the other:

> In foreignizing translation, the ethnocentric violence that every act of translating wreaks on a foreign text is matched by a violent disruption of domestic values that challenges cultural forms of domination, whether nationalist or elitist. Foreignizing undermines the very concept of nation by invoking the diverse constituencies that any such concept tends to elide. (147)

Thus domesticating translation practises the humanist function of offering up as natural and self-evident the values of the target language's domestic audience, by seeming to recover them from the translated text even as it installs them there itself. Foreignising translation, by contrast, opposes such a practice by drawing attention to its status as a translation, thus signifying not only the cultural alterity of the foreign original, but the arbitrariness of domestic cultural assumptions.

This is all very well, and Venuti, in his chapter on nineteenth-century translation, makes a plausible case for these as the terms in which his battle of the books was played out between Francis Newman – whose so-called foreignising translations of the classics were throwing down a clear challenge to the conceptions of a 'national English culture' (Venuti, 1995: 127) sponsored by a nationalist cultural élite – and the chief representative of that élite, Matthew Arnold, who replied with an attack on Newman in his *On Translating Homer* (1861). However, Venuti's overly-simplistic binary opposition between 'domesticating' and 'foreignizing' translations cannot accommodate a certain mode of what I shall term 'playful translation', which was common throughout the nineteenth century. Such translation seeks neither to be invisible – rather, it glories in its textuality and status as translation – nor to 'foreignize' by preserving the translated text's cultural alterity.

In Trollope's *The Last Chronicle of Barset* (1866–7), for example, we are told that one of the few bright spots in the Reverend Josiah Crawley's impoverished and mentally unbalanced existence comes when he is able to sell a playful translation that he has composed for his own amusement:

> In the course of the last winter he had translated into Greek
> irregular verse the noble ballad of Lord Bateman, maintaining the
> rhythm and the rhyme, and had repeated it with uncouth glee till
> his daughter knew it all by heart. And when there had come to him
> a five-pound note from some admiring magazine editor as the price
> of the same . . . he had brightened up his heart . . . (chap. IV)

This facet of Crawley's character is conventionally taken as an indication of his eccentricity, and of the lumbering abstruseness that makes
him so thoroughly unworldly. Even so, perhaps Crawley's translation
of *The Loving Ballad of Lord Bateman* (1839), a strange little ballad by
Cruikshank and Thackeray, with mock-erudite commentary by Dickens,
is not so eccentric as it might first appear. After all, Crawley is able to
sell his translation to an unnamed magazine editor, indicating some sort
of market for such productions. Indeed, in 'The Panjandrum', Trollope's
short story about an abortive attempt to establish a gentleman's magazine, the narrator is keen to include his friend Regan's Latin translation
of *Lord Bateman*:

> 'Bring it with you,' said I to him . . . He did bring it; but . . . [Mrs
> St Quinten, a member of the editorial committee] required to have
> it all translated to her, word by word. It went off heavily, and was
> at last objected to by the lady . . . Miss Collins . . . agreed with her
> friend in thinking that Mr. Regan's Latin poem should not be used.
> The translation was certainly as good as the ballad, and I was angry.
> Miss Collins, at any rate, need not have interfered. (Trollope, 1870)[15]

The dispute over the translation's inclusion in the magazine becomes a
contest between masculine and feminine notions both of what constitutes literature of publishable quality and of those whom the magazine
should be constructing as its ideal readers. For the narrator, Mrs St
Quinten and Miss Collins miss the point of the exercise, because the
translation needs to be retranslated back into English for them before
they can offer an opinion on its literary merit. *The Loving Ballad of Lord
Bateman* is itself a self-reflexive little squib that strives for its humorous
effect partly through the provision of its mock-erudite framework, thus
implicitly staking a claim for the literary worthlessness of the ballad
itself. Both Crawley's and Regan's respective translations of it thus reinforce this self-reflexivity, because such a playful translation exercise
demonstrates that the labour expended on the translation is dispropor-
tionate to the literary merit of the translated piece. The translation, thus,
principally directs attention to its own cleverness. If, as should by now

be readily apparent, the deployment of the classics in nineteenth-century literary culture is designed to perform one or many of a variety of discursive functions, then this observation logically extends to the sort of playful translations exemplified above. That they might signify the recollection of a formative community and the nebulous concept of 'gentlemanliness' can, I hope, by now be taken for granted: the fact that the women on the 'Panjandrum' committee are unable to understand Regan's translation or, indeed, see the point of it, reinforces yet again the claim that various cultural practices that stem from a classical education necessarily operate exclusively. More importantly, playful translation as a strategic practice weeds out those who possess but a superficial acquaintance with the classics.

There were, of course, plenty of playful translations from the classics into English. We have already seen some of the ways in which Trollope and Thackeray deploy and allude to Horace's ode 'Vixi puellis nuper idoneus'. In *An Autobiography*, Trollope goes one step further and, after quoting the ode's first stanza, offers his own verse translation:

> I've lived about the covert side,
> I've ridden straight, and ridden fast
> Now breeches, boots, and scarlet pride
> Are but mementoes of the past (1883: chap. XIX).

The translated verse performs many of the discursive functions assigned to classical allusion: it is retrospectively sentimental, as Trollope reaches the end of his life-story; it reasserts the cultural importance of a classical education; it excludes those to whom its mode of self-articulation is either alien or irrelevant.

Trollope's contemporary F.W. Farrar acknowledges the practice of amateur translation, both into and out of Latin, but for him it is just a potent example of the fatuous affectation that has made certain aspects of classical education culturally ridiculous:

> Those who know what leisure is, and who can afford to wile it away in writing Latin Verse, are apt in the beauty of the exotic to forget its costliness . . . The aspect of Latin Verse to the classical scholar who recurs to it as the light amusement of his manhood, is very different from that which it wears to the weary teacher, who has wasted so many of his own and his pupils' precious hours in the hopeless task of attempting to make poets of the many. (1868: 211)

For Farrar, the practice admits of no cultural importance because it is fundamentally useless to society: it is merely 'the light amusement' of those with leisure enough 'to wile it away in writing Latin Verse'. What is the point, he asks, of maintaining the whole edifice of classical education if one of its few post-educative manifestations is this practice of leisured translation, indulged in by a tiny minority of those who have received such an education? Farrar recognises that the practice is both class-based and increasingly inappropriate for a professionalised society; the passage implies that neither the artisan nor the professional has the time for such pursuits. If the leisured classes are becoming anachronistic as the nineteenth century progresses, so too are the cultural practices that occupy their very leisure.

Farrar's insight that the sort of belle-lettrist translation exemplified in *An Autobiography* has no function other than to parade the learning of the translator is not too wide of the mark. Playful translations of the classics, that is, translations that draw attention to their own status as translations, and therefore to the linguistic dexterity of the translator, were undeniably a common feature of the literary culture of nineteenth-century gentlemanly clubbability.

In *An Autobiography*, for instance, Trollope's version of the Horace stanza is printed alongside the original, to make explicit his incorporation of the ode into a different cultural sphere, and draw attention to its own figurative difference from that original. In other words, the translation makes no attempt to render the essential Horatian 'voice', by trying to efface its own textuality so as to give access to the 'authentic' Horace; rather, the translation's appropriation of the vocabulary of fox-hunting is juxtaposed with Horace's metaphors of the warfare of love so that the difference between the two versions is starkly apparent. Foregrounded in the reader's attention, then, is not so much the 'content', whether of the Horatian original or of its Trollopian rewriting, as the act of translating itself.

The deliberate self-referentiality of such translations is well demonstrated by Austin Dobson's twin versions, in 1877 and 1878, of the Horace ode 'Persicos odi, puer, apparatus',[16] which are deliberately juxtaposed in his collected *Poetical Works*:

Persicos Odi	Persicos Odi ('pocket version')
Davus, I detest	'Davus, I detest
Orient display;	Persian decoration;
Wreaths on linden drest,	Roses and the rest,
Davus, I detest.	Davus, I detest.
Let the late rose rest	Simple myrtle best
Where it fades away: -	Suits our modest station: -

Davus, I detest   Davus, I detest
Orient display   Persian decoration.'
Naught but myrtle twine
Therefore, Boy, for me,
Sitting 'neath the vine, -
Naught but myrtle twine;
Fitting to the wine,
Not unfitting thee;
Naught but myrtle twine
Therefore, Boy, for me. (1923: 324–5)

Here, the mere fact of the two translations' juxtaposition calls attention to their status as translations. Not only is the reader expected to have sufficient classical education to recognise the aptitude of the translations and their closeness to the original – and, presumably, to be aware that 'Davus' is the stock name in Latin literature for a slave; just as importantly, by setting the versions alongside one another, Dobson deliberately compromises any putative 'transparency' of language, whereby the translation could masquerade as the original Horace. This is further reinforced by the second version's parenthetic jocular subtitle, in inverted commas, drawing explicit attention to itself as an object-language. The blatant textual self-awareness of Dobson's twin versions ensures that the reader's attention is directed primarily towards the linguistic facility of the translator himself.

Thackeray's version of the same ode accomplishes something similar, making no attempt to translate the original, but rather transposing the Horatian dislike of Persian decorative and gastronomic excess into a dislike of 'Frenchified fuss':

Dear Lucy, you know what my wish is, -
    I hate all your Frenchified fuss:
Our silly entrées and made dishes
    Were never intended for us.
No footman in lace and in ruffles
    Need dangle behind my arm-chair;
And never mind seeking for truffles,
    Although they be ever so rare.
But a plain leg of mutton, my Lucy,
    I prithee get ready at three:
Have it smoking, and tender and juicy,
    And what better meat can there be? . . .
(Thackeray, in Saintsbury, 1912: 130)

Here again, the contemporary cultural values that Thackeray's version propounds, of middle-class, clubbable, cigar-smoking geniality, coupled with a healthy mistrust of Johnny Foreigner, are inscribed in such a way as to draw attention simultaneously to the similarities to, and differences from, the Horatian original. The implied reader-recognition of Horace's 'Persicos odi' presumably ensures that the reader will also perceive the verses' cleverness in transposing the ode wholesale into a contemporary cultural context. By transforming Horace's *puer* into 'Dear Lucy' and 'my Lucy', for example, Thackeray might be reinscribing in heterosexual terms the potential homoeroticism of the original. Thus the focus is put squarely on the performative aspect of Thackeray's imitation.

Taken together, these playful translations mount a challenge to Venuti's binary model of nineteenth-century translation practices. Playful translation has as its primary aim neither a 'domestication' nor a 'foreignization' of the translated text; rather, it seeks to act performatively as an index both of the translator's facility for translation and – by extension – of his rightful place within the community of gentlemen. It is in this context that the many buried translations from the Latin in Trollope's writings might be most helpfully situated. Although their 'playfulness' might be called into question, they nevertheless exist as instances of a mode of translation whose chief function is to display self-referentially the very ability to translate, and to invite the target reader concomitantly to recall a classical source-context through the correct identification of a buried translation. In short, the ability to translate from the classics, and to recognise translations as such, might provide a more fail-safe indication of one's gentlemanly status than the mere ability to quote from the classics directly. In this way, both playful translations and buried translations are part of a defensive strategy that implicitly and anxiously recognises the arbitrariness of associating gentlemanly behaviour with the ability to quote from the classics, and confirm, even as they seek to deny, the fragility of this particular discursive mode.

Such anxieties were not misplaced. As early as 1840, Thackeray's famous account of 'Going to See a Man Hanged' recognises the dangers of identifying the inner man, so to speak, from the outer man's propensity for muttering 'eheu fugaces' and the like at opportune moments:

> Honourable Members are battling and struggling in the House . . . Three hundred and ten gentlemen of good fortune, and able for the most part to quote Horace, declare solemnly that unless Sir Robert comes in, the nation is ruined. Three hundred and fifteen on the other side swear by their great gods that the safety of the empire depends upon Lord John; and to this end they quote Horace too. (Thackeray, 1879: XIV. 386)

The text here mocks the empty rhetoric and sterile ritualism of parliamentary procedure; the facility for quoting Horace unthinkingly in the House thus stands as a metonym for the hollowness of the parliamentarians. The interchangeability of the Whigs and Tories reflects their social uniformity and their unthinking philistinism. Thackeray's text reveals just how potentially insubstantial the trappings of a classical education might be as a signifier of the moral worth and social respectability that 'gentlemen of good fortune' are understood to possess. More ominously, the man on the street, 'Populus', is able to demonstrate his moral worth, or, perhaps, his potential gentlemanliness, without an ostentatious display of pseudo-learning:

> Talk to our ragged friend. He . . . has not been to Eton; and never read Horace in his life: but he can think just as soundly as the best of you; . . . he has been reading all sorts of books of late years, and gathered together no little information. He is as good a man as the common run of us; and there are ten million more men in the country as good as he, – ten million, for whom we, in our infinite superiority, are acting as guardians, and to whom, in our bounty, we give – exactly nothing. (Thackeray, 1879: XIV. 387)

Thackeray, writing at the beginning of the 'hungry forties', is giving an unmistakeable warning to his readers, and possibly himself, about the complacency of the gentlemen-amateurs of the House of Commons. While the Honourable Members bicker and quote Horace, there is a growing number of politically active plebs, who have a different set of cultural touchstones and modes of expression, whose very difference indicates the remoteness of the dominant class from those whom they purport to govern. Thackeray's text clearly positions the reader as hailing from this rarefied cultural élite and, like them, neglectful of, and inattentive to, the needs and opinions of the common throng. In this passage, the facility to quote from the classics again operates metonymically, to signify the blinkered self-satisfaction of those facing a real threat from the increasingly literate and politically motivated working classes.

'Going to See a Man Hanged' prefigures a debate that raged throughout the 1860s. This debate ultimately dealt a death-blow to the dominance of the cultural assumptions underpinning the presumed easy familiarity with the classics so often endorsed by the writings of Thackeray and Trollope; it can be taken as further evidence of the fragility at the time of classical education as a metonym for gentlemanliness. The debate concerned the advantages of a 'liberal education' – that is, an education covering a broad spectrum of disciplines – over against a classical education, and was widespread enough for Thomas Huxley to remark in 1868 that you cannot go anywhere without hearing a buzz of more or less confused and contradictory talk on this subject ... In fact, there is a chorus of voices ... raised in favour of the doctrine that education is the great panacea for human troubles, and that ... everybody must be educated. (1877: 27)

This constant questioning throughout the 1860s of the value of a classical education raised doubts, in the words of J.W. Hales, of 'the wisdom of the educational course at present followed in this country, – as to whether we avail ourselves satisfactorily of the means at our service, or rather, strangely ignore and neglect them' (Hales, in Farrar, 1868: 312), and played a huge part in establishing 'English Literature' as an academic discipline in its own right, and in achieving respectability for other disciplines. Henry Sidgwick, for example, in condemning the sterility of contemporary methods of teaching the classics, maintains that:

if the schoolmaster is ever to be ... a missionary of culture; if he is to develop, to any extent, the aesthetic faculties of other boys than those who have been brought up in literary homes, and have acquired ... a taste for English classics, he must make the study of modern literature a substantive and important part of his training. (1868: 107)

In a similar vein, near the end of Huxley's address to the South London Working Men's College, we find:

Literature is not upon the College programme; but I hope some day to see it there. For literature is the greatest of all sources of refined pleasure, and one of the great uses of a liberal education is to enable us to enjoy that pleasure. (Huxley, 1877: 52)

For Huxley and Sidgwick, then, the purpose and aims of education can be achieved without recourse to the classics; there is, Huxley continues, 'scope enough for the purposes of liberal education in the study of the rich treasures of our own language alone' (52). Lord Houghton is even more direct, arguing for a direct causal link between the classical education of 'our governing classes' and the 'self-satisfaction' of the 'present English gentleman'. The latter no longer has a place in an increasingly professionalised society, and his smugness is to be condemned rather than lauded:

the present English gentleman ... is exhibited to us as an ideal of humanity which it is almost sinful to desire to improve or transcend; and it is, if not asserted, continually implied that if he in his youth

were taught more or otherwise than he learns at present, some mysterious degradation would inevitably ensue . . . It is not pretended that
he pursues, or ever resumes, the study that has occupied a fourth
of his probable existence: . . . he may become a landed proprietor
without a notion of agriculture – a coal-owner without an inkling
of geology – a sportsman without curiosity in natural history – a
legislator without the elements of law: . . . he may frequent foreign
countries, without having acquired even a convenient intimacy with
their language, and continually incur that ridicule which is especially disagreeable to his nature; and yet, in the face of all these
admissions, every attempt to supply these deficiencies is regarded
as little less than revolutionary. (Houghton, in Farrar, 1868: 378–9)

Houghton's no-nonsense approach aims to demythologise the various
discourses informing the public school ethos and gentlemanliness,
arguing that the prestige it enjoys is an arbitrary construction that can,
and should, be dispensed with. It should be replaced by a different
set of cultural assumptions that will make good the 'deficiencies' of the
extant system. In this context, the assumed familiarity with the classics
that informed the writings of Trollope and Thackeray begins to look
increasingly affected, self-satisfied and marginalised. For, crucially, the
attack on the contemporary validity of the classics was not restricted to
a criticism on educational policy; it also manifested itself as a direct
assault on the cultural practice of quotation and allusion that operates
so unproblematically in Trollope's, and, to a lesser extent, Thackeray's,
writings: 'Men may not only go through the whole curriculum of a
university education, but take high honours in it, without the least intellectual advantage beyond the acquisition of a few quotations' (Payn,
1881: 39). Such was the journalist James Payn's dismissive intervention
into this debate, which, with contemptuous brevity, calls into question
the worth of such a practice. Payn, of course, was not alone in his
scepticism:

I was taught as a schoolboy that a false quantity makes a man ridiculous, and sticks to him for life . . . Considering that our entire method
of pronouncing Greek and Latin is radically wrong, I cannot pretend
to regard a false quantity in some rare word as otherwise than an
entirely venial error . . . Those people may hold the reverse who
think it worthwhile to learn Classics in order to understand 'graceful
quotations from Virgil and Horace' . . . The death-knell of all such
fastidious littleness will be the birth-peal of a nobler and manlier
tone of thought. (Farrar, 1868: 223)

F.W. Farrar's argument follows a similar trajectory to Lord Houghton's, by arguing that the pernicious lessons of one's schooldays will eventually prove fundamental to the way one perceives and inhabits the cultural formations of adulthood. Trivial mistakes of Latin pronunciation will signify only to those who have learned the classics so as to understand classical quotations in later life, and whose pleasure in those texts will be marred by mispronunciation. Such a practice is in itself, however, evidence of 'fastidious littleness'. This is a radically different answer to that offered, as we saw, in Trollope's *An Autobiography*. Trollope explicitly endorses, and naturalises as inherently masculine, the automatic ability to find 'canendo lapides' less soothing to the sensibilities than 'lapides canendo'. Farrar, by contrast, finds such exhibitions of what he terms 'taste' indicative merely of

> a certain delicate fastidiousness, a finical fine-ladyism of the intellect ... It is an exotic which flourishes most luxuriantly in the thin artificial soil of vain and second-rate minds. It cannot co-exist with robust manliness of conviction or of utterance ... It is the enthronement of conventionality, the apotheosis of self-satisfaction. (1868: 223)

Not only does Farrar find the cultural assumptions underpinning approval of the practice of quotation, in his damning phrases, 'the enthronement of conventionality' and 'the apotheosis of self-satisfaction'; more tellingly, his condemnation is couched in terms that strike at the very heart of the assumptions legitimating the various discursive practices surrounding classical education and quotation. Whereas Trollope and others depend on their education, and deploy classical quotation specifically to that end, to consolidate and perpetuate the public and domestic cultural dominance of the (gentle)man, Farrar bolsters his criticisms of such practices by portraying them as innately feminine. A largely pejorative vocabulary of terms, connoting femininity either directly ('finical fine-ladyism of the intellect') or by conventional and stereotypical association ('delicate', 'vain'), attacks such affected valorisation of classical education, a valorisation antipathetic to 'robust manliness of conviction or of utterance'. Farrar is, of course, no less concerned than Trollope to ensure that the assumptions that inform the dominant cultural beliefs should reflect and preserve male superiority. Nevertheless, his attack indicates yet again just how fragile, by the middle of the nineteenth century, the classical idiom as a space of male self-articulation actually was. The complacent yet powerful gentlemanliness that operates discursively in the writings of Trollope and Thackeray is just one – increasingly threatened – nineteenth-century construction of male subjectivity, as, on the subject of classical education at least, two different sorts of middle-class 'Englishness' emerge. On the one hand, one encounters the bonhomous cultural complacency signified by Trollope's 'omnes omnia bona dicere'; on the other, one encounters direct attacks on this very complacency, which acknowledge the extent to which the cultural impinges on, and helps buttress, the socio-political. The competing discursive modes of self-articulation of, say, Farrar and Trollope point to a struggle between two different discourses of middle-class identity, one emergent, the other in decline.

Classical allusion, then, becomes an inherently unstable signifier of a variety of competing forms of masculine identity: the formative public school community of the past; the pre-ordained League of Gentlemen of the present; class-based or gendered exclusivity; moral superiority; robust and manly philistinism; precious effeminacy. This multiplicity of possible significations reveals not only the importance of the twin cultural practices of classical allusion and quotation in certain fictions of the mid-Victorian period, but also the difficulty of establishing a fixed set of criteria by which the critic today can assess its various textual manifestations. However, to be even aware of the available competing discursive strategies for accounting for, and assigning meaning to, classical allusion in the mid-Victorian period, one must not approach the arch-realist Trollope's fiction determined to impose an aesthetic of representationalist linguistic self-effacement upon it. As this essay has argued, some of the most striking instances of the interpellation of their readers by Trollope's texts occur precisely at the moment when linguistic self-effacement is ruptured, and when Trollope's readership becomes implicated in the maintenance and affirmation of a vast network of intertextual references which performatively operate to construct that readership's subjectivity.

Notes

1. In this essay, unless otherwise indicated, quotations of, and translations of quotations from classical authors are taken from the Loeb editions of their works: Fairclough, 1926 (Horace), Sargeaunt, 1912 (Terence), Miller, 1917 (Seneca), Miller, 1984 (Ovid's *Metamorphoses*).
2. For a broad investigation into the poetics of allusion, see Meyer, 1968; Wheeler, 1979 (studying only eight novels, and neglecting Thackeray); Springer, 1983, McMaster, 1991 (writing on single authors); Clark, 1975, Tracy, 1982, and Epperley, 1989 (on Trollope, though the former badly underestimates the number of allusions and quotations to be found in Trollope's writings). For discussions of Victorian writers and their relationship to classical literature, see Skilton, 1988, and Vance, 1984, 1988 and 1993.

3. For the convenience of readers who have other editions of the works of Trollope, Thackeray etc. than those listed in the bibliography, all quotation from these works is given by chapter number only.

4. Horace, *Odes* III.xxvi,1–6: 'Vixi puellis nuper idoneus / et militavi non sine gloria; / nunc arma defunctumque bello / barbiton hic paries habebit, / laevum marinae qui Veneris latus / custodit.' [Till recently I lived fit for Love's battles and served not without renown. Now this wall that guards the left side of sea-born Venus shall have my weapons and the lyre that has done with wars.] The serial edition of the novel by Chapman and Hall (January 1864–August 1865), and the two-volume edition of 1865 (Chapman and Hall), both read 'Idoneus duellis' [fit for wars], a reading followed by nearly all subsequent editions.

5. Terence, *Andria* 96–8: 'omnes omnia / bona dicere et laudare fortunas meas, / qui gnatum haberem tali ingenio praeditum.' [all the town heaped congratulations on me and praised my good fortune in having a son endowed with such a character.]

6. The *Illustrated London News* wrote 'of an unnamed magazine under the control of Mr. Thackeray', and described him 'at Bordeaux, ordering first-class claret for his first-class contributors and second-class claret for his second-class contributors' (cited Ray, 1945–6: 369).

7. The most likely source is Horace *Odes* III.iii,1–8: 'Iustum et tenacem propositi virum / non civium ardor prava iubentium, / non voltus instantis tyranni / mente quatit solida neque Auster, / dux inquieti turbidus Hadriae, / nec fulminantis magna manus Iovis; / si fractus inlabatur orbis, / impavidum feriunt ruinae.' [The man tenacious of his purpose in a righteous cause is not shaken from his firm resolve by the frenzy of his fellow citizens bidding what is wrong, not by the face of threatening tyrant, not by Auster, stormy master of the restless Adriatic, not by the mighty hand of thundering Jove. Were the vault of heaven to break and fall upon him, its ruins would smite him undismayed.]

8. For an examination of 'gentlemanliness' as it relates specifically to Trollope, see Letwin, 1982, though her refusal to acknowledge any discursive context for the terms she deploys so freely, and her stress on 'individuality' as the necessary condition of the 'rational being', make her book unhelpful to the present argument.

9. See, for example, the following, from James Hain Friswell's *The Gentle Life* (1864): 'In this age of rivalry, money worship, and spurious equality . . . we all seek to be gentlemen and gentlewomen. The pursuit is laudable, the aim is noble; and what is more, in running this race, we may be all winners . . . To be a gentleman admits of such various interpretations, that . . . nothing is so easy' (quoted in Gilmour, 1981: 84).

10. An anonymous anecdote in the *Gentleman's Magazine*, entitled 'The Best Gentleman in Fiction', is worth recalling in this context: 'in the house of a well-known poet and dramatist . . . were gathered some of the most representative men in English literature . . . Casually, the question came up, "Who is the best gentleman in fiction?" . . . Slips of paper were handed round, and each one present wrote the name of the character he thought entitled to that distinction . . . To the surprise of all [fourteen present] the voting was unanimous[ly for] . . . Colonel Newcome . . .' (*Gentleman's Magazine*, 1884: 101).

11. Seneca, *Thyestes* 199: 'Novi ego ingenium viri / Indocile: flecti non potest, frangi potest' [I know the stubborn temper of the man; he may be broken but can ne'er be bent].

12. The Horace quotation in question is from *Epistles* I.xviii,69: 'percontatorem fugito: nam garrulus idem est' [Avoid a questioner, for he is also a tattler].

13. Horace, *Epistles* I.i,60–1: 'hic murus aeneus esto, / nil conscire sibi, nulla pallescere culpa' [Be this our wall of bronze, to have no guilt at heart, no wrongdoing to turn us pale].

14. The 'Mrs. Somerville' of this quotation is Mary Somerville née Fairfax (1780–1872), the Scottish scientific writer; 'Professor Playfair' is John Playfair (1748–1819), professor of natural philosophy at Edinburgh.

15. The story also contains a specimen of the translation: 'Tuam duxi, verum est, filiam, sed merum est; / Si virgo mihi data fuit, virgo tibi redditur. / Venit in ephippio mihi, et concipio / Satis est si triga pro reditu conceditur.' This (although the story doesn't indicate as much) is a translation of the penultimate stanza of *Lord Bateman*: 'O it's true I made a bride of your darter, / But she's neither the better nor the vorse for me; / She came to me with a horse and saddle, / But she may go home in a coach and three.' (Dickens *et al.*, 1839: 29.)

16. Horace, *Odes* I.xxxviii: 'Persicos odi, puer, apparatus, / displicent nexae philyra coronae; / mitte sectari, rosa quo locorum / sera moretur. / Simplici myrto nihil adlabores / sedulus, curo: neque te ministrum / dedecet myrtus neque me sub arta / vite bibentem.'

Chapter 5
'All the Others Translate': W.H. Auden's Poetic Dislocations of Self, Nation, and Culture

RAINER EMIG

Translation in Auden's Poetics

When W.H. Auden (1907–73) starts his poem 'The Composer' of 1938 (Auden, 1976: 148) with the line 'All the others translate' – all the other arts, that is, save music – he clearly implies that translation encompasses much more than the mere transposition of a text from one language to another. Translation, in fact, entails the entire problematic relation of life and art: 'the painter sketches / A visible world to love or reject ... the poet fetches / The images out that hurt and connect'. Music is miraculously exempt from the 'painstaking adaption' from 'Life to Art' in Auden's poem. Yet if Auden takes up the old Platonic idea of the proximity of music and eternal essences, he remains fully aware that there is a price to pay for ideal detachment. Only the 'inferior' arts that are, so to say, 'adaptations' are shown as capable of making statements about human existence. Even more dubious is the capacity of ideal, i.e. immediate and untranslated art, to right these injustices, as the poem's ambiguous conclusion implies: 'You alone, imaginary song, / Are unable to say an existence is wrong, / And pour out your forgiveness like a wine'.

In Auden's view that art is responsible not so much for eternal ideal essences and truths as for the realm of human existence and practice, translation is the key term. This realm of practice is determined by individual, often egotistical, positions, considered both in isolation and in their processes of human interaction, which are shaped by, and themselves shape and influence, larger cultural histories and norms. This interaction, 'The Composer' implies, is never a straightforward one, but always contains elements of adaptation, transposition, indeed of translation.

This essay investigates the changing role of translation in the development of Auden's poetics. It will not primarily scrutinise the technical details of his translations, an investigation that Nirmal Dass has undertaken from a theoretically informed position, even though his study concentrates on Auden's prose translations and devotes only one of the five chapters of his study to Auden's translations of poetry from Old Norse, Swedish, Russian and German (Dass, 1993). The present chapter will rather analyse the implications of Auden's approaches to translation for questions of subjectivity, linguistic and cultural identity. It will locate the benchmarks and problems of translation in key areas of Auden's aesthetics, such as the troubled constitution of the self and its placement in the historical and political context of a community, and the eventual transcendence of a cultural identity, initially defined and confined by Englishness, by the adoption of an altogether broader perspective, in which a sceptical humanism, based on an understanding of human interchange, communication, and community as identical with translation and dialogue, goes hand in hand with a position that strives to achieve the perspective of a global citizen.

Translating the Self

Auden's earliest translations, one is surprised to learn, do not involve the adaptation of foreign texts into English, but rather show a young Auden translating himself into a different linguistic and cultural framework, that of German. After having lived in Berlin for a mere few months, from autumn 1927 to summer 1928, Auden quickly started producing poems in this new language that he had hardly mastered and would indeed struggle with for the rest of his life (Constantine, 1990: 2). Christopher Isherwood describes them in the following terms: 'Their style can be best imagined by supposing that a German writer should attempt a sonnet-sequence in a mixture of Cockney and Tennysonian English, without being able to command either idiom' (Isherwood, 1966: 21). David Constantine has edited Auden's German poems and provided them with his own translations into English (1990: 1–15). The six poems are concerned with parting and separation, and most of them are written from a position of exile, looking back to the good time left behind when exchanging Berlin for Britain.

The biographical motivation for these odd poems is twofold. On the one hand, like many other writers of the 1930s – Isherwood and Stephen Spender, for example – Auden perceived Germany as the antithesis of the cultural preferences of his parents' generation, and his interest in

Germany became a necessary protest and means of emancipation. This was reinforced by the reputation of Berlin in particular for its loose sexual morals, a fact that was of special importance for the homosexual Auden. The second and more personal motivation for Auden's German poems is their role as poetic love letters to a boy he had left behind in Berlin when returning to Britain to work as a schoolteacher in Scotland (Carpenter, 1982: 90).

Yet, biographical background aside, these awkward and problematic translations – awkward because they are obviously flawed, and problematic because they have no fixed underlying source text, but are translations of Auden's favourite ideas and standard poetic formulas and images – contain strategies that throw an interesting light upon the role of translation in Auden's works as a whole. Even though they implicitly function as letters, these translations are not designed for dialogue. The first one, entitled 'Lacrimae Rerum', starts off with a 'Wir' [we] describing the minutes preceding the eventual farewell, then moves on to a general description of love's contingency and egotism in its second stanza, in order to conclude with an egotistical I telling the Other to leave: 'Mein Traum von Dir mit Dir hat nichts zu tun': in Constantine's literal translation, 'My dream of you with you has nothing to do' (1990: 4).

In the same way that the speaker of 'Lacrimae Rerum' is making all the running and dominating the argument, these German poems are attempts at taking possession of a different linguistic and cultural context. They do not expose a member of one linguistic community to the challenge of another – why would English or German speakers want to read poems in bad German? – but rather serve to ascertain that the challenge of the foreign is translated into assurance. If Auden is capable of writing in German, he signals that he is mastering both a foreign language and its connected culture. Evidence that the translation works in the direction of taking possession is, for example, the fact that the German poems are not primarily about Germany, but rather focus on Auden's detached position in Scotland. They thereby introduce yet another element of appropriation: Scotland as well as Germany is easily subsumed by an Audenesque style: 'Es regnet auf mir in den Schottische Lände / Wo ich mit Dir noch nie gewesen bin' [It is raining on me in the Scottish lands / Where I with you have never yet been (Constantine, 1990: 6)].

Translation serves to further a notion of self, here an artistic self that is determined by its stylistic capability. It is not a proper means of communication, but rather a thinly disguised outflow of a problematic narcissism, one that, like all forms of narcissism, creates closure to the outside to counter a feeling of threat. 'Nur dann wir können so zusammen sein / in diesem glauben dass wir sind allein', states poem number 3, which Constantine reproduces in a verse translation, with some liberties, as 'We cannot be together unless we know / We are alone with nowhere else to go' (1990: 8–9).

Freud remarks concerning this ambivalence: 'Narcissism in this sense would not be a perversion, but the libidinal complement to the egoism of the instinct of self-preservation, a measure of which may justifiably be attributed to every living creature' (Freud, 1984: 66). The terms 'ego-libido' and 'object-libido' that he employs in his essay on narcissism are of obvious relevance to translation. The question would then be: is the translation focusing, as if objectively, on the text-as-object, and attempting to do justice to its complexity and specificity, or it is concerned to assert the primacy of the target language and culture?

The assertive stylistic voice of Auden's early poems, one that even survives a translation into German, hides rather imperfectly the problem that the self that it refers to and creates is still in search of definition and location. These two essential poles of textual construction of the self are also the ones that are challenged by translation. When Auden starts his career with a very radical act of auto-translation, his writings acknowledge what is at stake, even when their author remains unaware of the gamble.

A similar form of translation happens when Auden turns his attention to what is at least seemingly his own cultural background. He had been fascinated for a considerable time by Old English and Old Norse texts, a passion kindled by his encounter with J.R.R. Tolkien in Oxford (Carpenter, 1982: 55). When he therefore undertook a translation of 'The Wanderer' in the 1930s, it did not come as a surprise. A second motive, for this translation of one of the earliest texts of English Literature into a modern format, might have been the already existing model for such an endeavour, Ezra Pound's translation of 'The Seafarer'.

Pound's poem forces the Old English original into an awkward style that mixes archaisms with classical modernist ruptures. Its beginning, 'May I for my own self song's truth reckon / Journey's jargon, how I in harsh days / Hardship endured oft', gives an impression of what Edward Mendelson describes as 'a farrago of misremembered and imaginary Englishes' (1981: 45). Pound's translation produces a strange text that hovers in an intermediate sphere between past and present:

> The Seafarer's world, for Pound, may be gone for ever, but its powers are recoverable in the poet's heroic transforming imagination, and only there. For Auden, in contrast, 'The Wanderer' is thoroughly available to the present. (Mendelson, 1981: 45–6)

Along with George Steiner, Susan Bassnett sees these endeavours as 'an attempt to "colonize" the past' (1991: 72–3). Yet Auden's poem at least realises that a seeming immediacy – which is very different from the preservation of an original's supposed intention, meaning, or merely flavour – is bought at a price. His celebrated view of the 'spongelike nature of imagination' (Hoggart, 1951: 14) permits an assimilation of the Anglo-Saxon source to his own style, yet at the expense of not so much translating it as rewriting it as an obviously Audenesque poem featuring the anxieties of the 1930s. What happens is indeed another auto-translation, this time not into German, but into Old English metrical patterns, alliterations, and kennings.

'Doom is dark and deeper than any sea-dingle / Upon what man it fall': so begins Auden's poem (1976: 62), and already this beginning shows that the poem's source does not lie exclusively in the Old English 'The Wanderer', which begins 'Oft him anhaga are gebideð, / Mehtude miltse' (Mitchell & Robinson, 1986: 255) [Often the solitary man enjoys /The grace and mercy of the Lord (Hamer, 1970: 174–5)]. In fact, Auden's initial lines derive from a Middle English prose homily, *Sawles Warde* (Watson & Savage, 1991), and only the central section of Auden's poem uses the Old English poem whose modern editorial title provided the title of Auden's text as late as 1966, 34 years after it was written (Mendelson, 1981: 44). Auden's 'translation' is evidently also a collage, and linguistic transposition is inseparable from historical and structural counter-projection. Translation, even when understood along the lines of Jakobson's tripartite model (1959) of intralingual (rewording), inter-semiotic (replacement by non-linguistic signs), and interlingual (transposition into a different language), becomes too narrow a term to contain the complexity of intertextual, historical, and discursive shifts that characterise poetics.

In terms of the discursive positioning of his text, Auden almost completely eliminates the religious framework that provides the introduction, conclusion, and recurring theme of the original 'The Wanderer' and similarly underlies *Sawles Warde*, as its very title indicates. Moreover, Auden changes the first-person narrative of the object text into an impersonal third-person one. Once again, the stress is not on personal experience, but on a general state of things in and by which the individual is subsumed. Nonetheless, several images from the Old English text reappear in Auden: hardships, enemies, the love of family and community. Yet in Auden's 'version' they assume very ambiguous roles whose complexity would have been unthinkable in Old English verse. An example of this is the treatment of the central trope of home against which the hardships of the wanderer are measured. In the Old English text, home is represented by the loving family and the security of the lord's hall. In Auden, however, one finds it first represented by the neutral term 'house' and then by the ambiguous comfort of intimacy: 'No cloud-soft hand can hold him, restraint by women'.

In the universe of Auden's early poetry we find a constant anxiety that the shelter of familiarity might merely be a disguise for an Oedipal attachment that prevents individual development and stifles existence. These frameworks of thought are obviously anachronistic in Old English poems, where psychological concepts of personality are never at stake, nor indeed make sense. The same applies to the concepts of gender and sexuality that Auden develops in the mock-heroic tones that parody, even as they echo, the Anglo-Saxon model. When Auden's 'The Wanderer' talks about the exile of its protagonist, it couches it in a crucial formula in stanza two, where the abandoned domesticity makes way for a very different kind of relationship: 'Kissing of wife under single sheet' is replaced by 'through doorway voices / Of new men making another love'.

The lines are usually read as advocating homosexuality, yet they can also be interpreted as a typical 1930s sentiment, expressing utopian ideals of equality and community in which questions of gender and sexual orientation become irrelevant. In any case, Auden's wanderer has by no means reached this ambivalent ideal. The wanderer realises that something new and strange is happening, but he remains excluded from it. He is an exile, but a rather different exile from the Old English wanderer. The Anglo-Saxon exile is an accident of fate, and is (over-)determined, like any figure of exile in the Middle Ages, by reference to the biblical Fall; by contrast, the modern one results from the exercise of personal choice inside larger historical developments. The two figures meet in what Eve Kosovsky Sedgwick (1985) terms a 'homosocial desire' for the company of other men. Yet in the Old English poem this desire is a yearning for a re-establishment of the *status quo*; in Auden it embodies an anxious hope for a cultural and political change, which might, obviously, include sexual politics.

Freud's essay 'On Narcissism' once again provides an interesting and unexpected background commentary. It claims:

> The ego ideal opens up an important avenue for the understanding of group psychology. In addition to its individual side, the ideal has a social side; it is also the common ideal of a family, a class or a nation. It binds not only a person's narcissistic libido, but also a considerable amount of his homosexual libido, which is in this way

turned back into the ego. The want of satisfaction which arises from the non-fulfilment of this ego liberates homosexual libido, and this is transformed into a sense of guilt (social anxiety). (1984: 96–7)

Auden's 'The Wanderer' therefore translates the Anglo-Saxon attachment of the individual into a protective group, by deflecting its own anxieties about self and family into a utopian notion of a modern community of fellow-men. Translation still serves as a narcissistic confirmation of the position of the translator, yet already it branches out from a purely individualist perspective into the problematic one of a group.

When, therefore, in its final stanza, Auden's poem lapses back into what appears to be an echo of the religiosity of the Old English model – when, that is, it prays 'Save him from hostile capture' and adds 'Protect his house' and eventually 'Bring joy, bring day of his returning' – it is not necessarily ending as a prayer addressed to the Christian God. The poem might equally well address the other great forces in Auden's early works, Marx or Freud or any of the Freudian psychologists that Auden was impressed by, and whom he usually calls 'healers'. The god of Auden's 'The Wanderer' is a secular one, and, to bring back the issue full circle to the Anglo-Saxon world, he is indeed very similar to a heroic overlord, with this difference, that in the 1930s leaders of men claim much greater status for themselves and achieve a much more dangerous significance than ever an Anglo-Saxon leader would do.

Auden's translation of the *Elder Edda*, which he undertook jointly with Paul B. Taylor (Taylor & Auden, 1969), can be regarded in a similar light to the odd 'travel book' entitled *Letters from Iceland* that resulted in 1937 from his journey to Iceland with Louis MacNeice and others. In the same way that 'The Wanderer' aims at establishing a quasi-mythological basis for a displaced self in the uncertainties of the 1930s, Auden's interest in Iceland and Old Norse literature is also based on an ultimately narcissistic desire. Auden fondly but falsely believed that his family had Icelandic roots. The claim is refuted as etymologically unconvincing by Carpenter (1982: 7). Nirmal Dass, however, takes at face value Auden's own tongue-in-cheek version of his family mythology, as expressed in the first edition of *Letters from Iceland*, where a section from 'Letter to Lord Byron' postulates: 'My name occurs in several of the sagas, / Is common over Iceland still' (1993: n. 156). What later editions of the poem retain, however, is a more realistic view of things: 'With northern myths my little brain was laden, / With deeds of Thor and Loki and such scenes' (Auden & MacNeice, 1967: 200).

Once again, it is not the source text that is of real interest, but the way in which it can be made to express contemporary anxieties. 'The

World of the Sagas', as Auden calls his collective mythology in one of his T.S. Eliot Memorial Lectures (Auden, 1968: 41–75), is appropriated as a stage on which the problems of the twentieth century can be re-enacted. It is therefore not surprising that, with blatant disregard for anachronism, Auden calls what he finds in texts such as *Njal's Saga* and *Hrafknel's Saga*, which date from as early as the thirteenth century, 'Social Realism' (51).

'The World of the Sagas' is of particular interest with regard to Auden's translations, since it is in part dedicated to discussing the technical difficulties both of writing in alliterative verse with complex technical rules and of translating such tightly knit texts into modern English:

> When we come to the Skaldic poetry the difficulties have become infinitely greater. The kennings are even more erudite, and, as in Irish and Welsh poetry, the technical complications of the verse forms are so formidable that one is surprised that the poets succeeded in saying anything. Certainly, it is absolutely impossible to translate them and remain in any way faithful to the metre. (Auden, 1968: 58–9)

The passage contains a notable contradiction: it is the claim, in the second sentence, that complicated poetic form leads to problems of signification. Such a claim is contradicted, blatantly, by the existence and considerable achievement of such poetry in the form of Skaldic poetry, as also, later, in the Irish and Welsh traditions that the lecture itself itemises: but also by Auden's verse. The claim once again explains why Auden calls the sagas social-realist texts: he is convinced that their technical complexity drives them towards prose. Yet this assumption is itself determined by the position of the translator. In effect, their complexity forces a modern English translation to adopt a prose style. An example of this used earlier in Auden's lecture is the intertextually determined character of kennings:

> while the epithet Homer applies to Diomedes, 'of-the-loud-war-cry', is straightforward description, no reader could guess that the kenning 'Grani's Road' means the River Rhine, unless he already knows the Völsung legend in which Grani is the name of Sigurd's horse, and Sigurd journeys down the Rhine. (1968: 58)

Two things become evident here that are theoretically important. They also have ideological implications when connected with the issues of dominance of target text over source text and of subject language and culture over their object equivalents. The kenning demonstrates that translation is always intrinsically multiple. It relies on pre-existent translations, for example in the shape of the intertextual transposition of one story or motif into another. Knowledge is thus determined by translation, and this translation is not a simple transposition from one fixed origin to another equally stable goal, but a chain of translations without identifiable origin and an unstable and evasive target. Second, the techniques of translation are determined by a simultaneous teleological forward movement from source to target, and by a backwards movement to remembered sources that ontologically precede source as well as target, yet whose own origins elude a fixing in the hermeneutic chain. Thus target and source stand and fall together, as the results of earlier translations.

That the act of translation is bilateral and without solid foundation is demonstrated by the paradox of Auden's claim that texts such as the *drottkvaett* are as good as untranslatable, while he then goes on to offer exactly such a translation:

> Hushed is the lake of hawks,
> Bright with our excitement,
> And all the sky of skulls
> Glows with scarlet roses;
> The melter of men and salt
> Admires the drinker of iron;
> Bold banners of meaning
> Blaze o'er our host of days. (1968: 58–9)

This translation, although certainly inferior to Auden's other poems, is nonetheless a hybrid or, in Jean Baudrillard's terminology, a simulacrum: it is a reproduction that has no original (Baudrillard, 1990: 11). Yet it is therefore not so much an exceptional or illicit example of translation as the prototype of all translations, at least when translation is taken out of the confines of a pragmatically reductive view. The 'bold banners of meaning' that Auden's modern English *drottkvaett* displays in an ironically self-referential way are also the cribs of translations that seemingly sport the securely established meaning. The question remains, however, whether this meaning is that of the source or of the goal, or whether it is displaced, somewhere in between the two. In ideological terms, this technical paradox also points at the fact that translation is incapable of establishing unproblematic historical and/or (auto)biographical links. As Nirmal Dass rightly points out, referring to Auden's translation of Goethe's *Italienische Reise*, Auden's translations are 'translating a translation, improving a crib' (1993: 55). Such works must eventually abandon the notion of translation as a return to an origin or the recovery, in and for the present, of historic facts and truths. These latter determine what Auden (1968: 41), borrowing the term from Tolkien, describes, in 'The World of the Sagas', as the 'primary world': the realm of the historian. The opposing 'secondary world' of the poet, however, is based on fiction. While Auden's lecture starts off by envisaging a possible union of the two, it ends with a vision of their irreconcilability. Translation is again of crucial importance here: it fails when regarded as the link between facts and facts, a view that still hovers over the established technical terms 'source' and 'target' and their objectifying associations. Yet when regarded as a crucial element of *poiesis*, it achieves a central position, not so much in the establishment of a meaningful relation between subject and object positions of translation and source respectively, as in their dislocation, one that leads to the need for negotiation and thus to the possibility of dialogue.

Auden takes up this challenge in several ways. First, he starts translating contemporary Scandinavian and Russian writers that he can no longer appropriate as spiritual or actual ancestors. Second, he begins to acknowledge influence as a form of dialogue, and abandons appropriation in favour of an opening-up to positions that cannot, after all, be translated into his established scheme of Englishness, but may be used as, often relativising, parallels. Goethe's *Italienische Reise* [*Italian Journey*] contains biographical analogies to Auden's post-war sojourns in Ischia. Yet its historical and cultural perspective is also obviously different.

A third and perhaps the most radical new form of translation in Auden's works entails translation between different media. His opera libretti show Auden self-consciously subjecting language to the demands of music. They also show him engaging with a number of cultural contexts – American, German, English – that force him to multiply his cultural perspective rather than to translate foreignness back into Englishness. The second half of this essay will therefore be concerned with the implications of Auden's 'contemporary' translations and those that display what recent German theory has termed *Intermedialität*, which translates, at best awkwardly, into English as 'intermediality'.

Translating the Other

Dass rightly traces a shift in Auden's poetic translations that leads him from an Englishing of the source texts, in his translations of the *Voluspa* and the poetry of Gunnar Ekelöf and Andrei Voznesensky, to an acceptance of their alterity. With reference to the early translations from Old Norse, Dass states:

> Auden has created a programmatic agenda and strategy (i.e. alliteration) from which he does not swerve. His translations are in fact a series of changes, omissions, and additions – all in an effort to fully recuperate and domesticate according to contemporary moral values, the source text's alterity. In short, Auden's fidelity lies with English and not with Old Norse, and therefore his translation seems blunted and often on the verge of cliché. The Voluspa is controlled and reworked in acquiescence to the target language. Anything that defies this control is expunged. (1993: 139)

Yet Dass's verdict ignores the fact that Auden's own poetry is characterised by cliché and the, often excessive, use of normalising rhetorical set-pieces. Its aim and effect is as much an acknowledgement of the dominance of cultural hegemony, the Englishness that Auden fails, or refuses, to shake off, as an attempt to deal with it in a critical and productive fashion. The question is indeed whether, in an ethics of translation, faithfulness to the source text would indicate an acceptance of its otherness or whether it would merely place the source in a fixed position of historical and cultural distance. Surely the target culture would be still actively at work, albeit in a disguised fashion, if the demands of the source material were seemingly met in this way? And what of these demands in a translation which is, after all, a communicative transference and dislocation?

The very fact that Auden chooses authors whose cultural as well as linguistic context is alien to him indicates that there is an opening of the cultural boundaries that define and safeguard individual as well as national identity. 'I know no Russian and have never been to Russia', he states in the foreword to his translations of Voznesensky (Auden *et al.*, 1966: vii), and, with reference to his translation of Dag Hammarskjöld's prose writings *Vägmärken*, 'It is no secret that I don't know a single word of Swedish' (1964: xxii). At the same time, the choice of these texts is obviously determined by individual interest. The themes of the authors that Auden translates are close to his own preoccupations.

In the case of Goethe, as earlier noted, there are biographical analogies that appeal to Auden. When, in 'Thanksgiving for a Habitat' in 1964, Auden calls himself 'a minor atlantic Goethe', he only semi-humorously links his own cultural migrations – from Britain to the USA, and back, via Italy and Britain, to Austria – to Goethe's uneasy position as a German classic with a penchant for Italy (Auden, 1976: 522). He also translates Goethe's established fame into a playfully exaggerated anticipation of his own, in the same way that he disrespectfully co-opts the title of Goethe's major metapoetic investigation, *Dichtung und Wahrheit*, for the title of 50 prose fragments with the subtitle 'An Unwritten Poem' in 1959. In this work he discusses, very much in the manner of Roland Barthes' *A Lover's Discourse: Fragments* several years later, the problem of expressing love in language. Translation here becomes the proof that language is indeed unnecessary:

> 'I love you'; 'je t'aime'; 'Ich liebe Dich'; 'Io t'amo' ... there is no language on earth into which this phrase cannot be exactly trans-lated, on condition that, for what is meant by it, speech is unnecessary. (Auden, 1976: 496)

Rather than establishing a complex link between different linguistic codes and historic and cultural settings, translation here functions on a purely semiotic level as the translation of one set of signifiers into another code. This seemingly pure form of translation, however, is instantly declared 'unnecessary'. Mere interlingual transference is not what the translation endeavour is about.

A complex intertextual connection, and not a mere semiotic one – the latter, one in which signifiers are transferred devoid of contexts – also shapes Auden's translation of the Russian poet Voznesensky: more precisely, a link between Auden's poem 'The Shield of Achilles' and Voznesenky's poem 'Akhillesovo Serdtse', the latter translated as 'My Achilles Heart'. Once again, Dass bluntly claims that ' "The Shield of Achilles" works as the controlling text, which predetermines Auden's choices, namely, additions, omissions, and changes' (1993: 147). Dass's evidence is that Auden orders the irregular source text into regular quatrains, suppresses its abruptnesses of expression and omits several of its dislocated lines. Yet Dass's explanation for this presumed manoeuvre is unconvincing. He claims that it serves to adapt the Russian source text to the dichotomy of arcadian and utopian that he believes is the theme of 'The Shield of Achilles' (147). He furthermore uses Auden's addition of the personal pronoun 'my' to the subjectless heart of the original title as a proof that the aim of this 'controlled' trans-lation is to support Auden's, rather than the original's, thrust, which is roughly to set arcadian harmony against a problematic utopian order.

Yet neither is there a utopian order in 'The Shield of Achilles', nor is there a coherent representation of arcadia that offers a model for actual existence. Rather, Auden's poem depicts the devastation of the twentieth century, embodied by war, propaganda, prison camps, urban dereliction and individual alienation. The 'arcadian ideal' is equally problematic, since it is meant to be depicted on a work of art, the shield, that is at the same time a weapon. Indeed, the shield fails to depict exactly what its sponsor, the goddess Thetis, expects: harmonic scenes of ideal civilisation. It shows instead 'An artificial wilderness / And a sky like lead'. There is no dichotomy between archaic ideal and contemporary malaise: the seeming contrast is merely a duplication and repetition.

In fact, Dass overlooks the fact that Auden's poem 'The Shield of Achilles' is itself an essay on translation, and the failures of translation to boot. The poem has as its theme the impossibility of translating suffering and injustice into a beautiful and reconciliatory work of art. It also emphasises the impossibility of translating the ideals of an earlier historical epoch into a recipe for positive developments in the present. Dass claims that

> there is, however, a contradiction implicit in this structuring in order to harmonize; for the kind of strict, utopian order repudiated is precisely what is being imposed upon the source text. Everything is radically ordered and reconstructed so that a strict discursive order can be imposed, and order predetermined largely by 'The Shield of Achilles'. What we end up with is complete domestication and recuperation: all elements and units which tend to wrinkle the spread of order are eliminated and displaced; phrases are denied their catachretic force in order to facilitate total order and recuperation. (1993: 148)

He thus misses completely the radical irony of what he sees as the controlling text, 'The Shield of Achilles', a text that concludes with the desperate stanza:

> The thin-lipped armourer,
>   Hephaestos, hobbled away,
> Thetis of the shining breasts
>   Cried out in dismay
> At what the god had wrought
>   To please her son, the strong
> Iron-hearted man-slaying Achilles
>   Who would not live long. (Auden, 1976: 455)

Auden's translation of Voznesensky, although evidently more structured than the original, still gives the impression of dislocation and chaos, as the following stanza illustrates:

> Are you still in pain? Do you act up at night?
> This defenseless extra is what saves me.
> Do not handle it roughly;
> The shudder would bring me down. (Dass, 1993: 145)

There is little evidence of a stylistic control by Auden's poem, even though the conclusion of the translation picks up the implicit theme of 'The Shield of Achilles', albeit in a very different shape: 'Our destruction is unthinkable, / More unthinkable what we endure'.

The problem of Dass's argument follows on from his attempt to base his thesis on a structuralist and poststructuralist position that, after Saussure, emphasises the separation of signifier and signifier and that, with Derrida, emphasises *différance* rather than a safe departure from a source and an equally secure arrival at a target. At the same time, he wishes to include in his thesis an ethical argument about appropriation of cultural difference. This second theoretical thrust forces him to ignore his own (post)structuralist premises, and to analyse texts in the traditional terms of faithfulness to their source. In short: his seemingly poststructuralist analysis becomes a hermeneutic one which eventually leads to value judgements.

This would still be justifiable if Auden's texts themselves did not incorporate in their own structures, images and themes much of the debate that Dass undertakes. In the same way as a psychoanalytic reading of Auden's works has to deal with the fact that Auden's writings are thoroughly informed by psychoanalytic teaching, and indeed often use it ironically and allegorically as clichés, Auden's ideas concerning translation shape his writings, and this encompasses obvious translation projects, as well as his own poetry and prose. While Dass acknowledges this in his introduction, he conveniently forgets the fact in his analysis. He also overlooks the irony embedded in Auden's foreword to the translation of Voznesensky's poems, in which, after having informed the reader about his ignorance of Russia and the Russian language, Auden claims that the poets engaged in the translations 'have tried to convey, in terms of their own poetic idiom and vision, the essence of what Voznesensky says in Russian to his compatriots' (Auden *et al.*, 1966: xxiii). A separation of translation from the idiom and vision (i.e. the linguistic and stylistic patterns, the preoccupations and concerns) of the translator is not possible, nor is it possible to think of translation as a simple reproduction of an original address. Whether this address is straightforward in poetry is highly questionable. Its complications become visible to an extreme degree in another genre, the dramatic one.[1]

Translating Translations: Auden's Writings between Media

Theatrical texts rely on multiple translations, that between a text and its production on stage and that between a particular production and its reception, none of which is simple and straightforward. The issue of translated theatre texts complicates matters further (Bassnett, 1991: 120–3). In the case of the theatrical translations that Auden undertook from the 1950s onwards with his partner Chester Kallman, yet another complication emerges, with the intersection of music and poetry in his opera libretti. Here, the issues of control and dominance, of music over text, meet issues of linguistic and cultural transposition.

It is not surprising that Auden as well as Kallman wrote extensively about the problems of translating poetry into opera. It is somewhat astonishing, though, that both their libretti and their statements on writing opera libretti still remain under-researched. Even Dass, who includes some of Auden's writings on libretti in his study on Auden's translations, eventually ties himself to the paradigm of 'proper' linguistic translation when he prefers to analyse in detail Auden and Kallman's collaboration with Brecht in *The Rise and Fall of the City of Mahagonny* (written in 1960, but published only after Auden's death) rather than Auden and Kallman's new libretto for Mozart's *Magic Flute* (1955); or the intermedial reworking of Hogarth's *The Rake's Progress* cycle of drawings into an opera libretti for Stravinsky (1947–8); or the rewriting of Euripides' *The Bacchae* in Henze's opera *The Bassarids* (1963).

That for Auden there was no qualitative or poetic difference between these different stage texts can be inferred from the treatment of Brecht's *Mahagonny* as a libretto, even though it was published without a musical score. Dass links this with Auden's insistence that music should be granted primacy in the translation of stage texts, a notion encountered in different form at the beginning of this essay. This 'melocentrism', Dass claims, leads Auden to impose 'his own ideology upon the source text' (Dass, 1993: 92). At the same time, however, Dass is aware of the dilemma already encountered in Auden's poem 'The Composer': the dominance of the word in translation processes – be these narrowly linguistic or most wide-rangingly cultural – inevitably creates a logocentric challenge. In Dass's words:

> as a result, the translator's sole concern is with verbal discourse . . . [T]he assumption is that if the words are 'properly' handled all the other show elements will 'naturally' fall into space. The Word retains its priority; all things are acted upon in order to accommodate it. And once again we fall back upon a self-authenticating presence: '. . . the translator has to trust his intuition and his knowledge of literature, both in the original tongue and in his own, of the period in which the opera is supposed to be set . . . the literary traditions of any two languages are so different that a puristic exactness is often neither necessary nor even desirable'. (1993: 89)[2]

Yet while there are undoubtedly remnants of essentialism in Auden's essay and his translation practice, they concern more the idealised figure of the translator as cultural expert whose intuitions are trustworthy and not unpredictable and idiosyncratic. As far as the primacy of language and therefore logocentrism is concerned, even the Auden quotation that Dass cites as evidence displays ambiguities. It shows an awareness of the difference, and indeed irreconcilability of context and history, of source and target languages, and therefore signals clearly that the translation will produce not so much an exact match as a new text. Auden wrote the above passage with the late eighteenth-century Italian of Mozart's *Don Giovanni* in mind. Yet even in the translation of a contemporary twentieth-century text, the German of Brecht's *Mahagonny*, into an equally contemporary English, differences emerge and create interesting difficulties.

One of the challenging elements of Brecht's original are its Americanisms and the use of an imaginary pidgin English to indicate a lingua franca of low life and capitalist corruption. Auden and Kallman reject this in their translation, since they doubt that the same effect can be achieved for an audience of native speakers of English (Dass, 1993: 95). Yet the effect of this normalisation, according to some critics, is that the topicality of Brecht's alienating Americanisms, designed for a 1920s Berlin audience, gives way to what amounts to a safe nostalgia that actually appeals to an American audience (95–6). Translation here neither reproduces the original faithfully – whatever this is supposed to mean – nor transposes subject matter into a relevant contemporary framework. It merely distorts and makes its results less relevant or, indeed, irrelevant. Despite all problematising notions of translations in terms of evasive objects and goals, this practice eventually questions the role of translation as communication.

Another problematic effect of Auden's normalisation is that it undoes the effect of Brecht's consciously detached and stilted German. Act II of *Mahagonny* contains the following refrain:

Spucke den Kaugummi aus.
Wasche zuerst deine Hände.
Lasse ihr Zeit
Und sprich ein paar Worte mit ihr. (Brecht, 1963: 46)

This is textbook German that has no connection with any colloquial idiom that would have been appropriate if the scene were designed to sound realistic: the grammatically correct forms of the commands 'Spucke', 'Wasche' and 'Lasse' would have been shortened in everyday speech. Brecht's artificial idiom is employed to inscribe a textual distance into the play which derives from his ideas concerning what he called epic theatre. Auden and Kallman's translation not only ignores this stiltedness; it actively colloquialises the passage through condensed forms and the insertion of the addressee, 'boy':

> Spit out your chewing-gum, boy.
> See that your hands aren't dirty.
> Give the girl time;
> A short conversation's polite. (Dass, 1993: 96)

Although the translation obviously has to follow the given number of syllables of the original to match a musical setting, there is no need for this stylistic adaptation which has obvious aesthetic, and ideological, consequences. A similar manoeuvre occurs in the summarising conclusion of the scene by the chorus of anonymous men. Here, the German original again employs awkward constructions that do not add up to poetic images or beautiful phrasing, but sound repetitive and mechanical and thus reinforce the theme of alienation:

> Erstens, vergesst nicht, kommt das Fressen
> Zweitens kommt der Liebesakt
> Drittens das Boxen nicht vergessen
> Viertens Saufen, laut Kontrakt.
> Vor allem aber achtet scharf
> Dass man hier alles dürfen darf.
> (Wenn man Geld hat.) (Brecht, 1963: 44)

A literal translation would reproduce the passage as follows:

> Firstly, don't forget, comes grub
> Secondly the act of lovemaking
> Thirdly don't forget boxing
> Fourthly getting pissed, according to contract.
> But most of all you must be keenly aware
> That one is allowed to be allowed everything here
> (If one has the money). [my translation]

Colloquial expressions such as 'Fressen' (grub) and crudely technical expressions, such as 'Liebesakt' (act of lovemaking) together with openly tautological constructions such as 'dürfen darf' (to be allowed to be allowed) add up to a simultaneously harsh and curiously unbalanced existential statement that represents the macho universe of the play but nonetheless stands on very uncertain (materialist) ground.

Nothing of this existential uncertainty, or of its links with proletarian speech and images, is left in Auden's version:

One means to eat all you are able;
Two, to change your loves about;
Three means the ring and the gaming table;
Four, to drink until you pass out.
Moreover, better get it clear
That Don'ts are not permitted here.
Moreover, better get it clear
That Don'ts are not permitted here! (Dass, 1993: 96–103)

While it would be unjust to read political intentions into Auden's translation, it is nonetheless evident that Auden's English version translates Brecht's lines not only into a different cultural context, but also into a middle-class perspective, where terms such as 'polite' act as markers of class and the technical crudeness of 'Liebesakt' has no room. As a result, the text has almost become nonsensical, because it finds itself in a cultural and linguistic vacuum where it loses its relevance and therefore its message. Although Auden translated the songs of Brecht's *The Caucasian Chalk Circle*, and he and Brecht embarked on another major collaboration, a reworking of Webster's *The Duchess of Malfi*, the latter project, as well as Brecht's idea that Auden should translate all the lyrics in his plays, came to nothing.

It is futile to speculate about the reasons for this, since biographers of Brecht and Auden provide conflicting explanations: the former claim that Brecht 'had a tremendous respect for Auden and would have liked to do much more work with him' (Berlau, 1987: 132–3); by contrast, the latter depend on comments such as the following by Auden: 'I've got a bit bored with old B.B. A great poet but he couldn't think' (Carpenter, 1982: 412). Yet, despite the flippancy of the latter remark, there seem to be indications that the collaboration suffered from an incompatibility of frameworks of thought and context of reference that eventually undermined the translation efforts. Despite the impossibility – and indeed undesirability – of locating translation somewhere between a fixed ontological starting point and an equally immobile teleological goal, translation obviously presents itself as an area of negotiation and struggle: not at all as a realm of an unproblematic free play of signification.

In their new version of Mozart's *The Magic Flute* of 1955, Auden and Kallman encountered no such cultural and ideological stumbling blocks as in their libretto for Brecht's *Mahagonny*. Mozart's opera is set in a semi-mythological fairyland, and what remains of historically specific frameworks of thought refers to Enlightenment ideals, such as the struggle between rationality and irrationality, the Apollonian and the

Dionysian. Nonetheless, Auden and Kallman are very much aware that the material is not entirely at their disposal, and the dedicatory verses hint at a debate on translation that becomes explicit in the preface and notes to the version:

> This Tale where true loves meet and mate,
> Brute, Brave, Grave, Laughter-loving, Great,
> Wee, Wise and Dotty translate
> To Music, we dedicate. (Auden & Kallman, 1993: 127)[3]

'Probably no other opera calls more for translation than *Die Zauberflöte*, and for a translation that is also an interpretation', begins their preface (129). In this preface the translators not only call the original text, by Schikaneder and Gieseke, 'peculiarly silly', but propose a reading of the text that very much assimilates it to the concerns of Auden's own works, and more specifically the concerns of Auden's mature writings as opposed to those of his early works. On the one hand, Tamino is quickly, and to a certain extent rightly, identified as 'the Quest Hero' (131), one of the central figures in Auden's early repertoire, already encountered earlier in this essay in 'The Wanderer'. To the fairy-tale framework is added a strange alternative reading, in which the characters of the opera are declared to possess 'a real history in which what happens next always depends upon what they choose now' (129). The interpretative translation thus inscribes in the magic plot an element of personal choice and responsibility and makes it ethical, moral, and even political to a degree that a fairy tale can hardly tolerate.

It is not so much *The Magic Flute* that is in need of these elements as Auden's own mature thinking. It is quite telling that the main reference point of his reading, the interpretation that shapes the eventual translation, is the key background text of his own mature poetry, Shakespeare's *The Tempest*. *The Tempest* is the text to which Auden's long philosophical poem *The Sea and the Mirror* of 1944 provides a poetic commentary, and in his preface to the translation of *The Magic Flute* some of Shakespeare's central characters reappear: Sarastro is equated with Prospero (130), and Monostatos becomes 'clearly another version of Caliban' (133).

What happens is a double translation, in which the first transposition makes Shakespeare's characters the representatives of Auden's emerging philosophy of reconciliation and negotiation of opposites – of reason and intuition, for example – and the second translation then projects the translated characters into a third text. Auden's emerging principle of dialogue finds expression in interpretation and translation that is based on statements such as the following, again from the preface to the libretto:

'What has been a relationship of antagonism, the war between the Queen and Sarastro, is finally replaced by a relationship of mutual affection and reconciliation, the marriage of Pamina and Tamino' (130). It is interesting that even this idyllic and seemingly mature reconciliation nonetheless contains traces of the early Auden, who in his 1930s poems firmly believed that solutions could only be found by replacing the 'Old Gang' with a new generation untainted by the corrupting influence of tradition.

In terms of translation, the problem is the one already encountered above: is translation, then, not merely another appropriation that subjects a source text to the demands of the target framework of thought? Such a consideration becomes especially poignant when this framework itself pretends to be concerned with acceptance and reconciliation, and there-fore opposes simple domination. Auden and Kallman indeed go so far as to change the sequence of scenes, in order, they claim, to make the opera more logical. The logic is, however, that of their interpretation and translation, and they rather clumsily seek a structural justification for it: 'Naturally, a change in order involves a change in key relation-ships. Were the music continuous, this would probably be a fatal objection, but it is not' (131). A little later they forcefully declare the autonomy of the translators of opera libretti:

> Translation is a dubious business at best and we are inclined to agree with those who believe that operas should always be given in their native tongue. However, if audiences demand them in their own, they must accept the consequences. Obviously, the texture and weight of the original words set by the composer are an element in his orches-tration and any change of the words is therefore an alteration of the music itself. Yet the goal of the translator, however unattainable, must be to make audiences believe that the words they are hearing are the words which the composer actually set, which means that a too-literal translation of the original text may sometimes prove a fal-sification. (133)

Something remarkable is going on in this passage. It culminates in the paradoxical demand that the correct translation is the one that tricks the audience into believing that they are hearing the original – or at least what the original intended. Apart from being based on an obvious inten-tional fallacy, the demand is also contradictory. Yet it goes hand in hand with the artistic reasons why Auden was interested in opera in the first place, and why he was even inclined to privilege it over poetry in certain respects: that is, its different way of connecting private and public spheres. In his lecture 'The World of Opera', Auden distinguishes poetry and opera in terms of the private and public nature of their respective audiences:

> in the primary world, most of our normal conversation is addressed to or elicited by another individual and thought of as private, that is to say, as concerning the speaker and the listener only, not an audience . . . The formalized art of poetry goes some way to meet our needs – a verse drama already involves the audience as well as the protagonists – but music goes much further. For singing is a form of public outcry: it is on the voluntary level what an *ouch* of pain or the howl of a hungry baby is on the involuntary. (1968: 76–7)

There is a critical consensus that the shift between Auden's earlier works and his mature writings happens to a large extent on this level of public and private utterance and relationships.[4] Auden's public poetry of the 1930s, whose most evident benchmark is the plural voice represented by 'we' and 'us', is increasingly perceived by its author as shallow, unfounded, and even potentially misleading and dangerous. This is not to say, however, that the mature Auden turned towards traditional forms of subjective and introspective lyric poetry. On the contrary, in terms of form his writings appropriate models that derive from the 'public' poetry of the Augustan period. However, his texts are careful to negotiate their speaking position and problematise not only their messages but also the reception situations they create. They become exercises in communicative interaction; indeed, they internalise some of the aspects and problematics of translation as the negotiating interchange between two communicative positions and contexts. 'Excuse, my lord, the liberty I take / In thus addressing you', starts Auden's *Letter to Lord Byron* of 1936, still ironically; his *New Year Letter* of 1940 begins to take the letter as a private and public form seriously.

Yet despite these poetic experiments, there remains a feeling of dissatisfaction in Auden's poetic works concerning poetry's public functions. His last poems tellingly opt for the private, as can be gathered from the titles of the collections in which they appear. While the explicitly private *About the House* of 1965 is followed by the more public *City Without Walls* in 1969, *Epistle to a Godson* of 1972 and the posthumous *Thank You Fog* of 1974 steer Auden's writings firmly into the private sphere. Early collections had titles such as *Look, Stranger!* (1936), *Another Time* (1940), and *The Enchafed Flood* (1950), which clearly express public concerns. What is the cause of this switch and the reason for Auden's disaffection with public writing, and what are the advantages that opera has to offer?

Again, in 'The World of Opera', Auden comes up with an interesting piece of amateur linguistics that has important implications for his translations:

> In verbal speech one can say, 'I love you'. Music can, I believe, express the equivalent of 'I love', but it is incapable of saying whom or what I love . . . A painting can portray someone as beautiful, loveable, etc., but it cannot say who, if anybody, loves this person. Music, one might say, is always intransitive and in the first person; painting only has one voice, the passive, and only the third person singular or plural.
>
> Both of them also have only the present indicative tense and no negative. For this reason, it makes no sense to ask of a piece of music or a painting: does the composer or the painter mean what he says, or is he just pretending? . . . [I]n a certain sense one might say that most verbal statements are in the subjunctive mood, that is to say, verifiable, if at all, by appeal to non-verbal facts. (1968: 79–80)

One could simplify this excursus as follows: music and painting cannot lie, because they are deictic and incapable of communicating intentions. By contrast, language can successfully pretend to be deictic and intentional; yet this capacity relies on the co-operation of the percipient. The dangers of self-deception and manipulation are evident; but what happens when language and music meet, as they do in opera libretti? Here, one could argue, an ideal is realised that Auden postulated for his first 'public' works, his attempts at verse drama: 'Ideally there should be no spectators. In practice every member of the audience should feel like an understudy'.[5] This creates an ideal reception situation, where the production of text and its interpretation are one. In theory at least this would overcome the dangers of misunderstanding and manipulation. It would also make translation unnecessary. Yet Auden quickly realises that this ideal cannot be put into practice. The constraints of staging cannot be fully overcome, nor is it possible to make participants the producers of texts. Yet one can trace an echo of this desired unity in the contradiction, earlier noted, that was triggered by the image of the successful libretto translation that simulates an original intention convincingly.

Opera, by employing the non-intentionalist medium of music, seems to be able to outbalance the vagaries and manipulative powers of language in Auden's thinking. It contains a public address in its reception situation, but includes private elements in its display of emotions.

It is a multiple translation, not merely in Bassnett's sense of translating text into performance, and spectacle into reception, but, according to Auden, in entailing a further translation of intention into spectacle. This intention becomes communicable, in the first place, through its links with established signifying practices, linguistic and otherwise, as also, and equally, through habitualised conventions of interpretation. Thereby an ideal communication situation is approached, in which individual utterance is guaranteed authenticity: an authenticity not of authorial intention, but of performance. At the same time, this individual utterance is prevented from becoming solipsistic and narcissistic by its integration into the practices of a communicative community.

It would not be stretching a point to compare this ideal of Auden's aesthetics – and an ideal it clearly is – with contemporary philosophical positions that stress the location of truths in communicative contexts. The German philosopher Jürgen Habermas, for example, has formulated such a position in his concept of 'communicative reason'. In his essay 'The Unity of Reason in the Diversity of its Voices', he speaks about the problem of the groundedness of this communicative reason in terms strikingly analogous to Auden's concepts of linguistic and intermedial translation and its recurring problems of groundedness, truth values, and justifiability:

> Transcendental thinking once concerned itself with a stable stock of forms for which there were no recognizable alternatives. Today, in contrast, the experience of contingency is a whirlpool into which everything is pulled: everything could also be otherwise, the categories of understanding, the principles of socialization and of morals, the constitution of subjectivity, the foundation of rationality itself. There are good reasons for this. Communicative reason, too, treats almost everything as contingent, even the conditions for the emergence of its own linguistic medium. But for everything that claims validity within linguistically structured forms of life, the structures of possible mutual understanding in language constitute something that cannot be gotten around. (Habermas 1992: 139–40)

In terms of Auden's translation endeavours, Habermas' claims reflect the insight that the bases from which the enterprise starts, and which provide the poles of orientation in the shape of source and target language and cultural context, are themselves the results of poiesis rather than transcendental essences. The interpretation comes first, as Auden and Kallman implicitly point out in the preface to their libretto of *The Magic Flute*, and it then generates the principles on which poetic translation and creation rest. But even this seemingly circular model of autopoiesis contains its touchstone of foundation in what Habermas calls 'the structures of possible mutual understanding in language'. Without breaking out of the linguistic turn, Habermas, as well as Auden, inscribes into the linguistic universe a personal as well as social dimension. This dimension is manifest exactly in translation, which, on the basis of significatory negotiation and interchange, establishes the modes of a possible understanding that motivates the poietic and foundational endeavours in the first place.

We have already traced this endeavour in *The Magic Flute*, where it assumes a fairly basic shape, reworking Enlightenment paradigms like rationality and irrationality in order to replace the logocentric insistence on binary oppositions and hierarchies with a model of negotiation and an attempted reconciliation that will still contain difference rather than positing dominance and enforcing homogeneity. In Auden and Kallman's libretto for Stravinsky's *The Rake's Progress* of 1947–48, this endeavour to establish a rudimentary philosophy of translation had in fact already gained a more radical shape. The media aspect of the translation is more pronounced, since the underlying model, Hogarth's cycle of engravings, is very different from the linguistic source text of an already existing libretto. Nonetheless, Auden groups painting together with music under the art forms that guarantee authenticity of gesture through renunciation of clear intention. The second radical aspect of Hogarth's works, as a starting point for Auden and Kallman's intermedial translation, is its obvious concern with morality, a morality that is of the eighteenth century and therefore provides a context potentially as challenging as that of Brecht's 1920s Berlin.

Yet rather than eliminating the obvious cultural and historical difference between the source text and the translation, as Auden and Kallman had done in their Brecht translation, they emphasise and complicate difference in *The Rake's Progress*. Hogarth's drawings are emblematic of eighteenth-century England. Furthermore, they represent the rather monocausal moral logic of vulgarised Enlightenment philosophy in the idea of the self-governing individual who is responsible for his actions and whose mistakes lead to his downfall. Auden and Kallman's libretto, however, inscribes a competing anachronistic logic into this linear morality. They create inside the Protestant Enlightenment ideology of self-determination and individual responsibility an older and contradictory teaching, the Catholic one of temptation through evil and salvation as the work of divine grace rather than human achievement. This countersource was originally meant to be even more pronounced, as Auden's statements, as reported by Alan Ansen, indicate:

There are to be seven characters – three men and three women, in addition to the hero. I think I'd like to connect it with the Seven Deadly Sins. The hero, of course, will represent Pride, the young girl Lust, I think. The rich old woman will be Avarice, the false friend Anger, the servant Envy and so on. (1989: 76–7)

In the end, Auden and Kallman primarily created the figure of Nick Shadow, who already in his name embodies the traditional devil. Yet equally clichéd, if not in a traditional religious sense, are the central roles of Tom Rakewell, the problematic protagonist, and Anne Trulove, his lover. Already in the first scene of Act I the audience is introduced to their essential differences of view that will keep them apart throughout the opera. In their introductory duet, the libretto shows them engaged in an act of interpretative translation that makes them view the spring afternoon in very different ways. Anne's part culminates in the orthodox view that 'With fragrant odours and with notes of cheer / The pious earth observes the solemn year'. Rakewell, on the other hand, translates the same scene into radically different terms that link sensual enjoyment with materialist ambitions: 'When swains their nymphs in fervent arms enfold / And with a kiss restore the Age of Gold' (Auden & Kallman, 1993: 49).[6]

Both positions – and this is the genius of Auden & Kallman's translation – are appropriate in eighteenth-century England. The conflicting ideologies that make up Enlightened England are exposed in this clichéd rendering, and so are their obvious gender implications: men are responsible for providing the materialist bases of life, women are in charge of maintaining moral principles. Tom and Anne's duet culminates in the line 'Love tells no lies', which restates the ambivalence of competing translation and interpretation: both positions are equally honest, yet mutually exclusive. Their apparent reconciliation occurs when the devil, in the shape of Nick Shadow, makes Tom believe that he is a rich heir, and thus supports his dislike of entering a profession. Yet even this Enlightenment ideal, that seemingly reconciles wealth and morality in the form of 'independent means', displays cracks when, as a result, Tom and Anne are parted, and Tom goes to London to settle his estate.

So Rakewell is delivered into the hand of brothel-keeper Mother Goose, and once again Enlightenment ideals are highlighted as prerequisites to downfall. When Tom declares in terms that resemble Rousseau's that he intends 'To shut my eyes to prude and preacher / And follow Nature as my teacher' (56), the brothel setting radically undermines the potential merit of this position. What Tom sees in Enlightenment terms as nature is interpreted by Nick Shadow in pagan terms as 'mysteries':

> Sisters of Venus, Brothers of Mars, Fellow-worshippers in the Temple of Delight, it is my privilege to present to you a stranger to our mysteries who, following our custom, begs leave to sing you a song in earnest of his desire to be initiated. (57)

Translation happens in ideological and moral terms inside the play as well, and it is the contradiction engendered by the possibility of multiple translation that, in fact, determines the plot of Stravinsky's opera. In the conclusion of Act I this becomes blatantly obvious when Tom and Nick's duet presents Tom's current ambition, the seduction of Baba the Turk, in two very different versions. While Tom mixes pride and libido in his view

> Of the wooing and wedding
> Likewise the bedding
> Of Baba the Turk,
> That masterwork
> Whom nature created
> To be celebrated,

Nick's sinister version asks 'What deed could be as great / As with this gorgon to mate?' (63).

Baba the Turk is another figure added by the libretto to the source engravings: in Hogarth, the Rake marries an ugly old woman for money. Baba is a further anachronism, yet she does not derive from the medieval tradition that generates Nick Shadow as the devilish seducer. She is a modern figure, a grotesque circus attraction: the Bearded Lady. She also relates to Auden's earlier works, more precisely to the character of the Man-Woman who appears in his earliest play *Paid on Both Sides* (1928). There, the androgynous character united the traditions of the mummer's play with Freud's concept of the phallic mother, the male wish-fulfilment fantasy that functions as an antidote to fears of castration. In *The Rake's Progress*, Baba is both a reminder of sexual instability and of the power issues that shape gender relations. It is she who is in control in the relationship with Tom Rakewell, and her control is a thoroughly modern one: 'You know you're bound / By law, dear' (67). She is also the revenge of the colonial object on the century that set the British Empire firmly in place: herself a translation from the exotic Orient, she turns the imperialist principles of acquisition upside-down, and translates symbolic representations of the colonisers into her miraculously autonomous

private sphere, in the same way that her seduction by Tom has led to
his enslavement. In Act II Scene 3 her aria summarises this reversal:

> Baba [*très vite without stopping*].
> As I was saying both brothers wore moustaches,
> But Sir John was the taller; they gave me the musical glasses.
> That was in Vienna, no, it must have been Milan
> Because of the donkeys. Vienna was the Chinese fan
> – Or was it the bottle of water from the River Jordan? –
> I'm certain at least it was Vienna and Lord Gordon.
> I get so confused about all my travels.
> The snuff boxes came from Paris, and the fluminous gravels
> From a cardinal who admired me vastly in Rome ... (69)

Rakewell only escapes from the imperialist clutches of Baba through
the economic collapse of their household; he allows himself to be taken
in by a deceptive machine that seemingly turns stones into bread –
another very vague allusion to Hogarth, who makes the philosophers'
stone the subject matter of one of his engravings. Once again, a foundational element of the Enlightenment, the technological revolution,
turns in on itself. To add to this relativising, Tom eventually gambles
for his soul with Nick Shadow, and in the traditional manner of the
Faustus legend – only more successfully than either Marlowe's or
Goethe's protagonists – has recourse to love to rescue his soul. And as
if this backward projection were not enough, the libretto recruits another
intertextual source that it translates into the plot. When Nick Shadow,
in a gesture of impotent revenge, makes Tom mad, Tom starts believing
that he is Adonis. In the lunatic asylum in which he ends up, he enacts
his own translation of Ovid's story, very likely read through the lens of
Shakespeare's *Venus and Adonis*:

> Prepare yourselves, heroic shades. Wash you and make you clean.
> Anoint your limbs with oil, put on your wedding garments and
> crown your heads with flowers. Let music strike. Venus, Queen of
> Love, will visit her unworthy Adonis. (87)

Tom's madness, however, is very aware of historical intertextuality and
its translation into contemporary contexts, as his address to his imagined fellow actors as 'heroic shades' implies. His madness is as much a
translation of earlier texts as the entire libretto of *The Rake's Progress* is
a multiple and consciously anachronistic translation. Yet this translation
also creates the tensions and problems in the plot, as the earlier analysis
of Tom and Anne Trulove's diverging world-views has demonstrated.

Consequently, when Anne visits Tom in Bedlam, she is moved by his protestations of everlasting love, but she is also aware that his love, translated into mythological settings, has nothing to do with her person. Her response is therefore: 'Tom, my vow / Holds ever, but it is no longer I / You need' (90). As much as translation can establish communicative connection and found communities, it can also inscribe distance and create rifts that are unbridgeable.

By translating a setting, itself anachronistic in a twentieth-century opera, into multiple anachronisms, Auden and Kallman make a statement about modernity as a mixture of competing traditions inside which translation plays a central negotiating role. These translated traditions are not merely of interest for textual scholars interested in intertextual source-hunting. On the contrary, since they encompass central ideological elements of Western culture, such as the ethical distinction of good and evil and the belief in an autonomous individual, as well as an insistence on the dominance of rationality and the ethos of progress and materialist gain, these translations challenge as much as they confirm. They no longer simply challenge the bases of individual autonomy or a narrow Englishness; their productive destabilising encompasses the entirety of Western culture since the Enlightenment. In a letter to Stravinsky, Auden summarised the central problems of these competing traditions, linking pleasure, free will, and the desire to replace God in a neat and concise way by relating them to the phases in the Rake's progress:

Bordel.	Le plaisir
Baba.	L'Acte gratuite.
La Machine.	Il désire devenir Dieu. (590)

Translation as Unravelling: Of Culture, Community, and Self

The libretto to Hans Werner Henze's *The Bassarids* of 1963 brings Auden and Kallman's intermedial translations to their utmost refinement. In a letter of September 1963 Auden expresses his conviction that 'it is the best libretto we have done so far' (Auden & Kallman 1993: 680). The libretto also reaches back furthest in the intertextual chain that Auden characterises, in his essay 'The World of the Sagas', as the foil of translation. By taking Euripides' *The Bacchae* as a source text, Auden and Kallman go back to classical Greek tragedy for a source of a modern opera libretto. Bassarids, an unusual term, was chosen by Auden, Kallman and Henze because it encompasses male and female followers of Dionysus, whereas 'Bacchae' refers only to women (Auden & Kallman, 1993: 682). But their use of Euripides is not simply a modernist borrowing of the most canonical of traditions, not even in the manner of Maud Ellmann's characterisation of a similar attitude in modernists such as Eliot and Pound as 'blasphemy' (Ellmann, 1987: 95). Auden and Kallman add a snippet from German modernist poet Gottfried Benn to the title page of their libretto, and this snippet already contains the first indication of the outlook of this problematic translation. It reads 'Die Mythe log . . .' [The myth lied . . .]. Why translate a source that is perceived as mendacious? Or does the quotation contain a first indication of a self-reflexive assessment of their intermedial translation endeavour?

The setting of the opera could not be more traditional ('The action takes place in the Courtyard of the Royal Palace in Thebes, and on Mount Kithairon'; Auden & Kallman 1993: 250),[7] and even the speeches imitate the *gravitas* of Greek tragedy ('Pentheus is now our lord. / Son of Agave and Echion, / May he walk in the ways / Of wisdom and right', 251). Yet already the detailed descriptions of the characters prepare for similar intertextual anachronisms and counter-projections to the ones encountered in *The Rake's Progress*. While Cadmon, Pentheus' grandfather, is to be dressed as 'the embodiment of legendary age: long white beard, staff, blue cloak and draped costume suggesting a Minoan rather than Hellenic past' (252), and therefore still corresponds, at least vaguely, to the historical background of the source, already with Pentheus' mother Agave a different intertext enters the libretto. She is dressed 'in the style of the French Second Empire' (253). Later, the Captain of the Guard appears in the costume of a fourteenth-century Frankish Knight (257). With the seer Tiresias, the libretto goes overboard completely:

> Tiresias is dressed in the complete get-up of an Anglican Archdeacon. He also wears dark glasses and taps with a cane to find his way. More than slightly inclined to an androgynous corpulence, he tends to cover his consciousness of his slightly comic failing with a hurried and portentous self-importance. In addition to his usual costume, his cane has been hastily decorated with fennel, and he carries a fawn-skin thrown over one arm . . . (253)

This grotesque Tiresias embodies the very translation processes at work in the libretto. He also adds an insistence on the Audenesque, since his outfit harks back to the many comical figures of authority in Auden's early writings, most notably, perhaps, the Vicar of Pressan Ambo in his play *The Dog Beneath the Skin* (1935). The plot of *The Bassarids* is also concerned with translation, and more specifically with the perils of translation in relation to cultural stability and its responsibility for a tradition that guarantees community. The appearance of the god Dionysus in Thebes is perceived by the forces of this tradition as a challenge to orthodoxy. Cadmus actually worries that Dionysus might be a test of their loyalty to Hera.

Dionysus is a god, but he is also an upstart. Tiresias describes him as

the youngest of the Gods; soon Hera
Will also befriend his might. On Olympus
Now and Delphi his place waits amongst Gods, the
God Dionysus! (254)

He represents culture as well as chaos, and worship of him is not a calm and dignified ritual, but enactment of excess. His position, identity, and role, are disputed. Cadmus in fact tries to find out who exactly Dionysus is, but the answers he receives are contradictory. Tiresias states that he is 'All he claims to be'; Agave calls him 'Nothing. A wine-skin / Emptied with its wine' (256). This is in stark contrast to the source text of the libretto, Euripides' play, in which Dionysus declares himself and his intentions in the very first line: 'I have come, the son of Zeus, to this land of the Thebans, / I, Dionysus, whom once Cadmus' daughter bore' (Kirk, 1970: 23). In Auden and Kallman's libretto, he is the principle of uncertainty, and yet he is to be feared, too. He represents cultural change and thereby also embodies translation: of stories, like those surrounding his own conception and birth; of allegiances; consequently, of power as well. It is not difficult to see in the figure of Dionysus an allegory of modernity turning away from firm doctrines of belief and towards convictions grounded in experience (the inheritance of empiricism and positivism) and ideals (the heritage of idealist philosophies and practice).

'Can they change, can the Gods change?' asks the sceptical Cadmus when confronted by the enthusiasm of the people of Thebes. Once more his question addresses both the issue of cultural change, over against the seeming stability of faith, and the mechanism that links the two and undermines them at the same time: translation. Translation, in this case the changing of affections, can turn men into gods, as Autonoe, Agave's sister, claims: 'A man might be thought a god were he loved / Enough' (259). She uses this insight to question one of the myths on which Thebes is founded, that of the love affair between her sister Semele and the god Zeus. This affair, according to the myth, killed Semele, but brought forth Dionysus. Foundation myths, this dialogue suggests, are themselves founded: on tradition and interpretation, between which translation negotiates. Yet, at the same time, the plot of the opera does not merely state its authors' loss of faith in traditional narratives. On the contrary, it also asserts the necessity of those narratives. The tragedy of *The Bassarids*, as much as that of its source *The Bacchae*, begins when the new king Pentheus tries to do away with myths altogether:

> We, Pentheus, King of Thebes, do hereby declare:
> Whereas certain idlers and babblers have deceived you with
>   their ridiculous inventions, impiously asserting that the
>   Immortal Gods do lust after mortals and strive jealously for
>   their favors, let all such blasphemers henceforth be
>   anathema.
> As touching our House, whoever shall say or think that the
>   Son of Chronos did abduct Europa from Tyre and ravish
>   her in a Cretan grove, let him be anathema.
> Whoever shall say or think that, in this very city, the Father of the
>   Gods had carnal knowledge of Semele, daughter of Cadmus,
>   and begot a child upon her, let him be anathema . . .
> We, Pentheus, the King, have spoken. (260–1)

When Pentheus appears shortly afterwards, he is tellingly

> spare, athletic, scholarly. In dress, monastic and soldierly: a medieval king in the sort of dress he might wear on a pilgrimage. He also wears a long cloak. The colour of his costume is that of undyed sackcloth. (261)

An ancient Greek Savonarola, he embodies an attempt to overcome the power of myth, and this means overcoming the power of stories. What this entails is also, in fact, the elimination of the story of his own dynasty, as is demonstrated by his grandfather Cadmus who, a little later, declares:

> Gods have stood before me and spoken.
> Their words are gone. Our city stands yet.
> And the radiance of their speech robes our endeavours
> Of stone and rich deed. And earth glows. (266)

Identity – and this means personal as well as communal identity – rests on stories, and the power of these stories depends on tradition, which means transmission as well as translation. In his attempt to create an identity purified from translation and its inevitable transformations, Pentheus undoes identity, that of his city and of himself, since, as king, his position is legitimised only through narratives of ancestry. As a result, he first has to ban his own grandfather, Cadmus, who refuses to give up his attachment to established myths. He then finds himself abandoned by his people and incapable of thought-policing them through his guards. Eventually, he has to endure a lecture by Tiresias, which offers him a run-down on the formation of myths and their proliferation through translation:

> Well then, Pentheus, as wine is born
> Each year from parched wry stems, like lightning shaped, so must
> Its God be born. So people think. So tales begin.
> So worship spreads . . .
> Now each can worship in his way. With Cadmus I
> Pretend to take this harmless tale as true in all
> Details; though you and he, the God himself, must know
> Much better, yes. And I. We see the facts, we know
> Our tongue, we know that anciently the words for 'pledge'
> and 'thigh' were similar . . . (273–4)

Later on, Tiresias repeats his sermon as a warning: 'Now Pentheus, you must not be too literal / About the Gods' (276–7). Pentheus' attempt to free knowledge from translation has actually deprived him of insight: he neither knows what he is doing, nor does he know himself. Thus it is not surprising when a worshipper of Dionysus denies him respect: 'Respect? The ungodly man who neither sees nor knows / The deed he does, the God he seeks, the man he is?' (279). Pentheus' helpless reply reiterates exactly the tales that he has sought to overcome: 'Slave, bow to Pentheus, son of Echion, King of Thebes' (279). After being introduced to the story of the discovery of Dionysus, his only response is to declare everything he hears a lie:

> Lies, lies, lies. Am I not King? . . .
> Lies! King Pentheus
> Is answered with a lie
> To his every question. Lies.
> What shall he call on? Where
> Is the One, the Good?
> The Heavens are dark with lies.
> And who would help him there?
> How will Perfection turn
> Into the Thunderer he needs
> If the King himself is not to become
> A lie, a lie, a lie? (280–1)

The radicalism of Pentheus' endeavour undermines even the endeavour itself. In order to succeed in his planned purification of knowledge, he relies on an authoritarian force that he himself can only envisage in the shape of a mythical story, Zeus as the Thunderer.

Pentheus' resistance to translation, and his eventual failure to escape its power, anticipate, in dramatic terms, Derrida's meditation on the biblical myth of Babel in his essay 'Des tours de Babel'. Here, Derrida speculates on the implications of the Old Testament story in terms that are strikingly analogous to Auden and Kallman's libretto:

> Telling at least of the inadequation of one tongue to another . . . of language to itself and to meaning, and so forth, it also tells of the need for figuration, for myth, for tropes, for twists and turns, for translation inadequate to compensate for that which multiplicity denies us. In this sense it [translation] would be the myth of the origin of myth, the metaphor of metaphor, the narrative of narrative, the translation, and so on. It would not be the only structure hollowing itself out like that, but it would do so in its own way (itself *almost* untranslatable, like a proper name), and its idiom would have to be saved. (1985: 165)

Auden and Kallman's libretto eventually goes so far as to undermine itself in order to retain this multiplicity, when the action is interrupted by an Intermezzo in a Rococo setting, in which Agave and Autonoe reappear as Marie Antoinette shepherdesses surrounded by liveried servants and musicians, and the Captain of the Guard returns as the object of their desires. They are disturbed in their attempted seduction when Tiresias enters and, expressing disapproval of their behaviour, suggests a charade to enact what he perceives as the problem of the set-up: the two women will soon fall out over their right to the Guardsman. Surprisingly enough, they agree, and soon the women assume the roles of the goddesses Venus and Proserpine, the Guardsman becoming Adonis, and Tiresias Calliope, the muse of epic poetry, to act as a judge.

This mock trial re-enacts the mythical dispute of the two goddesses over Adonis. Calliope's verdict is an early form of timeshare: one year Adonis will belong to Venus, the next to Proserpine, and every third year to himself. As casual as the verdict is the language used for it. When Tiresias in the disguise of Calliope simultaneously cautions that this Salomonic arrangement is unlikely to work, he couches his warning in colloquial terms: 'His chances of escape are dim: / Those girls will tear him limb from limb' (292). His prediction is no longer merely applicable to Adonis, but refers to the Guardsman as well, and, by extension, to Pentheus, whose fate is enacted at the end of the opera.

The Intermezzo not only introduces a further displacement and translation of mythical text into the eighteenth century. It also provides a play (the charade, incidentally another of early Auden's favourite models), within a play (the Intermezzo) within yet another play, the opera itself. What has been pointed out earlier about opera libretti as multiple translations is here brought to refinement, and so is the notion developed in Auden's essay 'The World of Sagas' that translation only ever happens inside a chain of intertextuality, even when here the chain is consciously ruptured and rendered anachronistic by jumping freely between Greek mythology and the Rococo. The choice of these two obviously antagonistic periods is itself motivated by their very different relation to signs, that is, their interpretation, and therefore again to translation. While classical culture interpreted signs in a monolinear way as standing clearly for something else, but only for *one* other meaning, to which they had an intrinsic connection – a good example is divination – the seventeenth and eighteenth centuries witness a proliferation of signs in excess of possible meanings, an explosion of signification and an undoing of the possibility of straightforward translation. In Derrida's words,

> it [translation] exhibits an incompletion, the impossibility of finishing, of totalizing, of saturating, of completing something on the order of edification, architectural construction, system and architectonics. (1985: 165)

A similar allegorisation of translation happens in the figure of Pentheus. The remorseful king is dressed by Dionysus in the clothes of his mother, Agave. He renounces his already lost identity for another equally dubious one, that of a woman, which he obviously is not. Of this dress, the stage instructions tell us mischievously, 'It is also obviously a bad fit' (295). 'Can this be the King? I see there a true daughter of Cadmus' is consequently Dionysus' ironic verdict. And indeed, the act of involuntary transvestism translates Pentheus' identity: 'suddenly coy and feminine' (in the words of the stage direction), he exclaims 'And I? Have I dressed myself well in truth? Yes? Like Agave?' (295). This is not merely the utterance of a mind in distress. Earlier on, the debates about the relative merits of truth and storytelling were conducted in terms of decking truth out in fictions, as a body is covered by clothes. Here identity is dressed in an obviously borrowed 'story', that of the mother. The Oedipal connotations are consciously employed.

When Dionysus plays his last trick on Pentheus and asks his followers, the Maenads, to hunt down and kill the spy in their midst, Pentheus gives himself away. The final dialogue between him and the Maenads is also the final expression of the conflicting demand to maintain identity and to deny it absolutely. In this dialogue it is important to notice that, after his reference to himself as his body, in the exclamation 'this flesh is me!' (301), has failed, Pentheus clings to his identity, exactly like the stories he tried to ban earlier on. He does this by reference to memory:

> PENTHEUS [*each line softer than the one before*]. Mother,
>   remember . . .
> MAENADS [*each line louder than the one before*]. No.
> PENTHEUS. Echion, my father.
> MAENADS. No.
> PENTHEUS. You loved him . . .
> MAENADS. No!
> PENTHEUS. And named me . . .
> MAENADS. No!
> PENTHEUS [*a soft whisper*]. Pentheus . . .
> MAENADS I [*a prolonged scream*]. NO!
> MAENADS II [*crescendo*]. Ayayalya . . .
> PENTHEUS. Ah! (301)

The story returns from the most universal foundation narratives, of creation and the foundation of cultures, to the smallest, Freud's *Urszene*, the family romance. Yet even there, the destructive voice of the Maenads, who do not respect history because they rewrite it constantly, denies safe points of orientation and therefore identity. When eventually even his name is taken away from him, Pentheus' dismemberment has already taken place on a symbolic scale before he is physically torn to pieces, and by no other than his mother Agave and his aunt Autonoe. Derrida links this dismembering potential of translation with his crucial theoretical endeavour of deconstruction (1985: 166).[8]

Yet the blindness of the two destructive women is only temporary. In the same way as culture contains blind spots in which order is suspended in order to keep its myth-making going, the plot of *The Bassarids* returns to normality, admittedly one of horror. Nonetheless, and despite Cadmus' mythical woe about the end of his dynasty through divine revenge, there is a contemporary element in this gruesome finale. While Cadmus perpetuates classical myth as an explanatory pattern imposed on events otherwise too monstrous to bear, Autonoe engages in a more mundane form of myth-making: 'I didn't want to do it. / Agave made me do it' (307), is her exculpatory refrain. The chorus of the Bassarids functions in the same way: 'We heard nothing. We saw nothing. / We took no part in her lawless frenzy. / We had no share in his bloody death' (308). In the context of the twentieth century, this self-exculpation is only too well known in the context of the atrocities of the holocaust and countless wars within and beyond national boundaries to need further comment.

And On . . . Contingent Foundations, Continual Translations

While seemingly taking us away from the narrower implications of translation, the extended discussion of *The Bassarids* has brought the analysis full circle back to the beginning of the investigation. Here, translation serves to support an identity that refuses to acknowledge its precarious status as an ungrounded process needing eventually to acknowledge its contingency. Translation, as appropriation of the discourse, linguistic and cultural, of the Other, serves to provide the self-enclosed individual with a sense of stability. That the narcissistic self thus created is a myth is indicated in Auden's self-deprecatory remarks about his infatuation with Old Norse sagas. In *The Bassarids* this mythic view of translation finds its allegory in the (self-)dismemberment of Pentheus when he strips himself not only of his borrowed clothes, but eventually of his borrowed identity. The borrowing happens precisely through translation, yet the reason why this translation cannot guarantee a stable identity is that it is itself forever in process, without firm origins and goals.

That translation, and the precarious identity that it creates, and on which it simultaneously rests, cannot be regarded without reference to their twinned contexts, is evident in Auden's translation of self into society. In embryonic shape this happens as early as in 'The Wanderer'; in more refined versions, his translations of contemporary twentieth-century texts display this intrinsic link that inevitably makes translation a social and political endeavour. This is evident even when the transposition fails, as it does, to a certain extent, in Auden and Kallman's translation of Brecht. In *The Bassarids*, Pentheus' failure derives precisely from his inability to accept that a cultural context, which is inevitably based on foundation myths, is necessary for communicative endeavours such as translation. Any attempt to eradicate this context, or reduce it to facts rather than narratives, themselves the result of translations in progress, leads to a severing of utterance from community, a divorce that has fatal consequences.

Translation enables Auden to work out his philosophical model of a reconciliation of differences that is not a homogenisation of those differences but a dialogue and negotiation between them, one that retains and respects difference. This becomes evident in the libretto to *The Magic*

Flute, which plays out Enlightenment concepts, such as rationality and irrationality, against each other, yet does not offer a solution in any easily established harmony. Integration always also means dispute and even struggle, and this is the recipe that Auden prescribes for dealing with binary opposites. The Program Notes for the first production of *The Bassarids*, which Auden and Kallman provided at the request of its composer Hans Werner Henze, clearly link Pentheus' failure to his lack of insight into this necessary negotiation:

> His attempt completely to suppress his instinctual life instead of integrating it with his rationality brings about his downfall. One might say that a similar fate would have befallen Sarastro, had there not been a Tamino and a Pamina to marry and so reconcile Day to Night (700).

Translation is the crucial strategy in this reconciliatory negotiation that is never a simple takeover and must indeed retain difference in order to function at all.

The complexity of modernity is largely founded on the simultaneous proliferation of these translations of texts and context and an awareness of this discursive explosion. This becomes evident in the multiple inter-textual schemes at work in *The Rake's Progress*. Here, the medieval belief in hell and salvation meets Enlightenment ideas both of nature as an intrinsic guideline and of human will as an instrument of domination and progress. These elements enter an even more contradictory alliance with twentieth-century concepts of gender struggle and Oedipal anxi-eties. In the same way, the translation from one to another very different medium, i.e. engraving and opera, creates technical and theoretical tensions, while at the same time enabling Auden to give expression to his desire to write works that function on both a private and a public plane.

An equally confusing multiple projection of contexts happens in *The Bassarids*. Here, the austerity of Greek tragedy meets the flamboyance of Rococo; the mythical inevitability of fate stands side by side with libid-inous charades. The recourse to foundation myths of Western culture is doubled when inside these myths the status of foundations itself is ques-tioned and allegorically torn to pieces. Culture itself is shown to be the result of translations, and these translations are depicted not so much as inevitable forces of history, but as individual acts that rely on their interplay with social and political contexts. Inside these contexts they often fail, and the consequences of these failures can indeed be fatal. But equally fatal is the attempt to ignore or even abandon translation as a crucial prerequisite of the formation of identity, be it personal, national or indeed cultural.

While Auden reaches the implicit ideal of his later works, the perspective of a global citizen, only in the ironic form of the self-applied label of 'a minor atlantic Goethe', and while his artistic ideal of reconciling private and public remains equally problematic, his works nonetheless demonstrate a keen awareness that, within the ungroundedness of culture and communication, translation acts both as a reminder of these contingent foundations and as a reassurance that inside this contingency communication can and must continue to be attempted.

Notes

1. Auden also translated the poems in Goethe's *The Sorrows of Young Werther and Novella*, trans. E. Mayer and L. Bogan (New York: Random House, 1971). Moreover, he translated one poem from Polish by Adam Mickiewicz which appeared in *Adam Mickiewicz 1798–1885: Selected Poems* (1957), ed. Clark Mills (New York: Noonday Press, 1956). For these details, see Dass, 1993: 157.
2. The concluding quotation is from Auden's essay 'Translating Opera Libretti' (Auden, 1963: 491).
3. All future references are to this edition and are given parenthetically by page number alone in the body of the text.
4. Compare, for example, Perrie, 1985: 63; Smith, 1985: 168–94; Callan, 1983: 252–67; Boly, 1991: 120–56.
5. Fuller, 1970: 13 (quoting from the programme note to Auden's *The Dance of Death* (1933)).
6. All future references are to this edition and are given parenthetically by page number alone in the body of the text.
7. All future references are to this edition and are given parenthetically by page number alone in the body of the text.
8. Like his model Walter Benjamin, however, Derrida also remains fascinated by the idea of what Benjamin calls 'Holy Writ', where 'meaning has ceased to be the watershed for the flow of language and the flow of revelation, [w]here a text is identical with truth or dogma, where it is supposed to be "the true language" in all its literalness and without the mediation of meaning' (Benjamin, 1973: 82). While in Benjamin the author's formalism (that finds expression in his denunciation of content over artistic form) meets his Messianism, in Derrida there is a psychoanalytically informed circumnavigation of 'the name of God the father' as 'the name of that origin of tongues' (Derrida, 1985: 167). While he eventually avoids a clear commitment to this transcendental ontology, its attraction as a counterbalance to the deconstructive flow is evident. Auden and Kallman's libretti, however, locate their ground within ungroundedness, in the more Habermasian location of communication itself, with all its problems, rather than in any transcendental presence.

Bibliography and Abbreviations

Note: in this bibliography, inconsistencies in the placing of the translator's name relative to the works and authors s/he is translating witness to the ambiguous status of the translator; major translators like Auden appear in their own right, as do translators of classical and medieval texts.

Agorni, M. (1994) Elizabeth Carter's translation of *Il Newtonianismo per le Dame* by Francesco Algarotti and the birth of the 'modern' reader. In *Cross Cultural Transfers* (pp. 1–10). Warwick Working Papers in Translation. Graduate Series I, H.G. Barbosa (ed.) [Coventry]: Centre for British and Comparative Cultural Studies, University of Warwick.

Alexander, N. (1968) *Elizabethan Narrative Verse*. London: Edward Arnold.

Algarotti, F. (1737) *Il Newtonianismo per le dame, ovvero dialoghi sopra la luce, i colori, e l'attrazione*. Venezia.

Algarotti, F. (1738) *Le Newtonianisme pour les dames, ou Entretiens sur la lumiere, sur les couleurs, et sur l'attraction*. (M. Du Perron de Castera, trans.). Paris. *See also* Carter.

Allen, R.S. (trans.) (1988) *Richard Rolle: The English Writings*. New York: Paulist Press.

Anon. (trans.) (1560) *The Fable of Ovid Treting of Narcissus*. London: Thomas Howells.

Anon. (1884) The best gentleman in fiction. *Gentleman's Magazine*, 256, 101.

Ansen, A. (1989) *The Table Talk of W.H. Auden*, N. Jenkins (ed.). London and Boston: Faber and Faber.

Aston, M. (1988) *England's Iconoclasts. Vol. I: Laws Against Images*. Oxford: Oxford University Press.

Aston, M. (1995) God, saints and reformer: portraiture and Protestant England. In *Albion's Classicism: The Visual Arts in Britain 1550–1660* (pp. 181–220), L. Gent (ed.). New Haven, CT: Yale University Press.

Auden, W.H. (1963) *The Dyer's Hand and Other Essays*. London and Boston: Faber and Faber.

Auden, W.H. (1968) *Secondary Worlds*. London and Boston: Faber and Faber.

Auden, W.H. (1976) *Collected Poems*, E. Mendelson (ed.). London: Faber and Faber.

Auden, W.H. and Kallman, C. (trans.) (1976) *The Rise and Fall of the City of Mahagonny*. Boston: Godine.

Auden, W.H. and Kallman, C. (1993) *Libretti and Other Dramatic Writings by W.H. Auden 1939–1973*, E. Mendelson (ed.). Princeton, NJ: Princeton University Press.

Auden, W.H. and MacNeice, L. (1967) *Letters from Iceland*. London and Boston: Faber and Faber.

Auden, W.H. and Mayer, E. (trans.) (1962) J.W. von Goethe. *Italian Journey 1786–1788*. New York: Pantheon.

Auden, W.H. and Sjöberg, L. (trans.) (1964) D. Hammarskjöld. *Markings*. New York: Knopf.

Auden, W.H. and Sjöberg, L. (trans.) (1971) *Selected Poems of Gunnar Ekelöf*. Harmondsworth: Penguin.

Auden, W.H. and Sjöberg, L. (trans.) (1975) P. Lagerkvist. *Evening Land: Aftonland*. Detroit: Wayne State University Press.

Auden, W.H. *et al.* (trans.) (1966) A. Voznesensky. *Antiworlds*, P. Blake and M. Hayward (eds). New York: Basic Books.

Auden, W.H. and Taylor, P.B. *See* Taylor.

Babcock, B.A. (ed.) (1978) *The Reversible World: Symbolic Inversion in Art and Society*. Ithaca: Cornell University Press.

Babington, C. and Lumby, J.R. (eds) (1865–86) *Polychronicon Ranulphi Higden Monachi Cestrencis*. 9 vols. Rolls Series 41. London: Longmans and Co.

Baker, M., and Malmkjær, K. (eds) (1998) *The Routledge Encyclopedia of Translation Studies*. London: Routledge.

Bakhtin, M.M. (1981) *The Dialogic Imagination: four Essays*, M. Holquist (ed.). Austin: University of Texas Press.

Bareham. *See* Trollope, *The Barsetshire Novels*.

Barkan, L. (1986) *The Gods Made Flesh: Metamorphosis and the Pursuit of Paganism*. New Haven: Yale University Press.

Barthes, R. (1979) *A Lover's Discourse: Fragments* (R. Howard, trans.). London: Jonathan Cape.

Bassnett, S. (1991) *Translation Studies. New Accents* (rev. edn; 1st edn. 1980). London and New York: Methuen.

Bassnett, S. (1998) *Constructing Cultures: Essays on Literary Translation*. Clevedon: Multilingual Matters.

Baswell, C. (1999) Latinitas. In *The New Cambridge History of Medieval English Literature* (pp. 122–51). (Full reference, Wallace.)

Bate, J. (1993) *Shakespeare and Ovid*. Oxford: Clarendon Press.

Baudrillard, J. (1990) *Fatal Strategies* (P. Beitchman and W.G.J. Niesluchowski, trans.), J. Fleming (ed.). London: Pluto Press.

Behn, A. (trans.) (1688) A discovery of new worlds. In *The Works of Aphra Behn*. Vol. 4. *Seneca Unmasked and Other Prose Translations*, J. Todd (ed.) (1993). London: William Pickering.

Benjamin, W. (1973) The task of the translator (H. Zohm, trans.). In H. Arendt (ed.) *Illuminations* (pp. 70–82). London: Fontana.

Bennett, C. (trans.) (1926) *Horace Odes and Epodes*. Cambridge, MA and London: Harvard University Press.

Benson, L.D. *et al.* (eds) (1988) *The Riverside Chaucer*. 3rd edn. Oxford: Oxford University Press.

Bergerac, Cyrano de (1961) *Histoire comique des État et Empire de la Lune*, C. Nodier (ed.). Paris: Club des Editeurs.

Berlau, R. (1987) *Living for Brecht: The Memoirs of Ruth Berlau*, H. Bunge (ed.). Trans. G. Skelton. New York: Fromm International.

Berry, L.E. (ed. and intro.) (1969) *Geneva Bible, Facsimile of the Edition printed by Rouland Hall, Geneva, 1560*. Milwaukee: University of Wisconsin Press.

Bhaba, H.K. (1994) *The Location of Culture*. London: Routledge.

Bland, C.R. (1992) John of Cornwall's innovations and their possible effects on Chaucer. In *The Uses of Manuscripts in Literary Studies: Essays in Memory of Judson Boyce Allen* (pp. 213–36), C.K. Morse *et al.* (eds). *Studies in Medieval Culture* XXXI. Kalamazoo, MI.: Western Michigan University, Medieval Institute Publications.

Bloom, H. (1975) *A Map of Misreading*. New York: Oxford University Press.

Blunt, J.H. (ed.) (1873) *The Myroure of Oure Ladye*. EETS ES 19. London: N. Trübner and Co.

Boer, C. de (ed.) (1920) *Ovide moralisé*. Amsterdam: Johannes Müller.

Boer, C. de (ed.) (1954) *Ovide moralisé en prose*. Holland: North Holland Publishing Company.

Boly, J.R. (1991) *Reading Auden: The Returns of Caliban*. Ithaca and London: Cornell University Press.

Bouwsma, W. (1988) *John Calvin: A Sixteenth-Century Portrait*. Oxford: Oxford University Press.

Braden, G. (1978) *The Classics and English Renaissance Poetry*. New York: Yale University Press.

Bray, G. (ed.) (1994) *Documents of the English Reformation*. Cambridge: James Clarke.

Brecht, B. (1963) *Aufstieg und Fall der Stadt Mahagonny*. Frankfurt am Main: Suhrkamp.

Brecht, B. (1979) *Collected Plays*, 2: 3, J. Willett and R. Mannheim (eds). London: Eyre Methuen.

Brooke, C. (1961) *From Alfred to Henry III 871–1272*. Edinburgh: Thomas Nelson and Sons Ltd.

Brown, P. (ed.) (2000) *A Companion to Chaucer*. Oxford: Blackwell.

Bühler, C. (1938) A Lollard tract: on translating the Bible into English. *MÆv* VII, 3, 167–83.

Burnley, J.D. (1992) *The History of the English Language*. London and New York: Longman.

Butler, H.E. (trans.) (1920–2) *Quintilian, Institutio oratoria*. 4 vols. London: Heinemann.

Callan, E. (1983) *Auden: A Carnival of Intellect*. New York and Oxford: Oxford University Press.

Calvin, J. (1949) *Institutes of the Christian Religion*. (H. Beveridge, trans.). London: James Clarke.

Calvin, J. (1960) *Institutes of the Christian Religion* (F.L. Battle, trans.). Philadelphia: Westminster Press.

Carpenter, H. (1982) *W.H. Auden: A Biography*. Boston: Houghton Mifflin.

Carter, E. (trans.) (1739) *The Philosophy of Sir Isaac Newton Explained, in Six Dialogues, on Light and Colours, Between a Lady and the Author*. London.

Castera, du Perron de. *See* Algarotti (1738).

Chance, J. (ed.) (1990) *The Mythographic Art: Classical Fable and the Rise of the Vernacular in France and England*. Gainesville: University of Florida Press.

Cheyfitz, E. (1991) *The Poetics of Imperialism: Translation and Colonization from The Tempest to Tarzan*. Oxford: Oxford University Press.

Clark, J. (1975) *The Language and Style of Anthony Trollope*. London: André Deutsch.

Clarke, M. (1959) *Classical Education in Britain 1500–1900*. Cambridge: Cambridge University Press.

Coleman, J. (1981) *English Literature in History 1350–1400: Medieval Writers and Readers*. London: Hutchinson.

Collinson, P. (1995) Protestant culture and the cultural revolution. In *Reformation to Revolution: Politics and Religion in Early Modern England* (pp. 33–52), M. Todd (ed.). London: Routledge.

Configurations = *Configurations: A Journal of Literature, Science, and Technology.*

Constantine, D. (1990) The German Auden: six early poems. In *W.H. Auden: 'The Map of All My Youth': Early Works, Friends and Influences*, K. Bucknell and N. Jenkins (eds). Auden Studies 1. Oxford: Clarendon Press.

Copeland, R. (1991) *Rhetoric, Hermeneutics and Translation in the Middle Ages: Academic Traditions and Vernacular Texts*. Cambridge: Cambridge University Press.

Courthope, W.J. (1897) *A History of English Poetry*. Vol. 2 (5 vols. 1895–1910). London: Macmillan and Co.

Crane, S. (1999) Anglo-Norman cultures in England. In *The New Cambridge History of Medieval English Literature* (pp. 35–60). (Full reference, Wallace.)

Crawford, P. (1996) *Women and Religion in England 1500–1720*. London: Routledge.

Cronin, M. (1996) *Translating Ireland*. Cork: Cork University Press.

Cummings, B. (1999) Reformed literature and literature reformed. In *The New Cambridge History of Medieval English Literature* (pp. 821–51). (Full reference, Wallace.)

Dass, N. (1993) *Rebuilding Babel: The Translation of W.H. Auden*. Approaches to Translation Studies 10. Amsterdam and Atlanta, GA: Rodopi.

Daston, L., and Park, K. (1998) *Wonders and the Order of Nature 1150–1750*. New York: Zone Books.

Deanesly, M. (1920) *The Lollard Bible and Other Medieval Biblical Versions*. Cambridge: Cambridge University Press.

Dear, P. (1990) Miracles, experiments, and the ordinary course of nature. *ISIS* 81, 663–83.

Derrida, J. (1978) *Writing and Difference* (A. Bass, trans.). London: Routledge and Kegan Paul.

Derrida, J. (1979) *Of Grammatology* (G.C. Spivack, trans.). London and Baltimore: John Hopkins.

Derrida, J. (1985) Des tours de Babel (J.F. Graham, trans.). In *Difference in Translation* (pp. 165–207), J.F. Graham (ed.). Ithaca and London: Cornell University Press.

Derrida, J. (1987) *Positions*. (A. Bass., trans.). London: Athlone.

Dickens, C., Thackeray, W. and Cruikshank G. (1839) *The Loving Ballad of Lord Bateman*. London: Charles Tilt.

Dobson, A. (1923) *Complete Poetical Works*. London: Oxford University Press.

Doran, S. (1994) *Elizabeth I and Religion 1558–1603*. London: Routledge.

Douglas, A. (1994) Popular science and the representation of women: Fontenelle and after. *Eighteenth-Century Life* 18, 2, 1–14.

Duffy, E. (1992) *The Stripping of the Altars: Traditional Religion in England c. 1400 – c. 1580*. New Haven: Yale University Press.

Duncan, T. (1998) The Middle English translator of Robert de Gretham's Anglo-Norman *Miroir*. In *The Medieval Translator* 6 (pp. 211–31). (Full reference, Ellis, Tixier and Weitemeier, 1998.)

Eagleton, T. (1976) *Criticism and Ideology*. London: Verso.

Easthope, A. and McGowan, K. (eds) (1992) *A Critical and Cultural Theory Reader*. Buckingham: Open University Press.

Edwards, A.S.G. (ed.) (1984) *Middle English Prose: A Critical Guide to Major Authors and Genres*. New Brunswick, NJ: Rutgers University Press.

EETS (ES, OS) = Early English Text Society (Extra Series, Original Series).

Eliot, George. *See* Evans, Mary Ann.

Ellis, R., Wogan-Browne, J., Medcalf, S., and Meredith, P. (eds) (1989) *The Medieval Translator* [1]. Cambridge: D.S. Brewer.

Ellis, R. and Oakley-Brown, E. (1998) The British tradition. In *The Routledge Encyclopedia of Translation Studies* (pp. 333–46). (Full reference, Baker and Malmkjær.)

Ellis, R., Tixier, R., and Weitemeier, B. (eds) (1998) *The Medieval Translator* 6. Turnhout: Brepols.

Elliott, A.G. (1980) *Accessus ad auctores*: twelfth-century introductions to Ovid. *Allegorica* 5, 6–48.

Elliott, A.G. (1985) Ovid and the critics: Seneca, Quintilian and 'seriousness'. *Helios* 12, 1, 9–20.

Ellmann, M. (1987) *The Poetics of Impersonality: T.S. Eliot and Ezra Pound*. Brighton: Harvester.

Epperly, E. (1989) *Patterns of Repetition in Trollope*. Washington, D.C.: The Catholic University of America Press.

Evans, Mary Anne (pseud. George Eliot) (1872) *Middlemarch*. (D. Carroll ed.) (1988). Oxford: Oxford University Press.

Fairclough, H. (trans.) (1926) *Horace Satires, Epistles, Ars Poetica*. Cambridge, MA and London: Harvard University Press.

Farrar, F. (ed.) (1868) *Essays on a Liberal Education*. London: Macmillan.

Feldhay, R. (1995) *Galileo and the Church: Political Inquisition or Critical Dialogue*. Cambridge: Cambridge University Press.

Findlen, P. (1998) Between Carnival and Lent: the scientific revolution at the margins of culture. *Configurations* 6, 2, 243–67.

Fisher, J.H. (1992) A language policy for Lancastrian England. *Publications of the Modern Language Association* 107, 1168–80.

Flint, K. (1993) *The Woman Reader 1837–1914*. Oxford and New York: Oxford University Press.

Fontenelle, B. le Bovier de (1687) *Discourse of the Plurality of Worlds*. (W.D. Knight, trans.). Dublin.

Fontenelle, B. le Bovier de (1803) *Conversations on the Plurality of Worlds*. (E. Gunning, trans.). London.

Fontenelle, B. le Bovier de (1637) *Entretiens sur la pluralité des mondes habités*. Intro. Th. Maulnier (1945). Paris: Les éditions de la nouvelle France.

Fontenelle, B. le Bovier de *see also* Behn.

Forshall, J., and Madden, F. (eds) (1850) *The Holy Bible . . . Made from the Latin Vulgate by John Wycliffe and his Followers*. 4 vols. Oxford: Oxford University Press.

Fowler, D.C. (1960) John Trevisa and the English Bible. *Modern Philology* 58, 81–98.

Fox, A. (1997) *The English Renaissance: Identity and Representation in Elizabethan England*. London: Blackwell.

Fradenburg, L.O. (1989) Criticism, anti-Semitism and the *Prioress's Tale*. *Exemplaria* 1, 1, 69–115.

Frazer, G. (trans.) (1931) *Ovid Fasti*. London: Heinemann.

Freccero, J. (1976) Dante's Ulysses. In *Concepts of the Hero in the Middle Ages and the Renaissance* (pp. 101–19), N.T. Burns and C. Reagan (eds). London: Hodder and Stoughton.

Freud, S. (1984) On narcissism: an introduction. In *On Metapsychology: The Theory of Psychoanalysis* (J. Strachey, trans.), A. Richards (ed.). The Pelican Freud Library 11. London: Penguin.

Fuller, J. (1970) *A Reader's Guide to W.H. Auden*. London: Thames and Hudson.

Galinsky, K.G. (1975) *Ovid's Metamorphoses: An Introduction to the Basic Aspects*. Berkeley: University of California Press.

Galloway, A. (1999) Writing history in England. In *The New Cambridge History of Medieval English Literature* (pp. 255–83). (Full reference, Wallace.)

Gentzler, E. (1993) *Contemporary Translation Theories*. Translation Studies. London and New York: Routledge.

Ghisalberti, F. (1946) Medieval biographies of Ovid. *Journal of the Warburg and Courtauld Institute* 9, 10–59.

Gillingham, J. (1995) Henry of Huntingdon and the twelfth-century revival of the English nation. In *Concepts of National Identity in the Middle Ages*, Leeds Texts and Monographs New Series 14 (pp. 75–102), S. Forde, L. Johnson and A.V. Murray (eds). Leeds: School of English, University of Leeds.

Gilmour, R. (1981) *The Idea of the Gentleman in the Victorian Novel*. London: George Allen & Unwin.

Golding, A. (trans.) (1567) *The XV. Bookes of P. Ovidius Naso, entituled Metamorphosis*. London: Willyam Seres. (Facsimile, W.H.D. Rouse (ed.), 1961. London: Centaur Press.)

Golding, L.T. (1937) *An Elizabethan Puritan: Arthur Golding*. New York: R.R. Smith.

Goodman, D. (1994) *The Republic of Letters: A Cultural History of the French Enlightenment*. Cornell: Cornell University Press.

Gradon, P., and Hudson, A. (eds) (1983–96) *English Wycliffite Sermons*. 5 vols. Oxford: Clarendon Press.

Gransden, A. (1974) *English Historical Writing in England*. 2 vols. London: Routledge and Kegan Paul.

Green, R.F. (1980) *Poets and Princepleasers: Literature and the English Court in the Late Middle Ages*. Toronto, Buffalo, London: University of Toronto Press.

Greenblatt, S. (1980) *Renaissance Self-Fashioning: From More to Shakespeare*. Chicago: University of Chicago Press.

Greene, T.M. (1982) *The Light in Troy: Imitation and Discovery in Renaissance Poetry*. New Haven: Yale University Press.

Gregerson, L. (1993) Narcissus interrupted: specularity and the subject of the Tudor state. *Criticism* 35, 1, 1–40.

Gregerson, L. (1995) *The Reformation of the Subject: Spenser, Milton, and the Protestant Epic*. Cambridge: Cambridge University Press.

Habermas, J. (1992) *Postmetaphysical Thinking: Philosophical Essays*. (W.M. Hohengarten, trans.). Cambridge: Polity.

Hales, J. (1868) The teaching of English. In *Essays on a Liberal Education.* (pp. 293–312) (Full reference, Farrar.)

Hamer, R. (ed.) (1970) *A Choice of Anglo-Saxon Verse.* London and Boston: Faber and Faber.

Hanna, R. (1989) Sir Thomas Berkeley and his patronage. *Speculum* 64, 878–916.

Hanna, R. (1990) The difficulty of Ricardian prose translation: the case of the Lollards. *Modern Language Quarterly* 51, 319–40.

Hanna, R. (1996) 'Vae octuplex', Lollard socio-textual ideology, and Ricardian-Lancastrian prose translation. In *Criticism and Dissent in the Middle Ages* (pp. 244–63), R. Copeland (ed.). Cambridge: Cambridge University Press.

Hanna, R. (1999) Alliterative poetry. In *The New Cambridge History of Medieval English Literature* (pp. 488–512). (Full reference, Wallace.)

Harbert, B. (1988) Lessons from the great clerk: Ovid and John Gower. In *Ovid Renewed* (pp. 83–99). (Full reference, Martindale.)

Hargreaves, H. (1955) The Latin text of Purvey's Psalter. *MÆv* 24, 73–90.

Hargreaves, H. (1969) The Wycliffite versions. In *The Cambridge History of the Bible* vol. 2 (pp. 387–414). (Full reference, Lampe.)

Harth, E. (1970) *Cyrano de Bergerac and the Polemics of Modernity.* New York: Columbia University Press.

Harth, E. (1990) The 'véritables Marquises'. In *Actes de Columbus: Racine; Fontenelle: 'Entretiens sur la pluralité des mondes'; Histoire et littérature* (pp. 149–60). (Full reference, Williams.)

Harth, E. (1992) *Cartesian Women: Versions and Subversions of Rational Discourse in the Old Regime.* Ithaca: Cornell University Press.

Hatim, B., and Mason, I. (1990) *Discourse and the Translator.* Language in Social Life. London and New York: Longman.

Hatim, B., and Mason, I. (1997) *The Translator as Communicator.* New York and London: Routledge.

Heinrichs, K. (1990) *The Myth of Love: Classical Lovers in Medieval Literature.* London: Pennsylvania University Press.

Henderson, M. (1985) *Borders, Boundaries and Frames: Essays in Cultural Criticism and Cultural Studies.* London: Croom Helm.

Hexter, R. (1987) Medieval articulations of Ovid's *Metamorphoses*: from Lactantian segmentation to Arnulfian allegory. *Mediaevalia* 13, 63–82.

Hinds, S. (1998) *Allusion and Intertext: Dynamics of Appropriation in Roman Poetry.* Cambridge: Cambridge University Press.

Hoggart, R. (1951) *Auden: An Introductory Essay.* London: Chatto and Windus.

Horace. *See* Bennett, Fairclough, Lytton.

Horstmann, C. (1888) '*Orologium Sapientiae* or *The Seven Poyntes of Trewe Wisdom.*' *Anglia* X, 323–89.

Houghton, Lord (Richard Monckton Milnes). (1860) On the present social results of classical education. In *Essays on a Liberal Education.* (Full reference, Farrar.)

Hudson, A. (1975) The debate on Bible translation, Oxford 1401. *English Historical Review* 90, 1–18 (repr. in Hudson, A. (1985) *Lollards and Their Books.* London: Hambledon).

Hudson, A. (ed.) (1978) *Selections from English Wycliffite Writings.* Cambridge: Cambridge University Press.

Hudson, A. (1988) *The Premature Reformation.* Oxford: Clarendon Press.

Hughes, J. (1988) *Pastors and Visionaries: Religion and Secular Life in Late Medieval Yorkshire*. Woodbridge: The Boydell Press.

Hughes, T. (1857) *Tom Brown's Schooldays*. London: Juvenile Productions (1944).

Hurstfield, J. (1973) *Freedom, Corruption and Government in Elizabethan England*. London: Jonathan Cape.

Huxley, T.H. (1877) *Lay Sermons, Addresses and Reviews*. London: Macmillan and Co.

Isherwood, C. (1966) *Exhumations: Stories, Articles, Verses*. London: Methuen.

Jacob, M.C. (1988) *The Cultural Meaning of the Scientific Revolution: New Perspectives on European History*. New York: Alfred A. Knopf.

Jakobson, R. (1959) On linguistic aspects of translation. In *On Translation*, R.A. Brower (ed.). Cambridge, MA: Harvard University Press.

James, E. D. (1987) Fontenelle: scepticism and Enlightenment. *Seventeenth Century French Studies* 9, 133–50.

James, E. D. (1990) Fontenelle's *Entretiens sur la pluralité des mondes* and their intellectual context. In *Actes de Columbus: Racine; Fontenelle: Entretiens sur la pluralité des mondes; Histoire et littérature* (pp. 133–48). (Full reference, Williams.)

James, H. (1883) Anthony Trollope. Repr. in *Anthony Trollope: The Critical Heritage*, (ed.) D. Smalley (1969). London: Routledge Kegan Paul.

JEGP = Journal of English and Germanic Philology.

Johns, A. (1998) *The Nature of the Book: Print and Knowledge in the Making*. Chicago: University of Chicago Press.

Johnson, I. (1989) Prologue and practice: Middle English lives of Christ. In *The Medieval Translator* [1] (pp. 69–85). (Full reference, Ellis *et al.* 1989.)

Johnson, L. (1917) *Poetical Works of Lionel Johnson*. London: Elkin Mathews.

Justice, S. (1999) Lollardy. In *The New Cambridge History of Medieval English Literature* (pp. 662–89). (Full reference, Wallace.)

Kalverkämper, H. (1989) Kolloquiale Vermittlung von Fachwissen im frühen 18. Jahrhundert. *Fachgespräche in Aufklärung und Revolution* (pp. 17–80), B. Schlieben-Lange (ed.). Tübingen: Max Niemeyer.

Kamuf, P. (1982) *Fictions of Female Desire: Disclosures of Heloise*. Lincoln: University of Nebraska Press.

Kant, I. (1848) *Critique of Pure Reason* (F. Haywood, trans.). London: Pickering.

Keach, W. (1977) *Elizabethan Erotic Narratives*. London: Harvester Press.

Keller, E.F. (1983) *Reflections on Gender and Science*. New Haven, CT: Yale University Press.

Kepler, J. (1609) *Kepler's Dream, with the Full Text and Notes of 'Somnium sive astronomicum lunaris Johannis Kepleri'* (P.F. Kirkwood, intro. and trans.) (1965). California: University of California Press.

King, J.N. (1982) *English Reformation Literature: The Tudor Origins of the Protestant Tradition*. Princeton: Princeton University Press.

Kirk, G.S. (trans.) (1970) *Euripides The Bacchae*. Greek Drama Series. Eaglewood Cliffs, NJ: Prentice-Hall.

Kirkpatrick, R. (1990) *Bullies, Beaks and Flannelled Fools: An Annotated Bibliography of Boys' School Fiction, 1742–1990*. London: Robert J. Kirkpatrick.

Kristeva, J. (1987). *Tales of Love*. Trans. L.S. Roudiez. New York: Columbia University Press.

Lacan, J. (1977) *Ecrits: A Selection*. (A. Sheridan, trans.). London: Routledge.

Lampe, G.W. (1969) (ed.) *The Cambridge History of the Bible*. Cambridge: Cambridge University Press.

Lanham, R. (1976) *The Motives of Eloquence: Literary Rhetoric in the Renaissance*. New Haven: Yale University Press.

Lawton, D. (1999) Englishing the Bible, 1066–1549. In *The New Cambridge History of Medieval English Literature* (pp. 454–82). (Full reference, Wallace.)

Lefevere, A. (ed.) (1992a) *Translation/History/Culture*. London: Routledge.

Lefevere, A. (1992b) *Translation, Rewriting and the Manipulation of Literary Fame*. London: Routledge.

Legge, M.D. (1963) *Anglo-Norman Literature and Its Background*. Oxford: Oxford University Press.

Letwin, S. (1982) *The Gentleman in Trollope: Individuality and Moral Conduct*. London and Basingstoke: Macmillan.

Leupin, A. (1989) *Barbarolexis: Medieval Writing and Sexuality* (K.M. Cooper, trans.). London: Harvard University Press.

Lewalski, B.K. (1986) Into the maze of the self: the Protestant transformation of the image of the labyrinth. *Journal of Medieval and Renaissance Studies* 16, 281–301.

Lipson, C. (1983) 'I n'am but a lewd compilator': Chaucer's *Treatise on the Astrolabe* as translation. *Neuphilologische Mitteilungen* 84, 192–200.

Locker, F. (Locker Lampson, F.) (1879) *Patchwork*. London: Smith, Elder and Co.

Lusignan, S. (1989) La topique de la *translatio studii* et les traductions françaises des textes savants au XIVe siècle. In *Traduction et traducteurs au Moyen Age* (pp. 303–15), G. Contamine (ed.). Paris: CNRS.

Lyne, R. (1996) Golding's Englished *Metamorphoses*. *Translation and Literature* 5, 2, 183–99.

Lytton, Lord (trans.) (1869) *Horace Odes and Epodes*. Leipzig: Bernhard Tauchnitz.

Machan, T.W. (1984) *Chaucer's Boece*. Norman: Pilgrim Books.

Machan, T.W. (1989) Chaucer as translator. In *The Medieval Translator* [1] (pp. 55–67). (Full reference, Ellis *et al.* 1989.)

MacIntyre, W.M. (1965) A critical study of Golding's translation of Ovid's *Metamorphoses*. PhD thesis. California: University of California.

MÆv = Medium Ævum

Martindale, C. (ed.) (1988) *Ovid Renewed: Ovidian Influences on Literature and Art from the Middle Ages to the Twentieth Century*. Cambridge: Cambridge University Press.

Martineau, H. (1864a) Middle class education in England: boys. *Cornhill Magazine* 10 (October), 409–26.

Martineau, H. (1864b) Middle class education in England: girls. *Cornhill Magazine* 10 (November), 549–68.

Matthew, F.D. (ed.) (1880) *The English Works of Wyclif Hitherto Unprinted*. EETS OS 74. London: Trübner and Co.

McKisack, M. (1959) *The Fourteenth Century 1307–1399*. The Oxford History of England V. Oxford: The Clarendon Press.

McMaster, R. (1991) *Thackeray's Cultural Frame of Reference: Allusion in The Newcomes*. London and Basingstoke: Macmillan.

McNiven, P. (1987) *Heresy and Politics in the Reign of Henry IV: The Burning of John Badby*. Woodbridge: The Boydell Press.

Mendelson, E. (1981) *Early Auden*. London: Faber and Faber.

Meyer, G.D. (1955) *The Scientific Lady in England 1650–1760: An Account of her Rise, with Emphasis on the Major Role of the Telescope and the Microscope*. Berkeley: University of California Press.

Meyer, H. (1968) _The Poetics of Quotation in the European Novel_ (T. and Y. Ziolkowski, trans.) Princeton: Princeton University Press.

Miller, F.J. (trans.) (1917) _Seneca Tragedies_. London: William Heinemann.

Miller, F.J. (trans.) (1984) _Ovid: The Metamorphoses_. 2 vols. London: Harvard University Press.

Minnis, A.J. (1988a) _Medieval Theory of Authorship_. 2nd. edn. Aldershot: Wildwood.

Minnis, A.J. and Scott, A.B., with Wallace, D. (eds and trans.) (1988b) _Medieval Literary Theory and Criticism c.1170 – c.1375: The Commentary Tradition_. Oxford: Clarendon Press.

Mitchell, B., and Robinson, F.C. (1986) _A Guide to Old English_. 4th edition. Oxford and New York: Blackwell.

Murray, J.A.H. (ed.) (1884–1933) _The Oxford English Dictionary_. 13 vols. Oxford: Clarendon Press. (2nd. edn. 1989).

Musgrave, P. (1985) _From Brown to Bunter: The Life and Death of the School Story_. London: Routledge and Kegan Paul.

Myers, K.S. (1994) _Ovid's Causes: Cosmogony and Aetiology in the Metamorphoses_. Ann Arbor: University of Michigan Press.

Nicolson, M.H. (1946) _Newton Demands the Muse: Newton's Opticks and the Eighteenth-Century Poets_. Princeton: Princeton University Press.

Nicolson, M.H. (1956) _Science and Imagination_. Ithaca, NY: Great Seal Books.

Niranjana, T. (1992) _Re-siting Translation: History, Post-Structuralism and the Colonial Context_. Berkeley: University of California Press.

Nissé, R. (1999) 'Oure fadres olde and modres': gender, heresy and Hoccleve's literary politics. In _Studies in the Age of Chaucer_ 21 (pp. 275–99). (Full reference, Scanlon.)

NLH = New Literary History.

Nuttall, A.D. (1988) Ovid's Narcissus and Shakespeare's _Richard II_: the reflected self. In _Ovid Renewed_ (pp. 137–50). (Full reference, Martindale 1988.)

Oakley-Brown, E. (1994) Translations of desire: English versions of Ovid's 'Salmacis and Hermaphroditus' 1480–1700. M.A. thesis. Cardiff: University of Cardiff.

Oakley-Brown, E. (1999) Subjects in translation: identity, representation and subjectivity in English versions of Ovid's _Metamorphoses_ 1480–1717. PhD thesis. Cardiff: University of Cardiff.

OED. See Murray.

Olmsted, W. (1996) On the margins of otherness: metamorphosis and identity in Homer, Ovid, Sidney, and Milton. _NLH_ 27, 167–87.

Olson, G. (1999) Geoffrey Chaucer. In _The New Cambridge History of Medieval English Literature_ (pp. 566–88). (Full reference, Wallace.)

Orgel, S. (1989) 'Nobody's perfect': or, why did the English stage take boys for women? _South Atlantic Quarterly_ 88, 7–29.

Ovid. _See_ Frazer, Miller, Showerman, Wheeler.

Owst, G.R. (1933) _Literature and Pulpit in Medieval England_. Cambridge: Cambridge University Press.

Parker, P. (1989) On the tongue: cross-gendering, effeminacy and the art of words. _Style_ 23, 445–65.

Parker, T.H. (1966) _English Reformers_. London: SCM Press.

Patterson, L. (1991) _Chaucer and the Subject of History_. London: Routledge.

Payn, J. (1891) _Some Private Views_ . . . London: Chatto and Windus.

Pearcy, L.T. (1984) *The Mediated Muse: English Translations of Ovid, 1560–1700*. Hamden, CT.: Archon.

Peend, T. (trans.) (1565) *The Pleasant Fable of Hermaphroditus and Salmacis with a Morall in English Verse*. London: Thomas Caldwell.

Perrie, W. (1985) Auden's political vision. In *W.H. Auden: The Far Interior*, A. Bold (ed.). London: Vision Press.

Pollard, A.W. (ed.) (1903) *Fifteenth Century Verse and Prose*. Westminster: Archibald Constable and Co.

Radice, B. (trans. and intro.) (1974) *The Letters of Abelard and Heloise*. London: Penguin.

Ray, G. (ed.) (1945–6) *The Letters and Private Papers of William Makepeace Thackeray*. 4 vols. Cambridge, MA.: Harvard University Press.

Richards, J. (1988) *Happiest Days: The Public Schools in English Fiction*. Manchester: Manchester University Press.

Robinson, D. (1997) *Western Translation Theory from Herodotus to Nietzsche*. Manchester: St Jerome Press.

Rosenberg, E. (1955) *Leicester, Patron of Letters*. New York: Columbia University Press.

Runsdorf, J.H. (1992) Transforming Ovid in the 1560's: Thomas Peend's 'pleasaunt fable'. *American Notes and Queries* 5, 124–7.

Saintsbury, G. (ed.) (1912) *Ballads and Contributions to 'Punch' 1842–1850, By William Makepeace Thackeray*. London, New York and Toronto: Henry Frowde/Oxford University Press.

Sargeaunt, J. (trans.) (1912) *Terence Plays*. London: William Heinemann.

Sargent, M.G. (ed.) (1992) *Nicholas Love's Mirror of the Blessed Life of Jesus Christ*. New York: Garland.

Scanlon, L. (ed.) (1999) *Studies in the Age of Chaucer* 21. Rutgers, NJ: New Chaucer Society.

Scase, W. (1994) *Reginald Pecock*. Authors of the Middle Ages 8. Aldershot: Variorum.

Sedgwick, E.K. (1985) *Between Men: English Literature and Male Homosexual Desire*. Guildford and New York: Columbia University Press.

Seneca. *See* Miller.

Shadwell, T. (1676) *The Virtuoso*, M.H. Nicolson (ed.) (1966). Lincoln: University of Nebraska Press.

Shaffer, E.S. (1984) Translation as metamorphosis and cultural transmission. In *Comparative Criticism: An Annual Journal* (pp. xiii–xxvii). Cambridge: Cambridge University Press.

Shapin, S., (1994) *A Social History of Truth: Civility and Science in Seventeenth-Century England*. Chicago: Chicago University Press.

Shapin, S. and Schaffer, S. (1985) *Leviathan and the Air Pump: Hobbes, Boyle, and the Experimental Life*. Princeton: Princeton University Press.

Shepherd, G. (1969) English versions of the Scriptures before Wyclif. In *The Cambridge History of the Bible*, vol. 2 (pp. 362–86). (Full reference, Lampe.)

Sheridan, J.J. (trans.) (1980) *Alan of Lille, De Planctu Naturae*. Toronto: Pontifical Institute of Medieval Studies.

Shoaf, A. (ed.) (1998) *The Testament of Love of Thomas Usk*. Kalamazoo, MI.: TEAMS Medieval Institute Publications, Western Michigan University.

Showerman, G. (trans.) (1914) *Ovid Heroides*. London: Heinemann.

Sidgwick, H. (1868) The theory of classical education. In _Essays on a Liberal Education_. (Full reference, Farrar.)

Silberman, L. (1995) _Transforming Desire: Erotic Knowledge in Books III and IV of The Faerie Queen_. Berkeley, Los Angeles, London: University of California Press.

Simon, S. (1996) _Gender in Translation: Cultural Identity and the Politics of Transmission_. London: Routledge.

Sinfield, A. (1983) _Literature in Protestant England, 1560–1660_. London: Croom Helm.

Sisam, G. (ed.) (1921) _Fourteenth Century Verse and Prose_. Oxford: Clarendon Press.

Skilton, D. (1988) Schoolboy Latin and the mid-Victorian novelist: a study in reader competence. _Browning Institute Studies_ 16, 39–55.

Smith, S. (1985) _W.H. Auden_. Rereading Literature. Oxford: Blackwell.

Smyth, A.P. (1995) _King Alfred the Great_. Oxford: Oxford University Press.

Somerset, F. (1999) 'As just as is a squyre': the politics of 'lewed translacion' in Chaucer's _Summoner's Tale_. In _Studies in the Age of Chaucer_ 21 (pp. 187–207). (Full reference, Scanlon.)

Southern, R.W. (1992) _Robert Grosseteste: The Growth of an English Mind in Medieval Europe_. Oxford: Clarendon Press (rev. edn; 1st edn, 1986).

Spencer, H.L. (1993) _English Preaching in the Late Middle Ages_. Oxford: Clarendon Press.

Springer, M. (1983) _Hardy's Use of Allusion_. London and Basingstoke: Macmillan.

Staley, L. (1994) _Margery Kempe's Dissenting Fictions_. University Park, PA: Penn State University Press.

Stanley, E.G. (ed.) (1960) _The Owl and the Nightingale_. London and Edinburgh: Thomas Nelson.

Stanley, E.G. (1988) King Alfred's prefaces. _Review of English Studies_ 39, 349–64.

Steiner, George (1975) _After Babel: Aspects of Language and Translation_. Oxford: Oxford University Press. (2nd edn, 1992.)

Steiner, Grundy (1950) Golding's use of the Regius-Micyllus commentary upon Ovid. _JEGP_ 49, 317–23.

Stewart, L. (1992) _The Rise of Public Science: Rhetoric, Technology, and Natural Philosophy in Newtonian Britain, 1660–1750_. Cambridge: Cambridge University Press.

Strohm, P. (1998) _England's Empty Throne: Usurpation and the Language of Legitimation, 1399–1422_. New Haven and London: Yale University Press.

Stubbs, W. (ed.) (1887–9) _De Gestis Regis Anglorum_. 2 vols. Rolls Series 90. London: Longman and Co.

Swanton, M. (trans.) (1993) _Anglo-Saxon Prose_. London: J.M. Dent; Vermont: Charles E. Tuttle.

Swinburn, L.M. (ed.) (1917) _The Lanterne of Liȝt_. EETS OS 151. London: Kegan Paul, Trench, Trübner and Co.

Szittya, P. (1986) _The Antifraternal Tradition in Medieval Literature_. Princeton, NJ: Princeton University Press.

Taylor, J. (1966) _The Universal Chronicle of Ranulf Higden_. Oxford: Clarendon Press.

Taylor, P.B. and Auden, W.H. (trans) (1969) _The Elder Edda: A Selection_. London: Faber and Faber.

Temple, F. (1860) The education of the world. In Temple, F. _et al. Essays and Reviews_ (pp. 1–49). London: John W. Parker and Son.

Terence. _See_ Sargeaunt.

Terrall, M. (1998) Heroic narratives of quest and discovery. *Configurations* 6, 2, 223–42.

Thackeray, W. (1848–50) *The History of Pendennis*, J. Sutherland (ed.) (1994). Oxford: Oxford University Press.

Thackeray, W. (1853–5) *The Newcomes*. A. Sanders (ed.) (1955). Oxford: Oxford University Press.

Thackeray, W. (1863) *The Roundabout Papers*. London: Smith, Elder and Co.

Thackeray, W. (1879) Going to see a man hanged. In *The Works of William Makepeace Thackeray in 24 volumes*. Vol. 14. (pp. 382–96). London: Smith, Elder and Co.

Tomkis, T. (1607) *Lingua*. London: Waterson. (Facsimile, in Old English Drama. London: 1913).

Tracy, R. (1982) 'Lana medicata fuco': Trollope's classicism. In *Trollope: Centenary Essays* (pp. 1–23), J. Halperin (ed.). London: Macmillan.

Trollope, A. (1858) *Doctor Thorne*, H. Osborne (ed.) (1997). London: J.M. Dent.

Trollope, A. (1860–1) *Framley Parsonage*, P. Edwards (ed.) (1980). Oxford: Oxford University Press.

Trollope, A. (1862–4) *The Small House at Allington*. J. Thompson (ed.) (1980). London, Harmondsworth: Penguin.

Trollope, A. (1864–5) *Can You Forgive Her?*, H. Osborne and D. Skilton (eds) (1994). London: J.M. Dent.

Trollope, A. (1865) *The Belton Estate*, J. Halperin (ed.) (1986). Oxford: Oxford University Press.

Trollope, A. (1865) Public schools. *Fortnightly Review*, 2 (October), 476–87.

Trollope, A. (1866–7) *The Last Chronicle of Barset*, D. Skilton (ed.) (1993). London: J.M. Dent.

Trollope, A. (1867) *The Claverings*, D. Skilton (ed.) (1986). Oxford: Oxford University Press.

Trollope, A. (1867–9) *Phineas Finn*, H. Osborne (ed.) (1997). London: J.M. Dent.

Trollope, A. (1870) The Panjandrum. In *The Collected Shorter Fiction*. (pp. 569–601). J. Thompson (ed.) (1992). London: Robinson Publishing.

Trollope, A. (1873–4) *Lady Anna*, S. Orgel (ed.) (1990). Oxford: Oxford University Press.

Trollope, A. (1878–9) *John Caldigate*, N. Hall (ed.) (1993). Oxford: Oxford University Press.

Trollope, A. (1879) *Thackeray*. London: Macmillan and Co.

Trollope, A. (1879–80) *The Duke's Children*, H. Lee (ed.) (1984). Oxford: Oxford University Press.

Trollope, A. (1880–81) *Ayala's Angel*, J. Thompson-Furnival (ed.) (1986). Oxford: Oxford University Press.

Trollope, A. (1881) *Dr Wortle's School*, J. Halperin (ed.) (1984). Oxford: Oxford University Press.

Trollope, A. (1883) *An Autobiography*, D. Skilton (ed.) (1996). Harmondsworth: Penguin.

Trollope, A. (1884) *An Old Man's Love*. Gloucester: Alan Sutton (1984).

Trollope, A. (1981) *Miscellaneous Essays and Reviews* (Michael Y. Mason, intro.). New York: Arno Press.

Trollope, A. (1983) *The Barsetshire Novels*, T. Bareham (ed.). London and Basingstoke: Macmillan.

Tupper, F. (1917) The envy theme in prologues and epilogues. *JEGP* 16, 551–72.

Turville-Petre, T. (1988) Politics and poetry in the early fourteenth century: the case of Robert Mannyng's *Chronicle*. *Review of English Studies* 39, 1–28.

Turville-Petre, T. (1996) *England the Nation: Language, Literature and National Identity 1290–1340*. Oxford: Clarendon Press.

Vance, N. (1984) Virgil and the nineteenth century. In *Virgil and his Influence: Bimillennial Studies* (pp. 169–92), C. Martindale (ed.). Bristol: Bristol Classical Press.

Vance, N. (1988) Ovid and the nineteenth century. In *Ovid Renewed* (pp. 215–32). (Full reference, Martindale 1988.)

Vance, N. (1993) Horace and the nineteenth century. In *Horace Made New: Horatian Influences on British Writing from the Renaissance to the Twentieth Century* (pp. 199–216), C. Martindale and D. Hopkins (eds). Cambridge: Cambridge University Press.

Van den Abbeele (1990) 'Fabula est Mundus': on the plurality of Fontenelle's worlds. In *Actes de Columbus: Racine; Fontenelle: Entretiens sur la pluralité des mondes; Histoire et littérature* (pp. 165–80). (Full reference, Williams.)

Venuti, L. (ed.) (1992) *Rethinking Translation*. London: Routledge.

Venuti, L. (1995) *The Translator's Invisibility: A History of Translation*. London and New York: Routledge.

Venuti, L. (ed.) (1998) *The Scandals of Translation*. London: Routledge.

Voigts, L.E. (1996) What's the word? Bilingualism in late-medieval England. *Speculum* 71, 813–26.

Voltaire, F. M. A. de (1738) *Elements de la philosophie de Newton*. R.L. Walters and W.H. Barber (eds). *The Complete Works of Voltaire*. Vol. 15 (1992). Oxford: The Voltaire Foundation, 1992.

Waldron, R. (1988) Trevisa's original prefaces on translation: a critical edition. In *Medieval English Studies Presented to George Kane* (pp. 285–99), E.D. Kennedy, R. Waldron and J.S. Wittig (eds). Woodbridge: D.S. Brewer.

Wall, S. (1988) *Trollope and Character*. London: Faber and Faber.

Wallace, D. (1999) (ed.) *The New Cambridge History of Medieval English Literature*. Cambridge: Cambridge University Press.

Watson, N. (1995) Censorship and cultural change in late-medieval England: vernacular theology, the Oxford translation debate, and Arundel's Constitutions of 1409. *Speculum* 70, 822–64.

Watson, N. and Savage, A. (eds and trans.) (1991) *Anchoritic Spirituality: Ancrene Wisse and Associated Works*. New York, Mahwah: Paulist Press.

Weber, R. (ed.) (1985) *Biblia Sacra iuxta Vulgatam Versionem*. 2 vols. Stuttgart: Deutsche Bibelgesellschaft.

Wheeler, A.L. (trans.) (1924) *Ovid Tristia ex Ponto*. London: Heinemann.

Wheeler, M. (1979) *The Art of Allusion in Victorian Fiction*. London: Macmillan.

Wilkins, D. (ed.) (1737) *Concilia Magnae Britanniae et Hiberniae*, 3 vols. London: R. Gosling.

Williams, C.G.S. (ed.) (1990) *Actes de Columbus: Racine; Fontenelle: 'Entretiens sur la pluralité des mondes'; Histoire et littérature*. Paris: Papers on French Seventeenth Century Literature.

Wind, E. (1958) *Pagan Mysteries in the Renaissance*. London: Faber.

Wither, G. (1635) *A Collection of Emblems*. London: Augustine Matthews. (facsimile: Scolar Press, 1968.)

Wogan-Browne, J., Watson, N., Taylor, A., and Evans, R. (eds) (1999) *The Idea of the Vernacular: An Anthology of Middle English Literary Theory 1280–1520*. Exeter Medieval Texts and Studies. Exeter: University of Exeter Press (co-published with Pennsylvania State University Press)

Woodmansee, M. (1994) *The Author, Art, and the Market: Rereading the History of Aesthetics*. New York: Columbia University Press.

Yates, F.A. (1964) *Giordano Bruno and the Hermetic Tradition*. London: Routledge and Kegan Paul.

Yolton, J.W. (1984) *Perceptual Acquaintance: From Descartes to Reid*. Oxford: Basil Blackwell.

Index

Abelard, Peter 90
Académie Royale des Sciences 88, 112
Addison, Joseph 82
Aidan, Bishop 26
Ailred of Rievaulx *see* Daniel
Alan of Lille: *De Planctu Naturae* 70, 84
Alfred, King of England 10-16, 21, 26,
    31, 33; tr. Boethius, St Gregory *qv*,
    Psalter 16; *Life of –, see* Asser
Algarotti, Francesco 3-5, 86-7, 110-19: *Il
    Newtonianismo per le Dame* 109, 111
Aline, Lady 35
Anne, wife of Richard II and Queen of
    England 33-4
Ansen, Alan 190
Antwerp 80
Arctic Circle 110
Aristotle 14
Arnold, Matthew 4: *On Translating
    Homer* 154
Arnolf of Orléans 84
Arundel, Thomas, Archbishop of (1)
    York (2) Canterbury 2, 5, 7, 32-4, 43,
    46: Constitutions 7, 40-43 *passim*
Asser: *Life of King Alfred* 13
Auden, Wystan Hugh 4, 167-204:
    About the House 187; *Another Time*
    187; *City Without Walls* 187; 'The
    Composer' 167; *The Dog
    Beneath the Skin* 195; *The Enchafed
    Flood* 187; *Epistle to a Godson* 187;
    'Lacrimae Rerum' 169; *Letters from
    Iceland* 173 (incl. 'Letter to Lord
    Byron' 173, 187); *Look, Stranger!* 187;
    'My Achilles Heart' 178; *New Year
    Letter* 187; *Paid on Both Sides* 192; *The
    Sea and the Mirror* 185; 'The Shield
    of Achilles' 178-80;'Thanksgiving
    for a Habitat' 177; *Thank You Fog*
    187; 'An Unwritten Poem' 178; 'The

Wanderer' 170-73 *passim*, 185, 202;
    'The World of Opera' 186, 188; 'The
    World of the Sagas' (T.S. Eliot
    Memorial Lecture) 174, 176, 194,
    200. *See also* Henze, Mozart,
    Stravinsky
Augustine, St 16, 18, 25, 28, 72: *De
    Doctrina Christiana* 28
Augustus Caesar 55

Bacon, Sir Francis 85-6
Bacon, Roger 17, 23, 27, 29, 45
Bakhtin, Mikhail 97
Barkan, Leonard 51
Barsi, Laura Maria Katherina 119
Barthes, Roland: *A Lover's Discourse*
    178
Basil, St 84
Bassnett, Susan 1, 171, 189
Bate, Jonathan 79, 83
Baudrillard, Jean 175
Beaumont, Francis 82
Bede, Venerable 14, 16, 20-21, 26-31
    passim: *Historia Ecclesiastica* 26, 46
Behn, Aphra 3, 5, 86, 102-7: *The
    Emperor of the Moon* 104
Benjamin, Walter 204
Benn, Gottfried 195
Bergerac, Cyrano de 91, 97, 119:
    Histoire comique 97
Berkeley, Thomas, Lord 7, 12
Berkeley Castle 14
Berlin 169, 190
Bhaba, Homi 84
Bible translations, general 3-7 *passim*,
    14-43 *passim*, 72, 80, 102; (English
    versions) Bishops' 82, Geneva 54-5,
    82, Great 82, King James 83,
    Wycliffite 17, 33, 46, 81 (incl.
    Prologue 2, 7, 16-24 *passim*, 27, 30,